INDIGENEITY AND LEGAL PLURALISM IN INDIA

As calls for reparations to Indigenous peoples grow on every continent, issues around resource extraction, dispossession, and displacement raise complex legal questions. What do these disputes mean to those affected? How do the narratives of Indigenous people, legal professionals, and the media intersect?

In this richly layered and nuanced account, Pooja Parmar focuses on indigeneity in the widely publicized controversy over a Coca-Cola bottling facility in Kerala, India. Juxtaposing popular, legal, and Adivasi narratives, Parmar examines how meanings are gained and lost through translation of complex claims into the languages of social movements and formal legal systems. Included are perspectives of the diverse range of actors involved, based on interviews with members of Adivasi communities, social activists, bureaucrats, politicians, lawyers, and judges. Presented in clear, accessible prose, Parmar's account of translation enriches debates in the fields of legal pluralism, indigeneity, and development.

Pooja Parmar is Assistant Professor in the Department of Law and Legal Studies at Carleton University. Her research on legal pluralism, indigeneity, human rights, and international law has been published in such journals as the *Australian Feminist Law Journal*, *International Community Law Review*, and *Osgoode Hall Law Journal*. Before entering academia, Parmar practiced law in New Delhi.

CAMBRIDGE STUDIES IN LAW AND SOCIETY

Cambridge Studies in Law and Society aims to publish the best scholarly work on legal discourse and practice in its social and institutional contexts, combining theoretical insights and empirical research.

The fields that it covers are studies of law in action; the sociology of law; the anthropology of law; cultural studies of law, including the role of legal discourses in social formations; law and economics; law and politics; and studies of governance. The books consider all forms of legal discourse across societies, rather than being limited to lawyers' discourses alone.

The series editors come from a range of disciplines: academic law, socio-legal studies, sociology, and anthropology. All have been actively involved in teaching and writing about law in context.

A list of books in the series can be found at the back of this book.

Indigeneity and Legal Pluralism in India

CLAIMS, HISTORIES, MEANINGS

POOJA PARMAR
Carleton University

CAMBRIDGE
UNIVERSITY PRESS

CAMBRIDGE
UNIVERSITY PRESS

32 Avenue of the Americas, New York, NY 10013-2473, USA

Cambridge University Press is part of the University of Cambridge.

It furthers the University's mission by disseminating knowledge in the pursuit of education, learning, and research at the highest international levels of excellence.

www.cambridge.org
Information on this title: www.cambridge.org/9781107081185

First published 2015

A catalog record for this publication is available from the British Library.

Library of Congress Cataloging in Publication Data
Parmar, Pooja, 1972– author.
Indigeneity and legal pluralism in India: claims, histories, meanings / Pooja Parmar, Carleton University.
pages cm. – (Cambridge studies in law and society)
Based on author's thesis (doctoral – University of British Columbia, 2013) issued under title: Claims, histories, meanings.
Includes bibliographical references and index.
ISBN 978-1-107-08118-5 (hardback)
1. Indigenous peoples – Legal status, laws, etc. – India. 2. Adivasis – Legal status, laws, etc. – India. 3. India – Scheduled tribes – Legal status, laws, etc. 4. Customary law – India. 5. Legal polycentricity – India. 6. Groundwater – Law and legislation – India – Kerala 7. Coca-Cola Company – Trials, litigation, etc. I. Title.
KNS2107.M56.P37 2015
342.5408′72–dc23 2015003108

ISBN 978-1-107-08118-5 Hardback

Contents

Acknowledgments

I have accumulated many debts in the course of researching and writing this book. I offer my gratitude first and foremost to all those who agreed to share with me many of their experiences and views. While not identified by their real names here, their words, their stories, and their silences inspired and challenged me as I wrote this book.

I offer my enduring gratitude to W. Wesley Pue, Karin Mickelson, and Renisa Mawani for their guidance, encouragement, enthusiasm, questions, and provocations that have each enriched and shaped my work. I am also thankful to Bruce Miller, Lorraine Weir, Ruth Buchanan, Margot Young, Doug Harris, and Benjamin Berger for reading earlier versions or parts of this book. Those who responded with comments, suggestions, and questions at various conferences and lectures are too many to name here, but I am grateful for all that I learned from each of those encounters.

I am thankful to several people who facilitated my fieldwork in India. I am grateful to Shiny Gopakumar for the enthusiasm she brought to her role as an interpreter, for her curiosity, and for her patience. I am indebted to Baby Siraj and P. M. Sirajuddin for providing me a home in Ernakulam and for their help throughout my stay in Kerala. Laila and Saifuddin Kitchlu made my research in Palakkad possible by welcoming me into their home and lives, and I am indebted to them for their kindness, concern, and care. I am also thankful to Dr. Koya in Palakkad; Shoma and Animon Ilias, Gopakumar S. Nair, Jiss Verkey and Robin in Thrissur; Preeti and Ravindra Gosain in Bangalore; Professors Chandan Gowda and S. Japhet at CSEIP in NLSUI Bangalore; Zainu Kitchlu and M. Balachandran in Palakkad; Dr. Sivanandan in Trivandrum; and Sreejith Nair, Praveen Hariharan, and Professor N. S. Soman in Kochi.

The University of British Columbia, the UBC Graduate Program in Law, the Centre for India and South Asia Research at UBC, and the Law

Foundation provided funds that made this research possible. I would also like to acknowledge the financial support provided by Carleton University during the latter phases of the preparation of this book. I am grateful to Jon Corbett for the time he spent creating the map for this book, and to Zorana Dimitrijevic for her assistance in formatting and tracking those last missing references. I am also grateful to the anonymous reviewers and the editorial team at Cambridge University Press for all their help in preparation of this book.

Special thanks are owed to my family and friends across three continents for their invaluable support while I worked on this book. I would like to especially acknowledge Prabh Bedi, Erika Cedillo Corral, Mary-Ann Chacko, Joanne Chung, Patricia Cochran, Emma Cunliffe, John Ferguson, Ian Greig, Varsha Gurha, Sandy Kaur, Asad Kiyani, Nikhil Kripalani, Don McIntyre, N. S. Negi, Padma Negi, Tavnit Parmar, Naayeli Ramirez, Kanan Rana, Chanan Singh, Harmandip Singh, Sukhchain Singh, Maymon Siraj, and the Gill and Manhas families.

Last but not the least I would like to acknowledge the people whose love has sustained me the most through the years of research and writing. I am indebted to my parents, Raji and Sukhjindar Singh, for too many reasons to list. Of the many things they have taught me, I hope the one lesson I have learned well is to never stop believing. I thank Navneet for being there through good times and bad, and for reading and responding to much of what I write. A special thank you to Arshia for the wonderful little notes and pictures she left on my desk on days I needed them most.

Glossary

Adivasi	Resident since earliest times, original inhabitant
Adivasi Maha Sabha	Adivasi Grand Assembly
Adivasi Samara Samithi	Adivasi Struggle Committee
Adivasi Samrakshana Samithi	Adivasi Protection Council
Anganwadi	Derived from the Hindi word *angan*, which means courtyard, *Anganwadi* translates as "courtyard shelter." Set up under the Integrated Child Development Services Scheme in India, *Anganwadi* centers provide basic health care to young children, offer advice on nutrition to parents, and function as preschools. *Anganwadi* workers/teachers also provide meals to children during the day.
Coca-Cola Viruddha Janakeeya Samara Samithi	Anti–Coca-Cola People's Struggle Committee
Dharna	Sit-in agitation
Samara pandal	Protest hut or shelter
Sirkar	The word generally refers to the government or a person in a position of authority.

1

Introduction

1.1. INTRODUCTION

Just write it as I'm telling it. You will understand.

That was eighty-six-year-old Adivasi woman Maariamma's advice to me the first, and only, time I interrupted her for a clarification while she narrated a story she had heard from her elders. Neither writing nor understanding has been easy for me. These words therefore haunted me as I struggled to do both. It is difficult to identify with any certainty when this book began to take shape, but it was most likely on a bus ride in rural Kerala in India that I started to understand some of what I present here. I was returning from a public meeting where many had spoken with passion about what is popularly known as the Plachimada Struggle.[1] As I watched the silhouettes of thatched roofs pass by in the fading light and reflected on what had been said by those who had started protests against Coca-Cola operations in the area and their many supporters, I began to understand that being the most dispossessed means much more than losing one's land and water. It is to experience an injustice that often, as in this case, goes unrecognized. This book is an attempt to identify and understand the violence of such injustice.

1.2. THE DISPUTE

In 2002 a dispute began with Adivasi protests against Hindustan Coca-Cola Beverages Private Ltd., a subsidiary of The Coca-Cola Company, in a village

[1] Plachimada is the name of one of the hamlets beside the Coca-Cola plant in Kerala and has become synonymous with the agitation against Coca-Cola.

in Kerala in south India. A *dharna*, or sit-in agitation, initiated by the Adivasis soon after the company bought 32 acres of farmland in Moolathara village and set up a beverage bottling plant in the middle of small hamlets is now in its thirteenth year. Adivasis who began objecting to the operation of the Coca-Cola plant have lived on and cultivated the farmlands in the area for generations. After some initial reluctance, and in some cases even strong opposition to Adivasi protests, other residents of the area, large farm owners, local activists, several political organizations, and civil society groups also joined in the protests. As a result of the agitations, operations in the bottling plant were suspended in 2004. The anti–Coca-Cola people's movement in Plachimada, with its focus on the excessive extraction of groundwater by Coca-Cola and the ways in which it has violated environmental and human rights of residents, has since received widespread local, national, and international support from committed activists, numerous social and religious organizations, and eventually also from the Government of Kerala.

More than a decade later, even as the litigation related to the dispute awaits final adjudication in the Supreme Court of India, and the central government disagrees with the Government of Kerala over the legality of a proposed law aimed at awarding compensation to those who suffered losses due to the operations of the beverage plant before it was closed, two Adivasi women continue to sit in protest outside the gates of the plant every day, waiting for the company to leave "their place."

The dispute continues to pose significant political and legal challenges, and much has been written about the Plachimada Struggle over the last decade in newspapers, online blogs, reports, research papers, administrative decisions, petitions, and judgments by various courts. This project began with critical questions that have not been raised in any previous engagement with the dispute: What does this dispute mean to those who started it? How do we understand the claims of the different protestors and the wrongs that they mean to draw attention to? These questions led me to a number of locations, such as the hamlets that are home to Adivasi protestors, the High Court of Kerala and the Supreme Court of India, the Kerala State Archives in Trivandrum and Ernakulum, National Archives of India in New Delhi, offices of various government departments and publications, offices of lawyers in Kerala and New Delhi, and other locations where I interviewed activists involved in the struggle against Coca-Cola.

I had set out with the hope that speaking with the protestors, their supporters, and those who claim to represent them in various capacities would offer a clearer understanding of the dispute, especially from the perspective of those who began it. I spoke at length with several Adivasis, as well as with non-Adivasi residents of the place, activists, local politicians, bureaucrats, lawyers, and judges. I found some answers, and more significantly, discovered more questions. I also found something I had not anticipated: incompleteness, uncertainty, anxiety, tears, guilt, anger, and affection. Through all of these emotions and reactions – mine and those of the people I met during my research – I have also learned to learn.

In this book I juxtapose the multiple accounts of this dispute as narrated by various people I spoke with, as well as the accounts that emerge from legal records and media reports. This juxtaposition enables a closer look at the ways in which meanings are gained and lost as Adivasi claims originating in contested, layered, histories and in the narratives of displacement and exclusion are translated into the stronger languages of social movements and the formal legal system. Many of the particular and situated meanings critical to the Adivasis' opposition to the operation of the Coca-Cola plant have been eclipsed in the accounts of their many supporters, more often than not in pursuit of justice *for* the Adivasis. Thus the purpose of this book is twofold: to demonstrate that when the Adivasi protests against Coca-Cola are understood on their own terms, in the context of their lives in the place, the meanings that emerge are quite different from the ones conveyed by the accounts of others; and to show that a recognition of this difference is important for a meaningful resolution of this dispute for the Adivasis whose lives have been most significantly affected by it.

By presenting the multiple accounts of the dispute in Plachimada, I attempt to draw attention to the violence done even before the Supreme Court of India decides the appeals before it, even before the central and state governments resolve their differences over the proposed law on compensation, and even before any claims for compensation lead to any actual money reaching the hands of any real people. These accounts reveal the injustice brought about by and through the very processes of the Adivasis' grievances being put forward for consideration, that is, in the very acts of re-presentation of their stories. Thus, regardless of which side "wins," the Adivasis who began the protests appear to have already "lost," because critical elements of what the dispute means to them have been eclipsed.

In addition to providing a deeper understanding of a particular dispute, the accounts presented here help us grasp the complex interplay of the global and the local in disputes of this nature, which are too often understood as isolated events. These stories also help us understand indigeneity in a broader context than the one offered by scholarship on states identified as settler-colonial and point to the urgent need for an interdisciplinary engagement with issues of access to justice raised by indigenous mobilization against ongoing appropriation of lands and resources. Before I turn to accounts of the dispute in Plachimada, I introduce concepts that have informed my understanding of this dispute and explain important themes that recur throughout this book.

1.3. ADIVASI

Several Adivasis I spoke with referred to themselves, as well as to each other, as "Adivasi." At times they also self-identified as "Eravalan" or "Malasar," which are two of the thirty-six communities recognized as Scheduled Tribes in the state of Kerala. For this reason perhaps, a few also self-identified simply as "ST," a reference to their membership of a Scheduled Tribe. Non-Adivasi residents of the area, local activists, politicians, and public officials almost always referred to the protestors as "Adivasi," but "Scheduled Tribe" and "tribal" were also used.

These terms – "Adivasi" and "Scheduled Tribe" – used interchangeably in everyday conversations in the country, are not, however, synonyms, but rather have distinct origins and invoke different histories.[2] The word "Adivasi" is a combination of the words "adi" and "vasi," which mean "of earliest times" and "resident" respectively, and is generally translated as "original inhabitant."[3] The phrase "Scheduled Tribes," on the other hand, refers to "tribes or tribal communities" that are explicitly identified as such in a periodically revised schedule of the Constitution of India.[4] During the debates in the Constituent Assembly, these communities were identified as "backward" and in need of "uplift" following the logic and language of the colonial administration.[5] It was felt that they had to be "developed" and "assimilated" in the new and "modern" India.[6] Inspired by this sentiment, as well as partly in response

2 See Pooja Parmar, "Undoing Historical Wrongs: Law and Indigeneity in India," *Osgoode Hall Law Journal* 49:3 (2012): 491.

3 See David Hardiman, *The Coming of the Devi: Adivasi Assertion in Western India* (Delhi: Oxford University Press, 1987), 13.

4 See *Constitution of India*, 1950, Articles 366(25) and 342.

5 These views were expressed several times during the debates of the Constituent Assembly. See Parmar, "Undoing Historical Wrongs," 505, 512–517.

6 Parmar, "Undoing Historical Wrongs," 505, 513. See also Ajay Skaria, *Hybrid Histories: Forests, Frontiers and Wildness in Western India* (New Delhi: Oxford University Press, 1999), xii. Skaria notes that "[t]he wildness of the tribe epitomized Indian backwardness, [which] had to be overcome for the nation to become modern, or simply for the nation to become." See also Nandini Sundar, *Subalterns and Sovereigns: An Anthropological History of Bastar, 1854–2006*, 2nd ed. (New Delhi: Oxford University Press, 2007).

to Adivasi demands to undo historical injustices, the Constituent Assembly approved a legal framework for the country's affirmative action policies, which include reservation of seats for members of Scheduled Tribes in educational institutions and public service employment.[7] A few laws enacted since then for preventing the commission of further "atrocities" on Scheduled Tribes, or for protecting their rights to access forests and natural resources, are also aimed at addressing some prevalent inequalities.[8]

As per the census data for 2001, 84.3 million or 8.2% of the total number of people in India are members of various recognized Scheduled Tribes.[9] In a judgment handed down in 2011, the Supreme Court of India notes that they are among the country's "most marginalized and vulnerable communities," with the everyday realities of their lives marked by a "high level of poverty, illiteracy, unemployment, disease, and landlessness."[10] This is confirmed by the latest available statistics compiled by the Ministry of Tribal Affairs: childhood mortality rates are higher among Scheduled Tribes than in any other social group in the country; a large percentage of men, women, and children suffer from "high nutritional deficiency" and are anemic; the literacy rates among these communities are much lower and school dropout rates much higher than the national averages.[11] Reports commissioned by the government as well as independent studies have repeatedly noted the connections between these conditions and processes of alienation from traditionally occupied lands, subordination of local economies, and erosion of indigenous laws and institutions.

The phrase "Scheduled Tribe" had replaced the word "aboriginal" in India's draft Constitution despite objections from Jaipal Singh, an Adivasi representative in the Constituent Assembly.[12] This "invented" phrase was preferred by the drafters of the Constitution over the word "Adivasi," which was favored by

7 See *Constitution of India*, Articles 46, 244, 244A, 330, 332, 335, 338A, and 339, and Fifth and Sixth Schedules.

8 See *Scheduled Caste and Scheduled Tribe (Prevention of Atrocities) Act*, 1989; *The Scheduled Tribes and Other Traditional Forest Dwellers (Recognition of Forest Rights) Act*, 2006; and *The Panchayat (Extension to Scheduled Areas) Act*, 1996. But see Apoorv Kurup, "Tribal Law in India: How Decentralized Administration Is Extinguishing Tribal Rights and Why Autonomous Tribal Governments Are Better," *Indigenous Law Journal* 7 (2008–2009): 87–126 for how some of these laws end up eroding traditional indigenous laws and institutions.

9 Government of India, "Census of India 2001," accessed August 3, 2014, http://www.censusindia.gov.in/Census_Data_2001/India_at_glance/scst.aspx.

10 *Kailas & Ors* v. *State of Maharashtra*, 1 *SCI* 94, (2011), para. 4.

11 Government of India, Ministry of Tribal Affairs, "Statistical Profile of Scheduled Tribes in India 2010," accessed August 3, 2014, www.tribal.nic.in, at 9, 11, 15, 18, 21, and 25.

12 See Parmar, "Undoing Historical Wrongs," 514–515. Note that some communities are still defined as "aboriginal tribes." See *The Andaman and Nicobar Islands (Protection of Aboriginal Tribes) Regulation*, 1956.

the Adivasi representative, because it was understood to provide a more "precise definition" of who the Adivasis were.[13] The word "Adivasi," it was said at the time, lacked legal specificity.[14] Consequently, the word "Adivasi" has no legal recognition in the country today. More significantly, this change serves to eclipse the histories of dispossession that Singh wanted to be acknowledged even as the legal foundations of the postcolonial nation-state were being laid.[15]

Unlike Scheduled Tribe, tribal, and Adivasi, the English word "indigenous" was not used to refer to the Adivasi protestors by anyone I interviewed, with the exception of one lawyer. Not only is the English word not commonly used in everyday conversations in India, the very "idea of indigenous peoples" is highly contested in the country.[16] While scholars continue to debate the applicability and relevance of the term "indigenous peoples" in India, raising several important questions of epistemology, history, and politics in the process,[17] the position of the permanent Indian mission to the United Nations is that the entire population of the country at the time of independence from British rule and their successors are indigenous.[18] This is a clearer articulation of the

[13] *Debates of the Constituent Assembly of India*, vol. VII (December 2, 1948) at 782.

[14] Ibid.

[15] See Parmar, "Undoing Historical Wrongs," 496–499.

[16] Virginius Xaxa, "Tribes as Indigenous Peoples of India," *Economic and Political Weekly* 34:51 (December 18–24, 1999): 3589.

[17] Scholars cite several reasons for caution in relation to the term. There are concerns over a lack of attention to particular histories of the region including the complex history of migrations into and within the subcontinent, as well as concerns over distinguishing with certainty "tribes" from other castes and communities classified by the colonial administration. Other reasons for caution include the long history of interactions and cultural exchange between various communities in the region, a questioning of colonial knowledge production and categorization, and the perceived imposition of a Western concept of "indigenous peoples." See generally Bengt G. Karlsson and T. B. Subba, eds., *Indigeneity in India* (London: Kegan Paul, 2006); Sumit Guha, *Environment and Ethnicity in India, 1200–1991* (London: Cambridge University Press, 1999); Irfan Habib, "The Formation of India: Notes on the History of an Idea," *Social Scientist* 25:7/8 (1997): 3; Virginius Xaxa, "Transformation of Tribes in India: Terms of Discourse," *Economic and Political Weekly* 34:24 (June 12, 1999): 1519. See also Kaushik Ghosh, "Between Global Flows and Local Dams: Indigenousness, Locality, and the Transnational Sphere in Jharkhand, India," *Cultural Anthropology* 21:4 (2008): 501–534. Ghosh argues that the terminologies "indigenous," "Adivasi," and "tribal" "roughly mark the transnational, national, and colonial histories through which indigenous populations have been bound to modernity" (p. 528, fn. 1). For more nuanced histories of the relations between Adivasis and non-Adivasis in particular regions of India and the ways in which colonial law and policies changed the balance of power between people categorized as "tribes" and others, see Sundar, *Subalterns and Sovereigns* and Skaria, *Hybrid Histories*.

[18] "Explanation by Mr. Randhir Jaiswal, First Secretary, on Position of India on the Report of the 9th Session of the Permanent Forum of Indigenous Issues to the ECOSOC," July 22, 2010, New York, accessed August 3, 2014, https://www.pminewyork.org/pages.php?id=997&page=5.

country's stand against recognition of any particular communities as Indigenous than that reflected in India's previous statement made at the time of its vote in favor of the UN Declaration on Rights of Indigenous Peoples in 2007.[19] Noting the long use of the word "Adivasi" to refer to particular communities in India, Xaxa associates the more recent critical examination of and opposition to the term "indigenous," which is basically an English equivalent of the Indian word, to the "internationationalisation of the rights and privileges associated with" the term "indigenous."[20]

Contests over indigeneity, or more specifically over who are Indigenous peoples, are not particular to India. The UN Declaration does not provide a definition of Indigenous Peoples even as it sets out their rights. In fact, there is no consensus among States as to whether a definition is even necessary.[21] The meaning of Indigenous Peoples and the contours of their rights are subject to fierce debates and disagreements in both international and domestic forums, driven to a considerable extent by anxieties over territorial integrity and state sovereignty.[22] Meanwhile, peoples making the claims of indigeneity continue their struggles to bring about real change in their lives and resist the accelerating destruction of their lands and livelihoods.[23] In such struggles indigeneity often emerges as a political tool.[24]

19 "Statement of Ajai Malhotra," September 13, 2007, New York. UN GA 10612, accessed August 14, 2014, http://www.un.org/News/Press/docs/2007/ga10612.doc.htm.

20 Xaxa, "Transformation of Tribes in India," 3590.

21 See Shin Imai and Kathryn Buttery, "Indigenous Belonging: A Commentary on Membership and Identity in the United Nations Declaration on the Rights of Indigenous People," in *Oxford Commentaries on International Law: A Commentary on the United Nations Declaration on the Rights of Indigenous Peoples*, eds Marc Weller and Jessie Hohmann (Oxford University Press, Forthcoming) accessed August 3, 2014, ///C:/Users/Win%207/Downloads/SSRN-id2360323.pdf, 1–3.

22 See Amelia Cook and Jeremy Sarkin, "Who Is Indigenous? Indigenous Rights Globally, in Africa, and among the San in Botswana," *Tulane Journal of International and Comparative Law* 38 (2009–2010): 93–130; Imai and Buttery, "Indigenous Belonging." In the case of India this anxiety is also reflected in its statement to the UN. See "Statement of Ajai Malhotra."

23 See Cook and Sarkin, "Who Is Indigenous?," 94–97. For complexities of determining tribal identity in the United States, see Matthew L. M. Fletcher, "Tribal Membership and Indian Nationhood," *Social Science Research Network*, accessed August 3, 2014, http://papers.ssrn.com/sol3/papers.cfm?abstract_id=2129813 and for Canada, see Pamela D. Palmater, *Beyond Blood: Rethinking Indigenous Identity* (Saskatoon: Purich Publishing Ltd., 2011).

24 Cook and Sarkin, "Who Is Indigenous?," 116. For an argument that the transnational discourse of indigeneity, when based on an essentialized idea of indigeneity, can be limiting and might even undermine local struggles, see Ghosh, "Between Global Flows and Local Dams," 501–534. On how contemporary politics of recognition might reproduce the relationships of colonial power that indigenous demands for recognition seek to transcend, see Glen Coulthard, "Subjects of Empire: Indigenous People and the Politics of Recognition in Canada," *Contemporary Political Theory* 6 (2007): 437–460.

Despite questions over the identity of the Indigenous peoples or original inhabitants of any particular region in the country, and the absence of formal legal recognition, the word "Adivasi" is widely used to refer to certain peoples in India today by "politicians, social workers, administrators and social scientists."[25] It is also a term preferred by Adivasis, for it signals "historical experiences and social consciousness [that] are markedly different from those" of other historically oppressed groups in the country, such as the *dalits*.[26] As such, it is not only a marker of a distinct identity but also an important political tool for articulating demands for empowerment and justice in the country.[27] The fact of such claim making and of actual references to certain peoples as "Adivasi" in particular locations, like Plachimada, also make its use a "social fact."[28]

In addition to the fact that the term is preferred by Adivasis themselves, I choose to use it because it allows recognition of a particular history. That is the history of "subjugation during the nineteenth century of a wide variety of communities which before the colonial period had remained free, or at least relatively free, from the controls of outside states."[29] Accounts of this subjugation do not often find a place in the official historical narratives of the postcolonial nation, and as such, the Adivasi identity can be understood as one grounded in "re-telling of the past."[30] Extending beyond the connotations of "autochthonicity" conveyed by its literal meaning, the articulation of "being Adivasi" in contemporary India is also "about shared experiences of the loss of the forests, the alienation of land, repeated displacements since independence in the name of 'development projects', and much more."[31] It is an articulation

25 Virginius Xaxa, *State, Society, and Tribes: Issues in Post-Colonial India* (New Delhi: Pearson Longman, 2008), 10. It is worth noting that the word "Adivasi" is used to refer to "tribes or tribal communities" in parts of central and south India and not to those in the northeastern states of Assam, Meghalaya, Tripura, and Mizoram. Tribes in the northeast have a different historical, political, and legal relationship to the Indian State. Tribes in that part of the country are governed by the Sixth Schedule to the Constitution of India, which also recognizes tribal areas in the region as autonomous units within the parameters of the Constitution.

26 Ibid., 5. The word "*dalit*" translates as "oppressed." Like the word "Adivasi," it invokes a particular history of oppression and subjugation of peoples once referred to as "untouchable" or the "lower castes" within the Hindu caste system.

27 See Xaxa, *State, Society, and Tribes*," 28–40.

28 Amita Baviskar, "The Politics of Being 'Indigenous,'" in Karlsson and Subba, *Indigeneity in India*, 36.

29 Hardiman, *Coming of the Devi*, 15.

30 See Stuart Hall, "Cultural Identity and Diaspora," in *Contemporary Postcolonial Theory: A Reader*, ed. Padmini Mongia (London: Arnold, 1996), 111. Hall urged that we understand identity as not one grounded in archeology, but rather in "re-telling of the past."

31 Skaria, *Hybrid Histories*, 281. See also Xaxa, "Transformation of Tribes in India," 3595.

of loss of autonomy. Understood thus, the term also refers to "a distinctive way of being outside the narratives of the Indian nation state."[32] It is a call to imagine the nation differently.[33]

As I have learned from my conversations with Adivasis in Kerala, claims to being an "original inhabitant" arise in particular contexts, in moments in time when experiences of having been wronged in a particular way in the past take on certain meanings in the face of inequalities and exclusions of the present. These claims and the injustices they seek to draw attention to can only be understood by paying attention to the complex relations rooted in layered histories of "original inhabitants," "settlers," and "outsiders" in particular locations like Plachimada, even as we acknowledge the many global connections.

1.4. LEGAL PLURALISM

Most simply, legal pluralism is the recognition of the simultaneous coexistence of multiple normative worlds, with the state being only one among other creators of legal meaning.[34] These worlds "of right and wrong, of lawful

[32] Skaria, *Hybrid Histories*, 281.

[33] See Parmar, "Undoing Historical Wrongs." Sundar has also suggested that struggles articulated as those over the choice between "backwardness" and "development" or "tradition" and "modern civilization" are better understood as struggles over different visions of democracy. Sundar, *Subalterns and Sovereigns*, front flap and p. 190.

[34] There is a vast body of literature on legal pluralism. Robert Cover's work was an important influence on my own understanding. See Robert Cover, "Nomos and Narrative," *Harvard Law Review* 97 (1983–1984): 4–68; Robert Cover, "Folktales of Justice: Tales of Jurisdiction," *The Capital University Law Review* 14 (1985): 179–203; Robert Cover, "Obligation: A Jewish Jurisprudence of the Social Order," *Journal of Law and Religion* 5 (1987): 65–74; and Robert Cover, "Violence and the Word," *Yale Law School Journal* 95:8 (1986): 1601–1629. As with any approach to law, there are numerous debates regarding the possibilities and limitations of legal pluralism. Some important work that helped me understand the early influences on the development of the concept, as well as appreciate its possibilities and limitations is: Lon Fuller, "Human Interaction and the Law," *The American Journal of Jurisprudence* 14 (1969): 1; Clifford Geertz, "Local Knowledge: Fact and Law in Comparative Perspective," in *Local Knowledge: Further Essays in Interpretive Anthropology* (New York: Basic Books, 1983); Marc Galanter, "Justice in Many Rooms: Courts, Private Ordering and Indigenous Law," *Journal of Legal Pluralism* 19 (1981): 1–47; Sally E. Merry, "Legal Pluralism," *Law and Society Review* 22 (1988): 869–896; Jeremy Webber, "Legal Pluralism and Human Agency," *Osgoode Hall Law Journal* 44 (2006): 167–198; Roderick A. MacDonald, "Custom Made – For a Non-Chirographic Critical Legal Pluralism," *Canadian Journal of Law and Society* 26 (2011): 301–327; Martha-Marie Kleinhans and Roderick A. MacDonald, "What Is *Critical* Legal Pluralism?," *Canadian Journal of Law and Society* 12 (1997): 25–46; Emmanuel Mellisaris, "The More the Merrier? A New Take on Legal Pluralism," *Social and Legal Studies* 13:1 (2004): 57–79; Gunther Teubner, "The Two Faces of Janus: Rethinking Legal Pluralism," *Cardozo Law Review* 13 (1991–1992): 1443–1462; Lauren Benton, "Beyond

and unlawful, of valid and void" are "constantly create[d] and maintain[ed]" by those who inhabit them through common understandings, rituals, language, myths, strong interpersonal obligations and commitments.[35] Histories and other common narratives are as much a part of a normative world as the formal rules and institutions of law.[36] In fact, within a normative universe, "law and narrative are inseparably related."[37] Narratives locate and give meaning to law within legal worlds.[38] Claims arise in particular legal cultures and are articulated in the languages of those specific cultures.[39] It is this understanding of inseparability of law from language and narratives that informs my understanding of the dispute in Plachimada.

In order to understand the nature of injustice experienced by those who began the protests against the operation of the Coca-Cola plant and, more critically, to understand how to meaningfully "right" those "wrongs," we have to begin by taking seriously what the protestors say, and attempt to make sense of it within all of that which comprises their normative world, including their accounts of their past, present, and future. These narratives have many forms: accounts of old and new unequal social relations, articulations of everyday experiences of injustice, stories about humans and nonhumans, personal life histories and oral histories of a community, as well as accounts of encounters with formal state law and legal institutions. All of these narratives

Legal Pluralism: Towards a New Approach to Law in the Informal Sector," *Social Legal Studies* 3 (1994): 223–242; Boaventura DeSousa Santos, "The Heterogenous State and Legal Pluralism in Mozambique," *Law and Society Review* 40 (2006): 39–76; Mitra Sharafi, "Justice in Many Rooms Since Galanter: De-Romanticizing Legal Pluralism through the Cultural Defense," *Law and Contemporary Problems* 71 (2008): 139–146. For the plurality of state-made law itself, especially in postcolonial contexts, see Merry, "Legal Pluralism," 869, and Shalini Randeria, "The State of Globalization: Legal Plurality, Over-lapping Sovereignties and Ambiguous Alliance between Civil Society and the Cunning State in India," *Theory, Culture, and Society* 24:1 (2007): 1–33.

35 Cover, "Nomos and Narrative," 4, 7, 9, 11, and 12. According to Cover, it is "the force of interpretive commitments" that not only holds together a normative universe, but also "determine[s] what law means and what law shall be" (Cover, "Nomos and Narrative," 7, and 44–60).

36 Cover, "Nomos and Narrative," 4, 5, and 19. See also Cover, "Obligation." See MacDonald, "Custom Made – For a Non-Chirographic Critical Legal Pluralism," 324, for the argument that production of formal legal rules is often an "indication of dissonance among different orders."

37 Cover, "Nomos and Narrative," 5.

38 Ibid.

39 See Cover, "Obligation," 65 for the suggestion that every "legal culture has its fundamental words" that are used to tell stories of law and justice. The example Cover used was of the word "rights" and he suggested that when we use the word "rights," we basically locate ourselves within a particular normative universe.

are relevant for understanding the normative universe of the Adivasi protestors, their claims, the meanings of their protests against Coca-Cola, and consequently, for arriving at a more meaningful resolution of the dispute for those who began it and have lost the most.

In situating this dispute in its broader social context and viewing it within the layered history of the place,[40] I have attempted to show that the stories that Adivasis tell about Coca-Cola cannot be separated from all the other stories they tell about the place, about themselves, and about their relationships with others in the place. My attempt here is to demonstrate that such narratives must be taken seriously in order to adequately understand the dispute. They are worthy of attention and respect because they offer insights into the normative world of the protestors and enable us to acknowledge their understanding of the past and their visions of future that in turn give meaning to their claims. While the focus of this project was this one dispute that began in a village in Kerala, the directions it has since taken and the insights it offers are relevant to Indigenous struggles emerging in other parts of the world.

An acknowledgment of a multiplicity of normative orders inevitably leads to questions about the manner in which these different legal orders interact, communicate, or collide.[41] My attempts to understand the dispute in Plachimada have also led me to look more closely at the interactions *between* normative worlds or traditions that offer multiple and alternative visions of a just future. These are the worlds of Adivasi protestors and their many supporters including activists, religious and social organizations, and legal professionals. I should clarify here at the outset that even as I reflect on how the perspectives of each of these have come to bear on their telling of the dispute in Plachimada, I do not treat any of these groups or the spaces they inhabit as bounded, homogenous, or unchanging, but rather as socially and historically constructed communities that are held together by common narratives and commitments at any given point of time.[42] Any consensus on commitments to particular norms

[40] See Michel Foucault, "The Subject and Power," *Critical Inquiry* 8:4 (1982): 777–795 on the significance of a historical awareness of the present and the need to examine particular context or "type of reality" in critical thought.

[41] See Teubner, "The Two Faces of Janus"; Webber, "Legal Pluralism and Human Agency"; Merry, "Legal Pluralism"; Benton, "Beyond Legal Pluralism"; Santos, "The Heterogenous State"; Randeria, "The State of Globalization"; and Cover, "Nomos and Narrative."

[42] See Akhil Gupta and James Ferguson, "Beyond 'Culture': Space, Identity and the Politics of Difference," *Cultural Anthropology* 7:1 (1992): 6–23; Nicholas K. Blomley, *Law, Space, and the Geographies of Power* (New York: Guildford Press, 1994); Susan G. Drummond, *Mapping Marriage Law in Spanish Gitano Communities* (Vancouver: UBC Press, 2006); and Galanter, "Justice in Many Rooms," 12.

within distinct communities is also always a result of contestation, a continuous ongoing process in any place.[43]

We are all familiar with the scenario where norms generated by different communities (including the State) compete for validation by courts – the formal institutional sites of such contestation and norm generation. Courts, as we know, choose certain narratives over others. This suppression of certain visions of law and the worlds it can create by courts led Cover to describe courts of the State as "jurispathic" even as he acknowledged that the "exiled narratives" – the ones that are not chosen – continue to "provide the normative bases" for distinct legal interpretations.[44] While moments of *collision* between multiple legal worlds in courts or other forums are certainly worthy of careful attention for understanding law, there are other moments of communication that are equally important. These are the moments of translation, linguistic slippages, and miscommunication between inhabitants of the various normative worlds – moments of strategizing, of receiving, framing, and naming claims – that precede the presentation of the various narratives for validation.[45]

Understanding these imperfect encounters between different normative worlds requires us to examine closely not only the narratives of the Adivasis who began the protests, and the courts that have so far handed down their decisions on the dispute, but also those of the many supporters and representatives of the Adivasi protestors. These multiple narratives drew my attention to the processes and practices of speaking, telling, listening, and re-telling by inhabitants of different normative worlds that precede and shape that final presentation of narratives. These are the processes and practices of translation that take place prior to, in anticipation of, or in preparation for that final presentation to those from whom a response is sought – a court of law, a State, an international forum, or a community.

1.5. TRANSLATION

The concept of translation is a useful one to understand the practices and processes that enable both the creation as well as the destruction of meanings

[43] See for example Webber, "Legal Pluralism and Human Agency," 182. Webber describes the process as one of "narrowing down of normative options."

[44] Cover "Nomos and Narrative", 40.

[45] For the importance of paying attention to the emergence and transformation of disputes, see William L. F. Felstiner, Richard L. Abel, and Austin Sarat, "The Emergence and Transformation of Disputes: Naming, Blaming, Claiming...," *Law and Society Review* 15:2–3 (1980–1981): 631–654.

as people inhabiting one normative universe receive, interpret, reorder, and re-present claims that arise in and are informed by legal cultures different from their own. It is a concept that offers a better understanding of how and why the most important elements of the dispute in Plachimada from the perspective of Adivasis are eclipsed as their various supporters continue to represent them. When presented with a different focus and emphasis, the Adivasis' stories and experiences of having been wronged are transformed into claims that hold little meaning for them.[46]

Translations – both literal and conceptual – facilitate communications across differences. Translation is not, however, a simple transference of information from one language to another, but rather, an attempt to bridge difference.[47] In a world of unequal languages, it is also often a "process of power."[48] Although translation of a particular experience into a recognized category of violation or "rights-talk" can sometimes be enabling,[49] when practiced as decontextualization, translation can also be an experience of loss.[50] The

[46] See Homi Bhabha, "The Voice of the Dom: Retrieving the Experience of the Once-Colonized," *Times Literary Supplement* (August 8, 1997) 14. In this brief review, Bhabha specifically mentions the fate of "the Dom" in an account by H. P. Foster as follows: "The Dom is left both culturally untranslated and legally unrepresented; he becomes voiceless in the very process in which he is supposedly spoken for, struck dumb by the State's claim to represent him." The Dom's "right to representation is literally lost in the practice of translation."

[47] Naoki Sakai, "Translation," *Theory Culture Society* 23 (2006): 71–86.

[48] Talal Asad, "The Concept of Cultural Translation in British Social Anthropology," in *Writing Culture: The Poetics and Politics of Ethnography*, eds. James Clifford and George E. Marcus (Berkeley: University of California Press, 1986), 148. See also Sally Engle Merry, "Transnational Human Rights and Local Activism: Mapping the Middle," *American Anthropologist* 108: 1 (2006): 40 for the argument that translation "takes place within fields of unequal power."

[49] See Sally Engle Merry and Rachel E. Stern, "The Female Inheritance Movement in Hong Kong: Theorizing the Local/Global Interface," *Current Anthropology* 46:3 (June 2005): 387–410.

[50] For the loss of meaning and intent of an original text in a translation that fails to pay attention to the former's specificities, see Gayatri Spivak, "Politics of Translation," in *The Translation Studies Reader*, ed. Lawrence Venuti (London: Routledge, 2000), 397–416. See also Gayatri Spivak, "Can the Subaltern Speak?," in *Marxism and the Interpretation of Culture*, eds. Cary Nelson and Lawrence Grossberg (Chicago: University of Illinois Press, 1987), 271–313. For the loss in meaning as social conflicts are translated into legal disputes through processes of legal abstraction and decontextualization, see Elizabeth Mertz, *The Language of the Law School: Learning to "Think Like a Lawyer"* (Oxford: Oxford University Press, 2007) and Elizabeth Mertz, "Teaching Lawyers the Language of Law: Legal and Anthropological Translations," *John Marshall Law Review* 34 (2000–2001): 91–117. See also Zenon Bankowski and Geoff Mungham, *Images of Law* (London: Routledge Direct Editions, 1976); Maureen Cain, "The General Practice Lawyer and the Client: Towards a Radical Conception," *International Journal of the Sociology of Law* 7(1979): 335; Maureen Cain, "The Symbol Traders," in *Lawyers in a Postmodern World: Translation and Transgression*, eds. Maureen Cain and Christine B. Harrington (Buckingham: Open University Press, 1994), 15–48; Christine B.

inequality in the power of languages and knowledges often enables the dominant languages to name violations, and in the process, appropriate and reorder narratives.[51] It is this difference in languages that belong to different normative worlds, the inequalities in the authority to speak and name, and the relationship of all of this to questions of justice and injustice, which the multiple stories I present here draw attention to.

It is in this context that I focus on the role of translators, especially that of committed social activists who continue to work tirelessly to ensure the dispute is not forgotten and the lawyers who are working to secure a just outcome in the litigation.[52] These are the people who have in many ways shaped the popular and legal accounts of the dispute. The stories they tell are framed in languages that are familiar to them and, more critically, are languages they often share with, and know will be recognized by their target audiences or those who will hear and respond to the claims.[53] Their strategic decisions and

Harrington, "Outlining a Theory of Legal Practice," in Cain and Harrington, *Lawyers in a Postmodern World*, 49–69.

51 See Jacques Derrida, *Monolingualism of the Other or the Prethesis of Origin* (Stanford, CA: Stanford University Press, 1996), 30; Asad, "The Concept of Cultural Translation"; Masamichi Inoue, "Comments," in Merry and Stern, "The Female Inheritance Movement," 387–409; Maria Tymoczko, "Translation in Oral Tradition as a Touchstone for Translation Theory and Practice," in *Translation, History and Culture*, eds. Susan Bassnett and Andre Lefevere (London: Pinter Publishers, 1990), 46–55; Couze Venn, "Translation: Politics and Ethics," *Theory Culture Society* 23 (2006): 82–84; Susan Bassnett and Andre Lefevere, "Introduction," in Bassnett and Lefevere, *Translation, History and Culture*; Piotr Kuhiwczac, "Translation as Appropriation: The Case of Milan Kundera's 'The Joke,'" in Bassnett and Lefevere, *Translation, History and Culture*; Michael Quigley, "Language of Conquest, Language of Survival," *The Canadian Forum* 52:723 (1982): 14–15; Spivak, "Politics of Translation." For reordering of narratives through and by the language of formal state law, see Mertz, *The Language of the Law School*. For the violence of this "transformation" of a narrative of "real historical experience" into a narrative of "abstract legality," see Ranajit Guha, "Chandra's Death," in *Subaltern Studies V: Writings on South Asian History and Society*, ed. Ranajit Guha (Delhi: Oxford University Press, 1987), 135–165. See also Shahid Amin, "Approver's Testimony, Judicial Discourse: The Case of Chauri-Chaura," in Guha, *Subaltern Studies V*, 166–202.

52 For lawyers as translators see Cain, "The Symbol Traders,"15–48; Harrington, "Outlining a Theory of Legal Practice," 49–69. See also James B. White, *Justice as Translation: An Essay in Cultural and Legal Criticism* (Chicago, IL: University of Chicago Press, 1990), 261. For the role of activists as translators who work within "established discursive fields that constrain the repertoire of ideas and practices available to them," see Merry, "Legal Pluralism," 40. See also Merry and Stern, "The Female Inheritance Movement," 387–409. For a particularly harsh view of the role of activists as "epistemic brokers" see Ronald J. Herring, *Epistemic Brokers, Authoritative Knowledge, and a Diffusion of Opposition to Biotechnology* (Cambridge: Cambridge University Press, 2010) and Ronald J. Herring, "Persistent Narratives: Why Is the 'Failure of Bt Cotton in India' Story Still with Us?," *AgBioForum* 12: 1 (2009): 14–22.

53 See Cain "The General Practice Lawyer and the Client," 335, 343. Cain describes lawyers (and judges) as both translators, as well as the "creators of the language into which they translate."

practices here are no different from translators of literary texts who strive to meet the expectations or the requirements of the "target culture/language."[54] Such are the practices of translation that I draw attention to.

My interest in and concerns over translation are, however, more personal than what may be evident from what I have said about it so far, and it is to my own role as a translator that I now turn. This is important for several reasons: my successes and failures in translating inform what I have written; the fact of my translation will inform your reading; and most crucially, all that I have learned in learning to translate and re-present has helped me think about law and justice in particular ways.

1.6. TELLING OTHER PEOPLES' STORIES

From the time I first conceived of this project as one involving long interviews with protestors and others connected to the dispute, I was concerned about issues that might arise in translation of Adivasi accounts that are central to this project. I do not speak any of the languages of the Adivasis and other residents of the area, and they do not speak any of mine.[55] The interviews in the village had to be (and were) conducted through an interpreter. What added to my concern was that most ethnographic accounts I studied to prepare for this research did not offer any advice in this regard.[56] In fact for a long time

They do not, however, translate into any language, but into "a meta-language in terms of which a binding solution can be found," a translation into the language of formal state law.

54 References to "source" and "target" cultures and languages are common in the body of scholarship referred to as Translation Studies. See for example Bassnett and Lefevere, "Introduction." For reference to reinterpretation of "source terms" so as to make them compatible with the "target discourse," see Derek Boothman, "Critique and Semantic Modification in Gramsci's Approach to Paradigmatic Translation," *Italian Culture* 24–25 (2006–2007): 118. For translators' attempts to meet the "expectations of the receptor culture," see Tymoczko, "Translation in Oral Tradition," 46–55. For "translation as appropriation" in order to meet the demands of the culture and language into which narrative is translated, see Kuhiwczac, "Translation as Appropriation."

55 The residents of Plachimada and neighboring hamlets speak Malayalam and Tamil. Adivasis also speak what appears to be a mix of the two but contains words that do not belong to either. They refer to this as their own language.

56 The one account I read that helped me understand the difference made by the identity and location of an interpreter vis-à-vis the community that comprises a researcher's "field" was published in 1962. See Gerrald D. Berreman, *Behind Many Masks: Ethnography and Impression Management in a Himalayan Village* (New York: Society for Applied Anthropology, 1962). For an early debate on the necessity of learning the "native language," see Margaret Mead, "Native Languages as Fieldwork Tools," *American Anthropologist* 41:2 (1939): 189 and Robert H. Lowie, "Native Languages as Ethnographic Tools," *American Anthropologist* 42:1 (1940): 81. I am grateful to Lawrence Rosen and Graham M Jones for bringing these two references to my notice.

I believed that researchers, especially anthropologists, never went into "the field" without learning local languages.[57] I was convinced about the importance of speaking with the protestors in order to better understand the dispute, but I agonized over my inability to converse with them directly. I may have given up had it not been for some very helpful conversations with other more experienced researchers.[58]

In Kerala I learned about interpreters who had assisted other researchers during visits to Plachimada, but I had some concerns about working with them given the different focus and approach of the other projects. I also wanted to avoid working with anyone who had a fixed idea about what the dispute in Plachimada is about. That, I realized quickly, was not going to be easy, as most people I met in Kerala "knew" what "Plachimada" was all about, even though opinions varied. As I considered my options, I met Shiny while visiting a friend. Even before I knew she was fluent in both Malayalam and Tamil, loved to travel, and would never complain about long bone-rattling bus rides, I knew I wanted to work with her because she had many questions about my project and about Plachimada. I was thrilled when she agreed to work with me. Like me, Shiny too brought to our conversations her prior knowledge, beliefs, ways of thinking about the world, and about people and events. But she was also open to listening, being questioned, and revising her opinions. That was most helpful as we constantly discussed our conversations and experiences in the hamlets, and transcribed the interviews together. Although the transcription took much longer because of this, it allowed me to understand not only what was said but also why she translated certain words and phrases differently at different times.

It was during one of these conversations that I learned that she translated the word "*samaram*" as "struggle" during our first few conversations in the village because I had been using the word. She had believed that was how my research required it to be translated. Had she not heard me use the English word repeatedly, she would have also translated the word as "strike" or "protest," which was a more suitable translation in some contexts. This and other such insights into the practices of translation thus became an unexpected reward for the many long hours we spent transcribing the interviews.

57 The fact that anthropologists in fact do work with interpreters, but do not often write about their experiences is acknowledged in Axel Borchgrevink, "Silencing Language: Of Anthropologists and Interpreters," *Ethnography* 4:1 (2003): 95–121.

58 I am especially thankful to Wesley Pue, Karin Mickelson, Renisa Mawani, Lawrence Rosen, and Laurie Patton.

In order to further minimize the loss of meaning and attain a deeper understanding, I have also tried to combine care in translation and transcription of narratives with attention to particular stories people choose to tell, the words they use to narrate their experiences and articulate their claims, the willingness to share certain fears and hopes, and decisions to not speak about certain things.[59]

Translation of unfamiliar stories narrated in unfamiliar languages into a familiar language does not, however, automatically lead to comprehension of lifeworlds. As Piya, a character in Amitav Ghosh's novel *The Hungry Tide*, observes, speech "was only a bag of tricks that fooled you into believing that you could see through the eyes of another being."[60] Humans, Ghosh tells us through his characters, have to make an effort to communicate in "our translated world."[61] Here Ghosh's reference is not simply to barriers posed by the existence of multiple languages in the human world, but our inability to see and experience the world as does another human being, living a different life. Ghosh's story is however, not merely about barriers to communication but also about communications that are possible between humans, and between humans and nonhumans, despite the limitations of language, translation, and understanding.

Acutely aware of my linguistic limitations, I also tried to be attentive to nonverbal modes of communication – a smile, a twinkle in the eyes, a shrug, a straightening of the back, a frown, a cautious glance in a particular direction, lowering of voices, and the silences. When understood in the context of all these, translated words can convey a lot more. But sometimes, we do not actually need words to communicate. I had an opportunity to reflect on this on a quiet afternoon in the samara pandal (protest hut) when Maya, a young Adivasi woman, suddenly asked me if I had spoken to my daughter the night before. She asked if my daughter cries when I call. On another afternoon, as I watched some toddlers playing nearby, she asked to see again a picture of my daughter she had seen before. It was passed around to other women present and many remarks were made and questions asked.

Both times I had in fact been thinking about my daughter when Maya mentioned her. I was stunned because I had not said anything. How could Maya have known that I was missing my child at that moment? Her response to the

[59] See Marjorie DeVault, *Liberating Method: Feminism and Social Research* (Philadelphia, PA: Temple University Press, 1999), 91 for listening "around and beyond words."

[60] Amitav Ghosh, *The Hungry Tide* (Boston, MA: Houghton Mifflin, 2006), 132.

[61] Ibid., 172.

question in my eyes was a smile. I could have spoken out the question, but I did not. At the time that communication had seemed enough to me. I have often wondered if she knew because perhaps she too thought about her two little children on quiet afternoons when they were away at school.

It may not always be possible to "see" the world as the other does or to re-present accurately what one does manage to see. But it is always possible to try. Sometimes communication across difference is also made possible by honest commitments to translate. According to Spivak, an ethical translation is an "act of hearing-to-respond."[62] It involves "listening with care and patience."[63] What we need therefore are "thick translations," attentive to reasons, motives, and histories of speakers *and* translators, and to the contexts of translation.[64] It is in this spirit of "trying to be faithful to the original" that I listened intently to all that was shared with me.[65] I have also reminded myself repeatedly of my own role as a translator even as I wrote about similar roles of others.

1.7. TRANSLATION AND JUSTICE

Anyone who speaks two or more languages must know that translation is never perfect.[66] There is always that particular expression that defies translation, an idea or a joke that is so rooted in a particular place, time, context, and history that its meaning and essence cannot be fully conveyed to those unfamiliar with those places, times, contexts, and histories even though it is possible to find in the language of translation words that have the same or similar meanings as the words in the source language. Much has been written about the difficulties of literal, conceptual, and cultural translations.[67] The difficulties

[62] Gayatri Spivak, "Translation as Culture," *Parallax* 6:1 (2000): 22.

[63] Ibid., 22. Spivak also mentions the "impatience of human rights interventions" as an example of failure of translation (Spivak, "Translation as Culture,"16).

[64] See Kwame Anthony Appiah, "Thick Translation," in Venuti, *Translation Studies Reader*, 432. See also Sakai, "Translation"; Bassnett and Lefevere, "Introduction," 11.

[65] See Spivak, "Politics of Translation,"14, where Spivak notes that "fidelity to the original" in any translation is something she believes in, "not because it is possible, but because one must try," pointing thereby to the significance of ethics in the practice of translation.

[66] For difficulties in translation and for the significance of context in translation, see Jacques Derrida, "Force of Law: The Mystical Foundation of Authority," *Cardozo Law Review* 11 (1989–1990): 925. Derrida notes that a translation "necessarily remains a translation," that is, "an always possible but always imperfect compromise between two idioms." See also Jacques Derrida, "Letter to a Japanese Friend," in *Derrida and Difference*, eds. David Wood and Robert Bernasconi (Warwick: Parousia Press, 1985), 1–5.

[67] Walter Benjamin, "Task of the Translator: An Introduction to the Translation of Baudelaire's *Tableux Parisiens*," trans. Harry Zohn, in Venuti, *Translation Studies Reader*, 75; Spivak, "Can the Subaltern Speak?"; Spivak "Translation as Culture"; Derrida, "Force of Law," 925; Asad, "The Concept of Cultural Translation"; Sakai, "Translation."

of translation, however, are not only the difficulties of transferring meaning but also the trouble we have in accepting the process of translation for what it is: imprecise, imperfect, and provisional, and our impatience with the imprecision and imperfection.[68] The problem with translation is our refusal to acknowledge that we do not all speak the same language and that in trying to translate, that is, communicate across difference, we often want to forget that we *are* in fact translating and that our language may not be able to represent fully what is expressed in a different language.

What does all of this have to do with justice? In thinking about the dispute in Plachimada and its various accounts shared with me, my thoughts invariably turned to translation and justice. These chains of thought, separate at first, converged at some point on the realization that both, in different ways, involved a coming to terms with incommensurability of difference and a simultaneous desire to overcome that difference. A meaningful understanding of both requires accepting the fact that both processes are imperfect, imprecise, context-driven and contingent even as we strive for perfection, precision, and certainty.

All possibility of justice, according to Derrida, lies in being able to "address oneself to the other in the language of the other."[69] The very fact of the otherness of the "other," however, requires us to think about translation. In *Justice as Translation*, James White suggested that justice, like translation, is a "form of talk," and that both acquired meaning in the context of specific communications and in the relations – connections as well as discontinuities – between languages and communities.[70] He saw much in the practice and process of translation that could in fact serve as "a model of law and justice."[71] The failure we experience in an attempt to translate, according to him, is a "necessary and instructive experience" because it is in trying to translate that we learn to recognize and respect the "other," even as we often "assert ourselves and our own languages" in relation to the other.[72] This experience of failure can, however, only be instructive if it is acknowledged.

[68] See Benjamin, "Task of the Translator," 17, 19. See also Tymoczko, "Translation in Oral Tradition," 46–55. Tymoczko suggests that the desire for "exactitude" and "objectivity" in translation is recent in human history and correlates with the general movement away from oral to text-based standards.

[69] Derrida, "Force of Law," 925. He further notes that this is not really possible, because we cannot in fact speak the language of the other.

[70] White, *Justice as Translation*, xiv, 229.

[71] Ibid., 230.

[72] Ibid. xvii. This is similar to Derrida's description of translation as an "experience of the impossible," and the connection he makes between translation and justice. See Derrida, "Force of Law," 925.

Just like desire for objective, timeless, and perfect translations of literary texts requires the invisibility of the translator, focus on objectivity and abstraction in legal processes diverts our attention from the roles of the authors of legal texts. It is indeed the invisibility of the translator that gives these texts their authority. Translation of human conflicts into legal disputes is a useful process that allows a court to recognize and respond to a claim. But this also leads to a belief that the translated story represents the entirety of the conflict. It leads to an unexamined assumption that the language of translation is fully able to represent all that was expressed in the source language.

It is only by accepting the limitations of one's own language to fully represent experiences and violations that originate in a language that belongs to and is informed by a different worldview, however, can we experience the impossibility that is a precondition for recognizing and respecting the "other." This is an experience of failure that, in its "potential to release us momentarily from the prison of our own ways of thinking and being,"[73] opens up the possibility of expanding our language as we try to understand and respond to other people's stories. It is only such moments of freedom from our "everyday habits of thought" that allow us to comprehend the multiplicity of lifeworlds that are "irreducibly not-one."[74]

It is with a similar hope that I draw attention to the practices of speaking, telling, listening, and re-telling that have shaped the various accounts of the dispute in Plachimada. When examined closely, these often overlooked critical moments of translation can be deeply unsettling for what they reveal – not only about the stories told and untold but also about the translators. They often expose an inability to listen, an arrogant unquestioned belief in some knowledges, the inadequacy of certain languages, and many unexamined habits of thought. An examination of such practices and processes of translation can offer critical insights into the many failures to respond highlighted here.

1.8. SOME NOTES ON RESEARCH METHODOLOGY AND METHODS

In placing the accounts of the Adivasis who started the protests against Coca-Cola at the center of my understanding of the dispute, I have followed the approach of those who seek to privilege experiences that have traditionally been marginalized within studies of societies, histories, and law.[75] My attempts

73 White, *Justice as Translation*, 257.

74 See Dipesh Chakrabarty, *Provincializing Europe: Postcolonial Thought and Historical Difference* (Princeton: Princeton University Press, 2000), 249.

75 For the ways in which "starting thought" from the lives of marginalized peoples might "generate illuminating critical questions that do not arise in thought that begins from dominant

to learn "from below" are influenced by my readings in Subaltern Studies, social history, postcolonial, feminist, and Indigenous scholarship, and Third World Approaches to International Law. My intellectual debts to these bodies of scholarship are signaled throughout the manuscript – in the text, in the many footnotes and references, and certainly in the ways I understand the dispute.

Not everyone may, however, be convinced of the usefulness of this interdisciplinary approach. One question that I have been asked several times during the course of this research and at conferences and other places by lawyers, officers of courts, law students, concerned friends, and others is about what specific "law" I meant to study or propose. Two social activists I interviewed were clearly disappointed that despite my legal training, I did not plan to use this opportunity to propose a new law. Although proposals for newer and better laws serve extremely useful purposes, questions such as the ones posed to me are often based on a narrow positivistic understanding of law and its separateness from other fields of knowledge. That they should continue to be raised both by those who are "inside" and "outside" law, despite the existence of substantial work that challenges these borders,[76] only points to the critical continuing importance of scholarship that attempts to understand law and legal processes in a broader context.

One conversation that I was most troubled and inspired by took place after I had presented my work in a law school. Three bright students of law, involved in the "law and society" group in their law school, and clearly committed to social justice (and much to my delight also familiar with the events in Plachimada), remained unconvinced about the necessity of speaking to "villagers." Their position was similar to that of others who had advised me

group lives," see Sandra Harding, "Rethinking Standpoint Epistemology: What Is Strong Objectivity?," in *Feminist Perspectives on Social Research*, eds. Sharlene N. Hesse-Biber and Michelle Yaiser (New York: Oxford, 2004), 45.

[76] See especially Margaret Davies, *Asking the Law Question* (Sydney: Law Book Co., 1994) for a critical questioning of the inside and outside of law. See also Margaret Davies, "The Ethos of Pluralism," *Sydney Law Review* 27 (2005): 89 for a suggestion that a pluralistic approach to law leads to better understanding of the "nature and limits of law in its conventional sense" as well as how law relates to "the social, political and moral spheres of life." See further Boaventura De Sousa Santos, *Towards a New Legal Common Sense: Law Globalization and Emancipation*, 2nd ed. (London: Butterworths, 2002); Robert M. Rich, "Sociological Paradigms and the Sociology of Law: An Overview," in *The Sociology of Law: A Conflict Perspective*, eds. Charles E. Reasons and Robert M. Rich (Toronto: Butterworths, 1978>). For the ways in which critical legal studies and feminist legal theory have challenged the separation of the political and the social, see Hillary Charlesworth, "The New Jurisprudences," in *Beyond the Disciplines: The New Humanities*, ed. K. K. Ruthven (Canberra: Australian Academy of the Humanities, 1992), 121–134.

to put my training to better use and focus on what was really important: How existing law can be better interpreted or which new legislation was needed. They were confident that "we" *know* what the dispute is about. In order to ensure justice for those who have suffered, we need to look at "the law," and how it can be made better. That is undoubtedly a very important exercise. I failed, however, to convince them of the importance of a prior question that I was pursuing: *Do* we know what the dispute is about? I hope the stories I present here show the importance of paying attention to *how* we know, and in what ways in failing to doubt our knowledge we limit our abilities to listen and respond. These insights are essential for understanding both the potential and limits of law and formal legal processes.

This multimethod project was designed to include a combination of qualitative research methods, such as long ethnographic interviews, recording oral histories, stories, participant observation, and analysis of texts.[77] Interviews with those who began the protests and those who support it are central to my understanding of the dispute and the processes of translation involved. Accordingly, most of my time during the six months I spent in Kerala and New Delhi was spent speaking with people. I had identified some themes and prepared a preliminary list of questions for each group of people I intended to interview, but I abandoned my lists soon after the first interview began. I realized, first to my frustration and then to my delight, that not everyone was interested as much in my questions as in telling the stories they wanted to share. I also began to see how my questions could limit all that the respondents may want to say and that their responses often got me interested in questions other than those on my list. Therefore, even the conversations recorded as "interviews" were not

[77] For the usefulness of long ethnographic interviews when one's focus is more on "shared meanings rather than individual affective states," on how long interviews create opportunities for recording and analyzing "the categories and logic" by which the interviewee "sees the world" and allow us to glimpse the lifeworld of an individual, see Grant McCracken, *The Long Interview* (New Delhi: Sage Publications, 1988), 7, 9, and 34. This method is also considered suitable for projects such as mine, where the researcher is not in a position to commit to "intimate, repeated, and prolonged involvement in the life and community" of the participants. For the usefulness of participant observation in ethnographic interviewing, see James P. Spradley, *The Ethnographic Interview* (New York: Holt, Rinehart and Winston, 1979). On ways in which life histories offer a deeper understanding of how individuals are "situated within networks concerning kinship, family, and community," all of which shapes the context in which people articulate particular claims, see Anne Griffiths, "Doing Ethnography: Living Law, Life Histories, and Narratives from Botswana," in *Practicing Ethnography in Law: New Dialogues, Enduring Methods*, eds. June Starr and Mark Goodale (New York: Palgrave Macmillan, 2002), 163.

structured or restricted by my questions but were open-ended. The lengths of these conversations varied from half an hour to several hours over days and months.

Of the eighteen residents of Plachimada and nearby hamlets who agreed to be interviewed for this project, fourteen identified as Adivasi, one as a member of a Scheduled Caste, two as members of a Hindu community included in the Other Backward Class category in Kerala, and one as Muslim.[78] I also interviewed two teachers who teach in government run preschools (known as anganwadis) in the hamlets.[79] These interviews were, in many cases, followed by many more conversations over the three months during which I lived in Palakkad town and visited the hamlets near the Coca-Cola plant almost every weekday, a few weekends, and holidays. I also interviewed six activists, six lawyers, two judges, two politicians, two government officers, and one former member of the local *panchayat* (village council). Conversations with others in the village, lawyers, a judge, few other officers of courts, and public officials in Kerala and New Delhi also added to my understanding of the dispute and proceedings.

Although many of those who agreed to be interviewed gave me permission to publish their names, I have decided to change all names (except that of deceased Adivasi leader Mylamma) in order to protect the identities and interests of several who may have to face, at the very least, the ire of those who disagree with what was shared with me. Some experiences in and around Plachimada that I have related in subsequent chapters also indicate that for some the consequences could be more serious than the disapproval of their peers. Due to the extensive media coverage of the dispute, especially in Kerala, identities of some individuals I have mentioned or quoted cannot be

[78] Other Backward Classes are groups of people classified as such by the Government of India based on certain socioeconomic criteria. For more information, see the Backward Classes Bureau under the Ministry of Social Justice and Empowerment, http://socialjustice.nic.in/aboutdivision4.php, accessed August 4, 2014; the National Commission for Backward Classes, http://www.ncbc.nic.in/, accessed August 4, 2014; and the National Backward Classes Finance & Development Corporation http://www.nbcfdc.org.in/main.html, accessed August 4, 2014.

[79] Derived from the Hindi word "*angan*," which means courtyard, *anganwadi* is translated as "courtyard shelter." Set up under the Integrated Child Development Services Scheme in India, *Anganwadi* centers provide basic health care to young children, offer advice on nutrition, and function as preschools. The teachers and their helpers in *Anganwadis* maintain records of births and deaths in the area and keep track of vaccination and other health requirements of young children. In addition to lunch and a snack provided to children who attend these preschools, specially packaged nutrition balanced foods for new mothers and toddlers are also distributed free of cost at these centers.

concealed effectively. I have, however, made an attempt to ensure anonymity to the extent possible.

While in Kerala, I also attended four public events. The first of these was a rally organized on August 25, 2009 outside the offices of the district administration (referred to as the Collectorate) in Palakkad town. A prominent local activist connected with the agitation in Plachimada spoke at this rally where numerous demands were presented on behalf of members of Scheduled Tribes and Scheduled Castes in Kerala. Two that were repeated numerous times and were also displayed on placards related to demands for reservation of prescribed spots in government-aided private educational institutions for members of these communities and for waiver of certain loans. The second was a meeting held on September 25, 2009 near Plachimada. This meeting was attended by Adivasi and a few non-Adivasi residents, mainly women. An officer of the local groundwater department and a visiting member of a government-appointed committee addressed the meeting. The third was a *gram sabha* (village assembly) meeting in Vijaynagar on October 7 that was attended by many Adivasi and non-Adivasi residents. At the meeting, names of successful applicants for various government loans were announced. The fourth event was a large public meeting on October 9, 2009 near the office of the Perumatty Panchayat (village council) called by the High Power Committee constituted by the Government of Kerala to examine the issue of compensation for those affected by the operations of the Coca-Cola plant. Adivasi and non-Adivasi residents of the area, as well as many activists, journalists, officers in the local administration, and members of several nongovernmental organizations attended this meeting. I learned much from the speeches and silences at these events.

Various texts also offered me a significant opportunity to understand the processes of translation. Some of these were archival records in the state archives in Kerala and New Delhi. Accessing court records of the litigation related to the dispute was more of a challenge than I had originally anticipated. Although my request for access was denied in the High Court of Kerala, I was allowed to look at some files in the Supreme Court of India on the condition that I do not publish the contents. I therefore used that opportunity primarily to note some important dates and names as well as to corroborate some information found elsewhere. Lawyers and activists provided most of the information about petitions and proceedings before courts. Records available in the office of Perumatty Panchayat and some government offices in Thiruvananthapuram were also an invaluable source.

I also studied a large number of media reports on events in Plachimada. Although many of these are available in the online English editions of national newspapers, I also collected important reports and analyses published in Malayalam. This material, and my conversations with those who translated them for me, also offered many insights that I would otherwise have missed. I also read several reports published by various government and nongovernmental organizations on the issue.

1.9. ORGANIZATION OF CHAPTERS

The following chapters present the available and eclipsed accounts of the dispute in Plachimada as well as the contexts and histories that are crucial for a fuller understanding of the dispute. The themes of plurality of normative worlds, narratives that give meaning to claims that emerge from these worlds, the potential and impossibilities of translation, questions of epistemology, the realities of "being Adivasi" in contemporary India, and the significance of all this to justice will emerge as the stories unfold. Before I present the multiple accounts of the dispute, I begin with an introduction to the place where it originated, situating it within the layered history of the region and its people in Chapter 2. Various communities who live in the area are introduced here, followed by a brief description of significant early events and overview of major subsequent developments. The histories presented in this chapter are based on available written histories. Other histories of the place, not always recognized as that, relationships of its people with the land, water, and with each other, connections with other places and people, as well as detailed accounts of specific aspects of the dispute emerge in the following chapters. This chapter shows why a meaningful resolution of such a dispute over water requires that it be understood within a wider context.

Chapter 3 presents the popular accounts of the dispute generally referred to as the Plachimada Movement or Plachimada Struggle. On the basis of interviews with non-Adivasi activists involved in the protests as well as analysis of reports and articles published in English and in the local language Malayalam, Chapter 3 highlights the concerns and commitments that underlie the immense support received by the Adivasi protestors over the years. The chapter also indicates how the commitments and strategies of various translators have shaped the powerful, popular understanding of the dispute.

Chapter 4 presents the official legal accounts of the dispute in Plachimada narrated by litigants and their lawyers as well as those found in the documents produced for or by courts. A closer look at the legal battles offers an opportunity to examine the processes and practices of legal translations as the specific and situated is re-presented and reorganized in accordance with the language, logic, concerns, and demands of a formal legal system. These accounts offer an opportunity to understand law's failure to respond in cases such as this one.

The two chapters that follow offer the accounts that have been thus far excluded from the available popular and legal narratives of the dispute. Based primarily on interviews with Adivasis in the village, Chapter 5 offers unexplored ways of understanding the Adivasis' opposition to the operation of Coca-Cola, as well as the reasons for their dissatisfaction with the popular movement. Chapter 6 presents a critical analysis of a litigation that emerged from the broader Adivasi struggle for restoration of alienated lands in Kerala. The Adivasi encounters with formal State law presented here alongside Adivasi oral histories and narratives of loss, displacement, and hope reveal yet another imperfect encounter between different normative worlds. They also offer an important opportunity to understand what lies at the heart of Adivasi movements, question the assumptions of lawyers, judges, activists, and policy makers about such disputes, and open up possibilities for further meaningful engagement with Adivasi perspectives.

1.10. "JUST WRITE IT AS I'M TELLING IT. YOU WILL UNDERSTAND"

Before turning to all the accounts of the dispute, I want to recall Maariamma's advice. I can never be sure about what exactly she wanted me to understand but I have thought about this a lot over the last few years. What I have learned is that understanding and writing all the stories I recorded is going to be a long and perhaps always an incomplete process. This lesson has been the hardest to learn, even as I continue to search for meanings in my many conversations. My inability to tie all the loose ends and smoothen the rough edges, all the experiences that I do not know how to translate into this book continue to bother me.

If I could write a novel instead, it would be about people on journeys, traveling on paths that sometimes intersect allowing them to see each other, offering a chance to acknowledge the journeys of the other in their sameness and across all the differences. If I could write a song, it would certainly be an unfinished one about incompleteness; a song of undefined incomplete connections with strangers, and incomplete inexplicable estrangement from what we imagine as ours (languages, disciplines, knowledges). Perhaps, a song about our desires to know more, even as we learn to recognize the limits of what can be known. This book is neither a song nor a novel, but it is an honest attempt to tell complex stories as best as I can. As the following chapters reveal, it is the complexity that is often eclipsed in the dominant narratives of this struggle against Coca-Cola. On some days I like to believe that is what Maariamma wanted a researcher who had so many questions to understand.

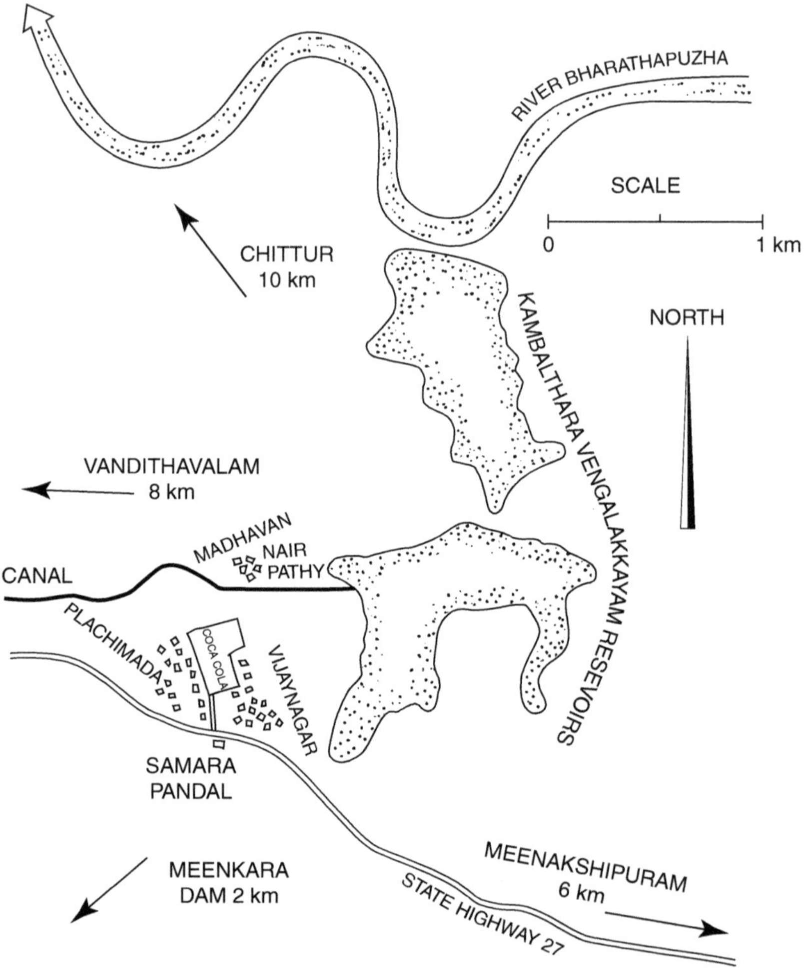

Location of the Coca-Cola beverage plant, the *samara pandal*, Plachimada, and other hamlets.

Map courtesy of Dr. Jon Corbett, University of British Columbia.

2

Locating a Dispute

In this chapter I introduce the place where the dispute began, situating it within the layered history of the region. I then briefly introduce the people who live in the area, followed by an account of how the dispute began, and an overview of major developments and events. Other histories of the place, relationships of its people with the place and with each other, connections with other places and people, as well as detailed accounts of specific aspects of the dispute will continue to emerge in the following chapters.

2.1. PLACES

2.1.1. *Plachimada*

Plachimada, the hamlet that has become synonymous with the dispute over operations of the Coca-Cola plant, is located in Moolathara village in Chittur, which is one of the five *taluks*[1] in Palakkad district of Kerala. Moolathara village is also part of Perumatty Grama Panchayat, which is one of ninety-one such elected village self-governance bodies in Palakkad district.[2] It is in Moolathara

[1] A *taluk* is an administrative subdivision in a district. Rural areas in each *taluk* or subdistrict are further divided into *panchayats* and villages for administration and revenue purposes.

[2] *Panchayat* literally means an assembly of five. *Panchayats* in India traditionally comprised elders who convened to resolve disputes in their village. Although these traditional *panchayats* still exist in some parts of the country, there is a separate contemporary constitutionally mandated system of local self-governance system referred to as the "*panchayati raj*" that was established in the country pursuant to the 73rd Amendment to the Indian Constitution. These village *panchayats*, such as the Perumatty Grama Panchayat, comprise elected members with a proportion of seats reserved for women and members of the Scheduled Tribes and Scheduled Castes. See Article 40 and Part IX of the Constitution of India for the basic legal framework, definition and composition of *panchayats*. Within this framework, state legislatures have enacted statutes that govern the functioning of *panchayats* within individual states.

that Coca-Cola decided to set up its beverage bottling plant. This decision, as it will become clear later, was a crucial one since it is Moolathara's location within the Perumatty Panchayat area that led to the Panchayat's involvement in the dispute. As set out in Chapter 5, a different *panchayat*, or a different president of the Perumatty Panchayat at the time, could have made a difference in how the litigation related to the dispute evolved, and the directions it has taken.

The road that goes from Palakkad town to Plachimada runs through miles of paddy fields, and bamboo, coconut, and palm trees. It passes through busy small towns and villages, rows of modest homes with thatched or tiled roofs, some old large unpretentious homes interspersed with new and larger brightly painted mansions with high boundary walls and imposing gates. A few kilometers shy of the border between the states of Kerala and Tamil Nadu on State Highway 27 are some hamlets where most of the Adivasis who began the protests against Coca-Cola live. The hamlets that surround the Coca-Cola plant are Plachimada, Vijaynagar, Madhavan Nair Pathy, and Thottichipathy. They are sometimes referred to as "ST colonies" because, as a local *panchayat* official explained to me, the majority of the residents belong to Scheduled Tribes.

Buses carrying passengers from Palakkad town to Meenakshipuram or further in the state of Tamil Nadu stop momentarily, almost reluctantly, near the few shops in Plachimada before they speed off to more important destinations. A few meters before the bus stop is the spot where brightly colored plastic pots are lined up for the "lorry *vellum*" or the lorry-water, which is the primary source of water for drinking and cooking in many homes in the area ever since the water in the wells was declared unfit for consumption. These pots are a familiar sight for anyone who has paid attention to the images of the Plachimada Struggle available on the Internet.[3] What those images of the bright pink, yellow, green, and blue plastic pots lined up for the lorry-water fail to reveal, however, is the absence of any marking on them that indicates that they are made of food grade plastic. Residents told me that the more traditional clay pots were not suitable for the new realities of being lined up on roadsides and frequent carrying. Not only did they break more often, but they also led to arguments because they looked the same.

The statute enacted in Kerala is the *Kerala Panchayat Raj Act of 1994*. For more information on statutes enacted by various states in the country, statistics, and plans, see the official web site of the Ministry of Panchayati Raj, Government of India, www.panchayat.gov.in.

3 See for example, http://www.flonnet.com/fl2715/stories/20100730271503300.htm and http://www.flickr.com/photos/csepictures/6725249965/, accessed May 20, 2012.

On the other side of the small shops, to the north of State Highway 27, is the imposing gate to the Coca-Cola premises that has clearly seen better times. The beverage plant itself has been locked since 2004 when operations were suspended due to the ongoing agitation. Across the road from here is a small structure made of bamboo, matted palm leaves, and a thatched roof known as the *samara pandal*.[4] It is the place where two elder Adivasi women sit in protest against the Coca-Cola plant everyday. The space between the large gate of the Coca-Cola premises and the *samara pandal* has been the site for numerous protest marches and sit-ins. A few meters further along the highway, adjacent to the eastern wall of the beverage plant, is another hamlet of thatched huts and a few concrete houses, named Vijaynagar. This place too has a designated spot where plastic pots await lorry-water.

A large locked gate, a protest shed, and rows of plastic pots are the popular symbols of a story that has been unfolding in Plachimada for more than a decade. This is not, however, how the story was supposed to turn out. At least not to many who viewed the setting up of a Coca-Cola plant as a sign of the arrival of much delayed "development" in Palakkad.

2.1.2. *Chittur*

As mentioned above, Plachimada lies in Chittur *taluk* of Palakkad district. Unlike other areas of Palakkad, however, it was not part of the British-ruled Malabar (a district in the Madras Presidency) before independence, but rather a part of the Cochin State. Before its merger, first with the state of Travancore and subsequently with Malabar, to form the present day state of Kerala, the Cochin State was made up of two disconnected parts.[5] The smaller of these was Chittur, which was ceded to the rulers of Cochin by the king of Palghat (Palakkad) in recognition of the former's help in driving back the "Ganga" or "Kongu" army that had invaded the territory of the latter in AD 917.[6] According to *The Cochin State Manual* published in 1911, at the time, Chittur *taluk* covered an area of 105 square miles and was "entirely encircled by British territory."[7] The *taluk* was further made up of two separated parts, with the eastern part lying in the center of the Palghat Gap. There is said to have been, at one time, a "magnificent teak forest" in this area that was entirely "assigned" for cultivation in the second half of

4 *Samara pandal* is translated most often as "vigil hut" or "struggle hut"; however, *samara* can also mean protest, movement, or strike.

5 *The Imperial Gazetteer of India* (Clarendon Press: Oxford, 1908) vol. X, 340.

6 C. Achyuta Menon, *The Cochin State Manual* (Thiruvananthapuram: Kerala Gazetteers Department, 1911), 55 and 472.

7 Ibid., 1.

the nineteenth century.[8] By 1911 there were several coffee and rubber plantation estates owned by Europeans and "natives" in some parts of the *taluk*.[9]

Unlike in the rest of Cochin, at the time, many people in Chittur spoke Tamil, Telugu, and Canarese in addition to Malayalam, which was the official language of the Cochin State.[10] In 1911, of the 89,549 residents of Chittur *taluk*, 75,939 were reported to be "Hindus," 7,201 "Muhammadans," 4,337 "Christians," and 2,072 "animists."[11] Despite the majority of Hindus in the *taluk*, there were reportedly "no Hindu temples of note" in the area.[12] Tamil Brahmans and Nayars are named as the predominant Hindu castes in the *taluk*.

The administrative headquarter of the *taluk* was (and still is) based in Chittur town. *The Cochin State Manual* also mentions "Mulattara," a village fourteen miles southeast of Chittur town. This, as far as I have been able to determine based on geographical location, and the fact that both words are pronounced the same, is the present Moolathara village where Plachimada and the Coca-Cola plant are located. The manual describes the village as "feverish," and suggests that it "would probably have remained uninhabited but for the irrigation works."[13] The population of the village in 1911 was reported to be "1,540, mostly Hindus."[14] The Moolathara village is presently home to 9,405 people,[15] even as it remains "feverish" in more than one sense of the word.

Because of Chittur's location near a natural pass or gap in the Western Ghats mountain range, it does not rain here as much as it does in other parts of Kerala. While there is considerable greenery, the air and soil are much drier than in other parts of Kerala. It was in fact often referred to as the driest region of the state. Since it does not receive as much rain, groundwater is the most significant source of water in the area.[16] Given repeated references to the area

8 Ibid., 471. Interestingly, according to a popular belief, Palakkad is named for the forest of *Pala* trees that is said to have existed in the region. Kkad or kkadu is often translated as forest, but several elders in Plachimada and Vijaynagar use the word for any land that is not cultivated, perhaps giving credence to another legend that the name "Palakkad" is derived from the word "palai," translated as dry, barren, or desert land.

9 Ibid., 475.

10 Ibid., 239.

11 Ibid., 472.

12 Ibid.

13 Ibid., 474–475.

14 Ibid., 475.

15 Government of India, Office of Registrar General and Census Commissioner, *Census Data 2001*, www.censusindia.gov.in.

16 This fact has been noted in various reports. See for example, "Report of the High Power Committee", March 22, 2010, 18–19, http://www.scribd.com/doc/80063693/Plachimada-High-Power-Committee-Report-PDF.

as dry and less green than other parts of Kerala, I was at first surprised to see miles of farmlands devoted to rice cultivation in the region.[17] Any deficit due to less rainfall is, however, made up by a vast irrigation network. The need for an alternate source of water for irrigation was recognized early in the region. The process seems to have begun in 1849 with the construction of an "anicut" in "Mulattara," which, appears to be a reference to the existing Moolathara Dam in Chittur, not far from Plachimada.[18]

The Coca-Cola plant is situated very close to two other reservoirs of water in the area: the Kambalthara reservoir beyond Vijaynagar to its east and the Meenakkara dam reservoir that is about three kilometers to its south. The Moolathara canal that flows from the Kambalthara reservoir at a distance of a few meters from the plant's northern boundary wall ensures a sufficient supply of water for irrigation to the surrounding farmlands.

It is in the middle of these farmlands that Coca-Cola bought thirty-two acres of agricultural land some time during 1998–1999. Some residents and activists believe the company chose this location, instead of the industrial area of Kanjikode (where incidentally a beverage plant owned by Pepsi is located), primarily because of the existence of a groundwater aquifer in the Plachimada area, which it could use for no cost other than what it spent on extracting the water. It is believed that this aquifer has replenished the numerous shallow wells that have been the only source of water for drinking, cooking, and other domestic chores in the area for centuries.

2.1.3. *Cochin State*

Cochin (*Kochhi* in some older records) was named after a port town with the same name that was at one time the capital of the Cochin State.[19] The port is said to have been given the name *Kochhi* after the formation of a harbour in 1341.[20] In circa 1500, the Portuguese set up a factory and then a port in the place, before being "driven out" by the Dutch in or around 1663.[21] The latter too began to lose their hold in the region after being defeated in a famous

[17] Rice accounts for 60 percent of the total food crops grown in the district. See, Department of Information and Public Relations, Government of Kerala, *District Handbooks of Kerala: Palakkad* (Thiruvananthapuram: KSAVRC Press, 2003), 18.

[18] Menon, *Cochin State Manual*, 314.

[19] *The Imperial Gazetteer of India*, 340.

[20] Menon, *Cochin State Manual*, 2–3.

[21] "Memorandum" prepared by T. A. Anantaramier, Government Advocate and Law Officer seeking legal opinion related to a dispute over the exact area comprising British Cochin (undated), Cochin, Kerala State Archives (M-35).

battle in 1741 by the ruler of Travancore (a kingdom to the south of Cochin).[22] While the Dutch lost most of their territory after that, the port town of Cochin was in their possession until 1795, when the East India Company took it over.[23]

Although the Cochin State (except for the port town of Cochin) remained independent as a Native State until its merger with independent India, as was the case with many other such states in the subcontinent at the time, it was not really free. The government in neighboring British-ruled Madras Presidency was involved in administrative and political matters of Cochin. Described in one source as a "petty State," Cochin reportedly "saved" more than two hundred thousand rupees from its annual revenue in 1844 and "invested" the same in the East India Company's securities.[24]

As the British gained "military and political supremacy" in the region during the nineteenth century, the political order established by the rulers of Cochin in the eighteenth century collapsed.[25] Driven by the interests and ideologies of the British Empire, the early part of the nineteenth century saw widespread legal, administrative, educational, and social changes in Cochin. Several new laws were introduced in the state that covered matters such as extension of the jurisdiction of civil and criminal courts, "imposition of stamp duty on documents evidencing sale, mortgage, etc.," "protection of Sirkar [government] monopolies," and "cattle trespass."[26] Experiments were carried out with the view of improving agriculture, and the cultivation of crops such as coffee and cotton was introduced and encouraged by the state in various areas including Chittur.[27] "European medical treatment" was also introduced in the second decade of the century.[28] In 1854, a reported 58,000 "slaves" owned by the "Sirkar" and "private owners" were emancipated following a "protracted discussion" on the matter that had been going on "since the time of Colonel [John] Munro," the British Resident and later the *Diwan* or Prime Minister of Cochin and Travancore.[29]

[22] Kesavan Veluthat, *The Early Medieval in South India* (New Delhi: Oxford University Press, 2009), 268.

[23] Anataramier, "Memorandum."

[24] Menon, *Cochin State Manual*, 215.

[25] Susan Bayly, "Hindu Kingship and the Origin of Community: Religion, State and Society in Kerala, 1750–1850," *Modern Asian Studies* 18:2 (1984): 180. For the manner in which British colonialism "disrupted the economic structure" in the region and changed social relations, see Prema Kurien, "Colonialism and Ethnogenesis: A Study of Kerala, India," *Theory and Society* 23:3 (1994): 385.

[26] Menon, *Cochin State Manual*, 202–203.

[27] Ibid., 203.

[28] Ibid., 368.

[29] Ibid., 213.

Regulation of forests was also strengthened during this time, with laws enacted for preventing "indiscriminate clearing for fugitive cultivation," hunting, fishing, and manure-gathering, among other activities.[30] Although the people whose lifestyles and economies centered around these outlawed activities do not find mention in the official records, many experiences of such people continue to survive in oral histories and community narratives. Some such accounts are presented in Chapter 6.

2.1.4. *Palakkad*

Almost everyone I met in Kerala before going to Palakkad (formerly also known as Palghat) referred to it as a "backward" district in the most "modern" state in India. Several people in Palakkad town itself echoed this view. Some explained this anomaly through references to the history of the region. It was pointed out that unlike parts of Kerala that were formerly the independent States of Cochin and Travancore, ruled by progressive local or native rulers concerned with the well-being of their subjects,[31] several parts of what is Palakkad today had long been ruled by "outsiders." These outsiders were at first Hyder Ali and his son Tipu Sultan, the rulers of Mysore who seized the area in mid-eighteenth century and ruled until 1792, thereafter the East India Company, and finally the British Crown.[32] In addition to this history, some residents of Palakkad also cited the influence of the neighboring state of Tamil Nadu, which they insisted was nowhere near as "progressive" as Kerala.

Despite differences over the reasons for its often-unspecified backwardness, Palakkad evokes a different response than the rest of Kerala when it comes to development. There appeared to be a popular consensus that the Palakkad district is certainly in need of development. This view seems to have played an important role in the initial enthusiastic reception of the Coca-Cola Company in the district by the state and local administration, as well as by many residents. According to some, it was felt at the time that the generation of revenue for the local administration as well as the direct and indirect creation of new jobs would go a long way in achieving both economic and social development

[30] Ibid., 334.

[31] The royal family of Travancore is held particularly in high regard by many people in Thiruvananthapuram for their emphasis on health care, education, and gender equality.

[32] For brief accounts of this history, see Centre for Development Studies, *Human Development Report 2005* (Thiruvananthapuram: Government of Kerala, 2005), 2–12; Department of Information and Public Relations, Government of Kerala, *District Handbooks of Kerala: Palakkad*, 6–7; Veluthat, The Early Medieval in South India, 385.

in the place. This perception seems to have translated into a welcome environment for Coca-Cola, with speedy clearances from various departments that allowed it to start production. As far as it can be determined from available records and my conversations, the fact that the Coca-Cola plant required large amounts of water to operate was not considered at the time.

2.1.5. *Kerala*

Although it has been noted that the processes of state formation had begun, in what is now known as Kerala, as far back as the ninth century,[33] until the 1740s, the region was "a patchwork quilt of shifting chiefdoms and principalities," and it was only in the eighteenth century that the kingdoms of Cochin and Travancore emerged, much like in other parts of the subcontinent.[34] In 1956, Travancore, Cochin, and the Malabar district merged to form the present state of Kerala. A coastal state in south India, Kerala is celebrated for what is widely referred to as the "Kerala model" of development.[35] Even as it is increasingly criticized for its inadequate focus on industrial development,[36] the state stands apart from all other states in India for its significant achievements in several areas that are commonly regarded as indicators of "human" or "social development," such as highest literacy rates in the country, wide access to health care, high life expectancy, a healthy gender ratio, low rates of infant mortality, and low population growth rates.[37]

This, however, is only part of the picture. Many residents of Kerala I spoke with expressed concerns over the increasing incidence of suicide and high levels of unemployment in the state. As is often the case, not everyone has benefitted equally from the changes in the state, including those brought about by the extensive land reforms carried out in the state since its formation.[38] Dalit groups have criticized the "Kerala model" for its inability to fundamentally

[33] Veluthat, *The Early Medieval in South India*, 249–276.

[34] Bayly, "Hindu Kingship,"181.

[35] See Govindan Parayil, "The 'Kerala Model' of Development: Development and Sustainability in the Third World," *Third World Quarterly* 17:5 (1996): 941; Govindan Parayil and T. T. Sreekumar, "Kerala's Experience of Development and Change," *Journal of Contemporary Asia* 33:4 (2003): 465; Centre for Development Studies, *Human Development Report* 2005; G. K. Leiten, "The Human Development Puzzle in Kerala," *Journal of Contemporary Asia* 32:1 (2002): 47; Jose Murickan and M. K. George, *Development-Induced Displacement: Case of Kerala* (New Delhi: Rawat Publications, 2003).

[36] Payaril and Sreekumar, "Kerala's Experience of Development."

[37] See Centre for Development Studies, *Human Development Report* 2005.

[38] See Parayil and Sreekumar, "Kerala's Experience of Development."

change the "upper-caste dominance" in the state.[39] A large number of Adivasis have been displaced from forests and other areas that have been acquired for various development projects in the fields of water resource management, forest conservation, wildlife protection, and creation of national parks.[40]

Despite their willingness to criticize the policies of successive governments in Kerala since its formation, most residents proudly point to the emphasis on education and high levels of political awareness and engagement as the reasons for the state's success. The state's commitment to fostering a culture of transparency and accountability in its various public departments was obvious during my visits to some offices in the state capital Thiruvananthapuram as well as in Kochi. For these and other reasons, residents who generally describe Kerala as a "modern" state, are proud of the state's many achievements, even as they point to many things that can be improved further.

2.2. PEOPLE

2.2.1. *Adivasis*

The lands surrounding the Coca-Cola plant in Moolathara are home to Adivasis and non-Adivasis. Some of them have lived here for generations, while others have moved to the area more recently. As mentioned above, the hamlets near the plant are also referred to as "ST colonies" since a majority of residents are members of Scheduled Tribes. The rows of homes adjacent to the eastern and western boundary walls of the Coca-Cola plant are known as Plachimada and Vijaynagar, respectively. As per information available in the Tribal Extension Office in Chittur, half of the families in Vijaynagar are Adivasi whereas in Plachimada the number of Adivasi families is a little more than one-third.

To the north of the company's premises, beyond the Moolathara canal and some rice fields, is a coconut grove. Nestled within this is Madhavan Nair Pathy. All the families here self-identified or were described as Adivasi. There are other small- and medium-sized hamlets nearby: Kocchikkad, Sarkarpathy,

[39] Gail Omvedt, "Disturbing Aspects of Kerala Society," *Bulletin of Concerned Asian Scholars* 30:3 (1998): 31. A senior bureaucrat I spoke with in Thiruvananthapuram also mentioned that "untouchability" is still practiced in at least one area in the state.

[40] See Murickan and George, *Development-Induced Displacement*. See also Smitu Kothari, "Whose Nation? The Displaced as Victims of Displacement," *Economic and Political Weekly* 31:24 (1996): 1476; Anjan Chakrabarty and Anup Dhar, *Dislocation and Resettlement in Development: From Third World to World of the Third* (Oxford: Routledge, 2010).

Thottichipathy, Kunjemenonpathy, and Nellimedu. Many Adivasis who live here are related by blood or marriage. They often refer to all of these "colonies" collectively as "here" or "this place." Specific place names are offered only when asked for. The administrative divisions of their "place" into colonies, wards, villages, and *panchayats* seem to hold little meaning or use for them, except for when required to be entered in forms for government loans, ration cards, pensions, and so on.

A majority of Adivasis in this area belongs to the Eravalan tribe. The rest belong to the Malasar tribe. As stated before, both communities are recognized as Scheduled Tribes in Kerala. Most Adivasis I spoke with self-identify as Eravalan. The few who identified as Adivasi or "ST" could have been either Eravalan or Malasar. According to oral history shared with me by an Eravalan elder (set out in Chapter 6), they arrived in this place when there was no one else here. There is, however, no mention of the Eravalan or Malasar people in the list of people who, as per *The Cochin State Manual*, resided in Moolathara village,[41] or in other records of the history of the place. In all likelihood, they were included in the category of "animists" who lived in Chittur at the time in accordance with the census policy of the time. They could also constitute the "other classes" listed in early twentieth century administrative records prepared in Chittur: the ones who were not "Europeans," "Eurasians," "native Christians," "Hindus," or "Muhammadans." Their presence (and that of other communities that lived in the forests and hills in the region) can also at times be sensed on pages of old records that describe the need for increased state control over forests, as the unnamed people who were no longer allowed to clear lands for cultivation or to fish, hunt, or gather forest produce as the state increased its control over forests. The consequences of centuries of lawmaking, which enabled these dispossessions and the ways in which the ideas from those old records shape contemporary life experiences of Adivasis today, are set out more fully in Chapter 6.

2.2.2. *Eravalans and Malasars*

Among the few written records of Eravalans and Malasars that I was able to locate is Iyer's *Cochin Tribes and Castes*, which according to its author, "deals with all the Malayali and animistic castes, the members of which pollute the high-caste men at various distances, and cannot approach the outer walls of the temples of the higher castes."[42] Passages from Iyer's account of "Eravallens"

[41] Menon, *Cochin State Manual*, 475.

[42] L. K. Ananthakrishna Iyer, *Cochin Tribes and Castes*, vol.1 (Madras: Publication for the Government of Cochin by Higginbotham & Co. London, Luzas & Co., 1909), viii–ix.

were also reproduced in Edgar Thurston's *Castes and Tribes of Southern India*.[43] Eravalans, also referred to as "villu vedans" or "hunters using bow and arrows," are described by Iyer as "a wild and inoffensive jungle tribe found in Chittur Taluk of the Cochin State."[44] Their language is reported to be Tamil, although it is noted that some spoke Malayalam. They are described as "very poor" with "no titles among them."[45] Further, they were seen as "rude timid primitive people like the other jungle tribes of the State [with] no knowledge of their origin."[46] Their status is reported to have improved "under the civilizing influence of their masters."[47] They lived in villages called "pathies" (a sufix that follows names of several "ST colonies" in the area today), and they addressed their elders as "*Muthans* (elderly men) and *Pattans* (grand-fathers)."[48]

The rest of the entry describes their clothes, jewellery, customs, and ceremonies including those for marriage, pregnancy, childbirth, and death. Customary rules of marriage, divorce, and inheritance are also mentioned. The record also mentions that there was no "tribal assembly" and disputes "seldom occur[ed]."[49] It is indicated that they followed the rules of "pollution" prevalent in the region at the time, and although they "bathed when touched by" members of certain castes, they also "recognize[d] their social inferiority to the Brahmans and Nairs, and [stood] at a distance from them to avoid polluting them."[50]

A section titled "Religion" describes Eravalans as being "pure animists," who believe that "demons" reside in trees, rocks, peaks, and so on.[51] A few "gods" are also mentioned, each believed to protect certain places or certain aspects of life. "Kannimar (seven maidens)" were among the "family deities" who watched over the welfare of the tribe.[52] Kannimari, a place next to Plachimada where an interstate sales tax check-post is situated today, appears to be named after this deity. Another deity "Kali" is said to have been "adored" by the Eravalans in order "to obtain her protection for themselves and their families while living in the forest."[53]

[43] Edgar Thurston, *Castes and Tribes of Southern India*, vol. 2 (Madras: Government Press, 1909), 210. In this volume the name of the tribe is spelled as "Eravallars."

[44] Iyer, *Cochin Tribes and Castes*, 43.

[45] Ibid.

[46] Ibid.

[47] Ibid.

[48] Ibid.

[49] Ibid., 47.

[50] Ibid., 49.

[51] Ibid., 47.

[52] Ibid.

[53] Ibid.

Eravalans were recognized as skilled hunters who knew the forests well.[54] They hunted porcupines, hare, wild hogs, and birds, with "the game equally divided."[55] However, their main occupation at the time was agriculture, dominated by cultivation of grains (that several Adivasis told me are not grown anymore). They were reported to be "attached to farmers" for whom they worked for daily wages paid in measures of paddy.[56] At times they borrowed money from the farmers "to improve their condition," and those who were unable to repay the loans reportedly "willingly mortgage[d] themselves to their masters or to some other person."[57] The author notes, however, that "[w]omen never surrender themselves to work in a state of bondage, but are independent day labourers."[58] The section on Eravalans ends with a note that they are "certified by their masters to be always truthful, honest, and faithful" and, unlike members of another tribe, they never "ungratefully run away from their employers."[59]

As mentioned before, Malasar is the other tribe whose members reside in and around Plachimada. The earliest available written record of this tribe appears to be an account by Buchanan that dates back to 1807.[60] Buchanan's description of Malasars is reproduced in a volume of Edgar Thurston's *Castes and Tribes of Southern India*.[61] The volume also includes information from the Madras Census Report of 1901. Malasars are described as a "rude tribe" that lived in the forests in Coimbatore district and Cochin State, and spoke a "mixture of the Tamul and Malayala languages."[62] To Buchanan, the "Malasirs" seemed "better looking than the slaves," but also "ill-clothed, nasty, and apparently ill-fed."[63] Like the Eravalans, Malasars too lived in "pathis" that were essentially small clusters of huts "situated in the skirts of the woods on the hills of Daraporam, Ani-malaya, and Pali-ghat."[64] To their observers, Malasars

54 During one of our conversations, Maariamma mentioned the fact that their ancestors used to hunt in the hills. She explained that this was the reason why bows and arrows are still an important part of their rituals and ceremonies including those performed during weddings.

55 Iyer, *Cochin Tribes and Castes*, 48.

56 Ibid., 49.

57 Ibid., 49–50.

58 Ibid., 50.

59 Ibid.

60 Francis Buchanan, *A Journey from Madras through the Countries of Mysore, Canara, and Malabar* (London: T. Cadell and W. Davies, 1807).

61 Thurston, *Castes and Tribes of Southern India*.

62 Ibid., 394.

63 Ibid.

64 Ibid.

appeared to prefer to live in their "rude huts" and seemed to have "an objection to well-built houses."[65] A "Malasar forester," it was reported, preferred the "rude huts" to "Government quarters."[66] The elders in Plachimada and Vijaynagar still prefer the thatched roofs to the ill-conceived brick and cement structures promoted by the administration, which according to the Adivasis are not properly ventilated.

Their god, according to Buchanan was represented by a "rude idol" that was a stone "that is encircled by a wall, which serves for a temple."[67] There is a deity represented in a small black stone in Vijaynagar very close to a boundary wall of Coca-Cola. According to Adivasi residents, it guards the boundary of their place. An elaborate annual Adivasi ceremony involving this deity was described to me by the *anganwadi* teacher in Vijaynagar and mentioned by some other non-Adivasis, but Adivasis were reluctant to speak about it. An account in the Madras Census Report that came about a hundred years after Buchanan's account, also mentions Kali and Mariamman as the gods worshipped by Malasars along with their "special deity."[68] Whereas Kali, also described as an Eravalan goddess above, is today widely regarded as a Hindu deity across India, Mariamma seems to be a local deity. She is generally regarded as a goddess of smallpox in the area (and in some other parts of rural Kerala) by many Hindu communities as well. An Adivasi elder in one of the hamlets also mentioned both of them, while suggesting that there was some tension between those who wished to build a temple to one goddess and those who would rather have one built for the other. It is unclear, however, whether Buchanan, who only referred to the "rude stone idol," had missed some "gods" or whether the community had acquired (or were seen to have acquired) additional "gods" over the hundred years after which the second available record was produced.

According to Buchanan the "puddies" (also spelled "pathies") and its inhabitants were "considered the property of some landlord," who farmed out their labor and all they collected from the forests to traders.[69] The traders had the "exclusive right" to purchase anything the Malasars collected and gave them, in return, "a subsistence" and supplied "salt and other necessaries."[70] He also notes, however, that Malasars practiced a form of slash and burn cultivation

65 Ibid., 396.
66 Ibid.
67 Ibid., 395.
68 Ibid.
69 Ibid., 394.
70 Ibid.

"in the woods" for themselves and their neighboring farmers.[71] In the latter case they were paid for the labor.

The Madras Census Report of 1901 also records the chief occupation of most Malasars to have been "hill cultivation and day labour,"[72] but unlike a century ago when Buchanan passed through the region, in 1901 they were seen to be growing food-crops for themselves on land "given" to them "free of rent" by "landlords."[73] In return, they worked for the "landlords" who exercised "absolute control over them."[74] Instead of gathering herbs, food, and other items from the forests, they were now employed for "game-tracking" and taming wild elephants. Several of them were now also engaged as "baggage coolies."[75] They were also, according to the Report, "proverbially lazy" and spending a large proportion of their wages on alcohol.[76] They were reportedly "not to be depended on in any way," as they were said to "desert *en masse* on the smallest excuse."[77] Several Malasar communities were also by now feared for committing "dacoities" near roads on the foot of hills.[78]

The fact that these "forest tribes" were two among many such peoples who were being, and would continue to be, dispossessed of the lands they lived and worked on as a result of social, legal, political, and economic changes that had been going on for several centuries is not acknowledged in any of these written historical records.[79] These written records are not, however, the entire or only histories of the Eravalans or Malasars. In fact, as will become clear from the oral histories presented in Chapter 6, this is not exactly or entirely how they remember and narrate their pasts. Meanwhile, the disposession continues.

71 Ibid.

72 Ibid., 395.

73 Ibid., 396–397.

74 Ibid., 397.

75 Ibid., 396.

76 Ibid., 397.

77 Ibid., 396.

78 Ibid. The word "dacoit" is used for bandits in India and is the anglicized version of the Hindi word "daku."

79 See Darley J. Kjosavik and N. Shanmugam, "Property Rights Dynamics and Indigenous Communities in Highland Kerala, South India: An Institutional-Historical Perspective," *Modern Asian Studies* 41:6 (2007): 1183–1260, where the authors offer a brief overview of the manner in which Adivasi dispossession in certain regions of Kerala began with land being brought under the control of temples between the sixth and fifteenth centuries and how it continued under the landlord-chieftain regime (1400–1766), the Mysore regime (1766–1792), the colonial period (1792–1947), and postcolonial India.

2.2.3. *Settlers and Others*

Among other residents of the two hamlets are members of the Scheduled Castes,[80] as well as some Muslim and Ezhava families. The last two are included in the category of Other Backward Classes (OBC) in Kerala.[81] Most of these non-Adivasis are referred to as "settlers" by Adivasis. Most recent settlers have built homes on small pieces of land allotted by the state government under various schemes introduced in furtherance of its "land to landless" policy. Although some residents are the original allottees, others have bought lands sold by allottees. Some moved here a couple of decades ago, whereas others only a couple of years ago.

Different communities among the "settlers" who have arrived over the last few decades are sometimes referred to as "malayali," or "mappila." The word "malayali" generally denotes the linguistic identity of people who speak the Malayalam language.[82] In Plachimada it is used mostly while referring to non-Adivasi Hindu settlers. Occasionally it was used to refer to Muslim settlers in the area. Otherwise, the word "mappila" is used to refer to Muslims in the area.[83] Many settlers have or are in the process of building brick walls for their homes, although many currently have thatched roofs. A couple of settler families who recently bought land or started small businesses around the plant live in modest concrete homes.

Unlike the "settlers," the other group of non-Adivasis who live in the area are the wealthy landowners who have been in the area for generations. The

[80] Scheduled Caste is defined in the Indian Constitution as "such castes, races or tribes or parts of or groups within such castes, races or tribes as are deemed under Article 341 to be Scheduled Castes for the purposes of this Constitution." See *Constitution of India*, Article 366 (24). Several groups included in this administrative category that identifies target groups for affirmative action belong to castes formerly referred to as "lower castes" or "untouchables." Many such groups, however, self-identify as *dalit*, translated as oppressed or broken.

[81] The category of Other Backward Classes identifies groups and communities for affirmative action within individual states in the country. As in the case of Scheduled Tribe and Scheduled Caste, a group or community may be classified as an OBC in one state but not in another.

[82] In the rest of the country, especially in north India, the word "Malayali" is generally used to refer to a person who belongs to the state of Kerala. The Adivasis, at least in these hamlets, do not refer to themselves as Malayalis, even though the hamlets are in Kerala, and most of them can converse in Malayalam. Similarly, Adivasis who speak primarily Tamil do not refer to themselves as Tamilians.

[83] The words "mappila" or "mopla" are frequently used in Kerala. A Gazetteer published in 1908 describes "moplas" as a "race of converts to Islam" that lived in the Malabar. See Edward Thornton, *A Gazetteer of the Territories Under the Government of the Viceroy of India 1799–1875*, revised and edited by Roper Lethbridge and Arthur N. Wollaston (London: Allen & Co., 1886), 557.

Hindu landowners with "upper caste" last names common in Kerala are referred to either by their individual names or as *jenmi*.[84] Muslim landowners are also referred to either by individual names or as "Rauther,"[85] or "Pattanis."[86] More recent Hindu landowners of Tamil origin are referred to as "Gounder" or "Goundon." A large concrete house with brightly painted exteriors located almost at the edge of Plachimada colony belongs to a family that is said to own substantial farmlands in the area. They were described as "upper caste" Hindus. The men in the family are simply referred to as "Gounder" by the residents of the colonies.[87] Some of these landowning groups have their own histories that go back a century or more in the area. For example, the Muslim "Pattani" landowners, as per local legend, arrived in this area in the early to mid-eighteenth century when the area was ruled by Hyder Ali, the emperor of Mysore, and later his son, Tipu Sultan. None of these groups of non-Adivasis in the area is referred to as "outsiders" by the Adivasis. That word is used for nonresidents such as researchers like me, activists, news reporters, and various other kinds of visitors who have made their way to Plachimada over the past decade.

The relations between all these groups of people – Adivasis, settlers, *jenmis*, *pattanis*, Gounders – are inevitably complex and dynamic. Class, caste,

84 *Jenmi* or *janmi* is a reference to one of the stakeholders in land or one of the persons who had hereditary authority over land under the traditional system in regions now known as Kerala. In addition to these "upper caste" landholders, other stakeholders were the intermediaries who managed the lands, the actual cultivators, and finally *adiyars* or bonded laborers considered to have been attached to the lands they worked on. The privileges and rights exercised by *jenmis* as well as the obligations of other stakeholders were governed by local custom in each area or village, with no standardized form across what is now known as Kerala. *Jenmis* were not absolute owners of land to the exclusion of other stakeholders to begin with, especially before the nineteenth century when the British colonial administrators misinterpreted the land tenure system in the region. See K. N. Ganesh, "Ownership and Control of Land in Medieval Kerala: Janmam-Kanam Relations During the 16th–18th Centuries," *Indian Economic Social History Review* 28 (1991): 299. See also B. A. Prakash, "Agricultural Development in Kerala from 1800 AD to 1980 AD: A Survey of Studies," (working paper number 220, Centre for Development Studies, Trivandrum, (June 1987), 8, 16.

85 Rauther was generally used to refer to Muslims who speak Tamil and follow Tamil cultural practices.

86 As per a local legend the word "pattani" is a derivative of the word "pathan," which in turn refers to the Pashto-speaking Pashtun people of what are now parts of northern Pakistan and Afghanistan. A young woman I met near Plachimada traced the ancestry of her family to *pathans* with a sense of pride. The evidence that she and others pointed out to me in support of this is the extremely light skin tones of *pattanis* as compared to others in the area, and their traditional skills as horsemen. Pattanis have a significant presence in parts of Palakkad and Chittur.

87 "Gounder" or "Koundan" was described to me as a caste title. Gounders are said to belong to a Tamil community. In this region they are mostly landowning farmers.

religion – all constitute multiple combinations of "us" and "them" here, as they do elsewhere. Marriages between members of different castes and between Adivasis and Hindu and Muslim "settlers" are not common but do take place. One fact that emerged from my many conversations in the area is, however, that many non-Adivasis here (as in other parts of the country) believe that Adivasis need to change in order to become like everyone else. Several Adivasis too think they have to "learn" from the "malayalis" and the "settlers." The accounts in the following chapters reveal more about the past and present relations between these groups of people as well as the interesting ways in which the protests against Coca-Cola has brought all of them together on a common platform.

2.3. CHANGE

Every Adivasi elder and a very large proportion of the younger members of the community I met in the various "colonies" either works or has worked on the farms in the area. Their relationship to these lands and their understanding of their work and that of their ancestors is a more complex story recounted in Chapter 6. Now they receive daily wages for working on the farms, but many remember the time when they received a measure of grains every week that more often than not did not last a week. Several non-Adivasi "settlers" in the colonies also either work on farms in the area or find work on construction sites in nearby towns. A few work in what was referred to as a "thread factory" not far from the place, whereas some others have found jobs as drivers or are engaged in other similar temporary work. For many of these residents, the rumors of a "factory" being set up in the area had held the promise of permanent and better-paying jobs close to home.

While Coca-Cola obtained the necessary administrative approvals, certificates and clearances under an expedited Single Window Clearance process introduced in Kerala in 1999,[88] none of the residents of Plachimada or Vijaynagar were consulted or even informed of the proposed plans to set up a beverage plant right next to their homes, on land many had lived and worked on for as long as they remembered. Some residents heard that "a company" had bought the land. Some recall rumors of a "big company"

[88] The *Kerala State Single Window Clearance Boards and Industrial Township Area Development Act of 1999* mandated that Boards set up for the purpose at state and district levels provide necessary clearances to industries within a period of 45 days. This expedited and simplified process is aimed at attracting industry to the state. See the web site of the Kerala State Industrial Development Corporation: http://www.ksidc.org/.

being set up in the area. No one, however, had any idea about what the company produced at the time, or more critically, what it would extract. Ramesh, a man who sold a small part of the total land bought by Coca-Cola mentioned that an agent negotiated the sale, and that he learned of the identity of the buyer only at the time of registration of the sale.[89] According to him, at the time he and the other small landowners were given to understand (it is not clear by whom) that the company would employ those who sell their land. He now feels cheated as this did not happen.

Some Adivasis in the area who were also approached refused to sell the very small pieces of land on which they live. That appears to be the reason Coca-Cola ended up with an irregular eastern boundary wall that goes some way around the Adivasi homes in Vijaynagar. Kecharan, an Adivasi man, told me that they refused to sell their land simply because "[t]his is the place where [they] have been living."[90] He said that money offered by the company did not matter as they "cannot go and live in another place."[91] Even with regard to the situation today, he says that while *they* cannot leave this place, the company can easily buy land elsewhere. Several other Adivasis echoed the same sentiments. These repeated references to living and dying "here" were an early indication to me about the significance of questions of land and displacement in the protests against Coca-Cola. As will be clearer in Chapters 5 and 6, the Adivasis' insistence on not leaving relates to who they are and how they understand their lives as an inseparable part of the place and everything else that belongs here, including the land, water, and trees.

Maariamma belongs to one of the Adivasi families who had been working on the lands bought by Coca-Cola since what she describes as "the time of our fathers," a general reference to their ancestors.[92] Work on the land was the only source of income for most members of these families – men, women, elders, and until some time ago, children. They were therefore concerned about losing their livelihoods. The former owner, who according to Maariamma had to sell the land because the family needed money, reassured them before he moved his family to their "family home" in a nearby town.[93] He had said they would continue to *live with the company as they had been living with him*. Some others in the hamlets recall being told that the company would even

[89] Interview with Ramesh.
[90] Interview with Kecharan.
[91] Ibid.
[92] Interview with Maariamma.
[93] Ibid.

pay more wages. None of them however knew anything about what those jobs would be or even when they would be available.

After the lands were sold, some Adivasi men went to other places to find work temporarily. Some men and women found work on nearby lands. Meanwhile, the work on what was now the "company land" began with clearing and leveling. Maariamma recalls that the "tamarind trees were cut down from their place" and "big rocks removed."[94] And then, she recalls: "[t]hey brought in [a vehicle] and made the paddy fields and the *kkad* as one."[95] *Kkad* here refers to the land not under paddy cultivation. She had earlier explained that groundnuts were grown on some of the land, although a small part of it was also covered with shrubs. To an eighty-six-year-old woman who has worked on this land all her life, this was clearly not just a piece of land, or *any* piece of land. It was a place with particular trees and rocks she lived around; it was a place where she and others in her family, as their ancestors before them, had sown and harvested crops. Despite being enclosed by walls now, the company's land was a part of, and connected to, the same *place* as the small plots of land on which the Adivasis live. It was part of the same place where their wells are.

It is clear from my many conversations in the hamlets that in those early days no one expected things to go wrong as they ultimately did. Maariamma's face lit up when she spoke about the bright lights on the company's premises. Her expression conveyed the excitement of that time. "We were very happy," she declared, "when all these lights were put up."[96] After all, as she explained, there were no lights there "for all these years."[97] For others, especially the young men in the hamlets, the prospects of working in a company held out new possibilities for their future. In the words of Ottukan, an Adivasi man, "[p]eople thought that they will be respected when they go to work in the company."[98] He further explained that society values people working in a company more than it values people who work on farms. Jobs in a company were regarded as more prestigious.

At the time, many Adivasis were "willing to go there for work," just like the non-Adivasi residents of the area.[99] Initially a few of them found temporary employment on daily wages while the plant was being constructed. But they

94 Ibid.

95 Interview with Maariamma. The word *kkad*, as I have explained before, is often translated as forest, but it was also translated as uncultivated land, barren land where only dry shrubs grow, and it is even used to describe a grove.

96 Ibid.

97 Ibid.

98 Interview with Ottukan.

99 Interview with Maariamma.

quickly learned that there would be no jobs for those who had no or little formal education. Some say the company was only willing to hire those who had passed grade ten. This basically meant that a majority of the Adivasis, who had dropped out of school at an early age to work on the farms in order to help their families make ends meet, were ineligible.

Some non-Adivasis who were employed by the company, however, say that jobs were available and not just for people with formal education. They, as most other "settlers" in the two colonies, were initially opposed to any action against Coca-Cola. Some readily acknowledge this fact, even as now almost everyone in the area is "with" the struggle against the company. Many of the non-Adivasi residents were initially happy with the company and what came with it, namely, a more prestigious and possibly permanent "company job," electricity, and televisions. All, however, confirmed that this was before their water turned bad.

Every Adivasi I spoke with insisted there were no jobs for them. Attukaran, a young Adivasi man, recalls that initially there was talk of some jobs for residents of the hamlets, but after about six months it was clear that the company was hiring only those with a "degree" or "qualification."[100] The following words of Rajan, a sixty-five-year-old Adivasi man, essentially echo what most others said:

> I didn't know that the company was offering jobs at first. Later I learned that there are no jobs for our people since we have no proper education. We were told that only people with proper education would get jobs. People who have gone to school.[101]

The manner in which several Adivasis spoke about this exclusion suggests a sense of betrayal and injustice. They had, after all, expected to live "with" the company, as they had lived with the farmers who sold the land to Coca-Cola. Most of them, who had been born on that land and had been working on it for as long as they could remember, found it hard to understand how they could be separated from it. The meaning of "living with" for Adivasis will become clearer in the context of Adivasi lives and histories in this area presented in the following chapters. I mention it here to indicate the early sense of betrayal they experienced and to flag that this separation and this betrayal have particular meanings within their normative universe.

Since they did not have a real choice in the matter of their formal education (or the lack thereof), and no say in the change of the land use from agricultural

[100] Interview with Attukaran.

[101] Interview with Rajan.

to industrial, they naturally see the denial of jobs as unfair. Having lived and worked on these lands for generations, their lives are inseparably connected to the place. Being forced to look for work farther away from their homes, especially work for which they often do not have the skills, has had serious consequences for the community. A few younger men have been forced to move to other places, leaving behind aging parents who are unable to find any employment in the area. Others, who cannot imagine a life away from this place, try to find daily wage work in nearby fields or construction sites. Many women with young children, who could earlier carry their children with them as they worked on farms all around their homes, are now unable to find work. Elders, who were also working on the land earlier, now find it extremely difficult to find suitable work.

Despite the sense of betrayal, however, there appears to have been no anger or resentment against the company over the denial of jobs initially. As with the other things the "outside world" (an expression the Adivasis use often) seems to be telling them – about their clothes, rituals, beliefs, attitudes – they seem to have decided to accept this exclusion from job opportunities, at the time, as another thing that indicated that they are responsible for what is perceived as their "lack." Several said to me that they are trying to learn the ways of the "settlers," and repeatedly referred to the community's commitment to formal education for their children.

Formal education, however, cannot be separated from their lives. I will return to the topic of formal education, especially the State's attempts at making it available to Adivasis in Chapter 6. Here I note that an education that does not respect their past, their beliefs, and their vision for the future would hold little meaning for many of them. As some Adivasi elders and leaders emphasized, to continue to live together as a community is very important for them. Kothandan, an elder in Madhavan Nair Pathy, said: "[a]long with education, community living – living with others – makes a difference."[102] His meaning becomes clearer with what he said next: "[p]eople in the company are selfish."[103]

Formal education, no matter how "proper" it may be considered by the rest of the world, becomes meaningless when it fails to teach people to live together. Unlike the Adivasis who thought they could live "with" the company, Coca-Cola, despite all the formal education acquired by those who run it, did not come here to live with anyone. It came here for the land and for the water. This is not the kind of education the Adivasi elders wish for their

102 Interview with Kothandan.
103 Ibid.

children when they say: "[t]he coming [next] generation should get a better life. This *samaram* is not for us."[104]

2.4. HOW IT ALL STARTED

Sudha, a teacher at one of the local *anganwadi* preschools in the area, remembers the day several parents came to the school accusing her assistant of feeding undercooked meals to their children. They said that many children had been sick because the lunch served in school was not cooked well. Some parents even shouted at the teaching assistant. That was when Mylamma, a well-respected Adivasi woman, described by Sudha as a woman who "people listened to," intervened.[105] In the course of the discussion that followed, everyone acknowledged that lately the food did not cook well in their homes either. That is how, Sudha recalls, it all started.

Attukaran, an Adivasi resident of Vijaynagar, says: "[a]t first we didn't feel anything. After some time, there were small changes in the water."[106] Several people describe the same changes that residents had begun to notice. At first, it was the food: rice took much longer to cook, and, unlike before, rice cooked in the morning spoiled by afternoon. They also started noticing a white residue on the insides of the cooking pots. And then the water in their wells began to look, feel, and taste different.

Wells are the traditional source of water in this region. There is a common "panchayat well" in Vijaynagar,[107] but many of the Adivasi homes have shallow open wells beside them. Most of these wells are described to be only about "two-men" deep,[108] but they have been a perennial source of water for drinking, cooking, washing, bathing, and other domestic purposes. Madhavan Nair Pathy, the cluster of huts to the north of the company land, also has a well. There are some wells near Plachimada as well. People living closer to the highway used to walk to a well near the Kannimari check-post to fetch water. Those who live further away from the state highway, mostly Adivasis, have been drawing water from nearby wells. The canal that passes by the fields, to the north of Plachimada, the Coca-Cola plant, and Vijaynagar, is used primarily for irrigation. On some days, young women and children can be seen bathing in the canal as well – a welcome break, no doubt, from the

[104] Interview with Ottukan.
[105] Interview with Sudha.
[106] Interview with Attukaran.
[107] This is the deepest well in the hamlet and is maintained by the Perumatty Grama Panchayat.
[108] Interview with Attukaran.

heat. The "canal-water" is, however, not used for drinking or cooking by the Adivasis. For these purposes, they only trust the "well-water." Some said this was because one could not be sure of what might be present in the water that comes from another place.

Every person I spoke with in the hamlets said water in their wells (some of which are located a few meters from the boundary wall of the Coca-Cola plant) was affected some time after the company began operations. Everyone – Adivasis and non-Adivasis, those who worked for the company at the time and those who did not, people who decided to do something about it and others who were against any action, the ones who blame the company and want it out of the place and the very few who choose not to ascribe responsibility – agrees that their water changed some time after the company started functioning.

Amma, an Adivasi elder woman whose niece lives near the Coca-Cola plant, recounted how at first they thought that the bitter taste of the water from the well next to her niece's home was due to the leaves of a tree beside the well. They cut off the overhanging branches of that tree to prevent any leaves from falling into the well. Since that didn't change anything, they started discussing the matter with others in the hamlet. That is when it was realized that it was not just the water in that one well that had turned bitter. Everyone else felt the water tasted different as well. Not only was it not sweet as before, it also felt different. The water now made their hair "stick together."[109] Soon even adults began to complain of stomachaches. Some even began to notice rashes on their skin.

A man, whose wife watered plants in the Coca-Cola premises for some time, mentioned how her hands and feet were infected in places that came in contact with that water. Everywhere the water came in contact with her skin it caused discoloration and itching. He also remembers a foul smell from the water he saw being filtered inside the premises. Several others talk about the unfamiliar smell in the area generally, while many describe the increasing frequency of rashes. There also appeared in the area at the time some "big leeches" or leech-like creatures that no one had seen before.[110] And then, the levels of water in their open wells reduced drastically. No one remembers the water level falling to that extent ever in the past.

After a while, in the words of Amma, an Adivasi elder, "[t]here was a situation like even though water is there but nobody can drink it."[111] There were

109 Interview with Amma.
110 Interviews with Sudha and Rajan.
111 Interview with Amma.

many signs that indicated that their water had changed. This is how Amma explained some of the changes:

> If water is there, there will be fish in it. If fish is there, there will be frogs. There will be all living things that live in water. The fish in the water was dying. Frogs dying.[112]

What they had now was water that they could not drink. She added that it was "just like dead water."[113]

2.5. WATER

Water sustains life – a fact known to everyone. It is repeated like a mantra countless times at conferences addressing the global water crisis. The fact is emphasized in innumerable articles and books on water. Water is described as pure or polluted, potable or not. It is possible to figure out the exact quantity of impurities and specify at which point it becomes unsafe for consumption. Water can be a torrential rain or a picturesque waterfall. I know, like everyone else, that water gives life, and that it also takes life, but I had never thought of water as a live or dead member of a place, in the manner described by Amma. Her meaning becomes clear not only in the words she used but also in the manner she spoke. She spoke of water as if she were talking about a person, not a thing. This became even clearer as the interview with her was being transcribed. On listening to the interview later on, it emerged that although Amma had used the words "dead water," the words were interpreted at the time of the interview as "dead body." It seemed, at the time, that she was speaking about a person, leading to a significant mistranslation during the interview.

When Amma says, "a *nadu* cannot survive without water,"[114] she understands, as does anyone who knows about the interconnectedness of life on earth, that water is essential for life. But her understanding differs in a significant way. That water is essential as it sustains life and water is a living member of a place are two different ways of relating to water. In understanding water as a live member of a place, Amma believes it should "live" for that reason too. Making water "just like dead water"[115] is not simply violence to the humans and animals who need it to live, but more crucially, for Amma, it appears to

112 Ibid.
113 Interview with Amma
114 Ibid.
115 Interview with Amma.

be a violence to water itself. In the normative universe she inhabits, that violence matters.

This understanding is significant in order to appreciate why water is not simply water here. It holds meanings that are connected to lives in ways that are not always clear, unless one listens carefully. It took me a while to notice that while I spoke about water, people I was speaking with always referred to particular waters. It is not water as such that they spoke about, but well-water, lorry-water, canal-water, dam-water, tap-water, and of course, the company-water. Each of these has a distinct meaning and significance. These waters could not be treated at par, as if they were all *just* water.

These distinctions, never clearly articulated, but always present in responses to particular questions, explain a lot about Adivasis in this place and their responses to the changes in the place after Coca-Cola's arrival. It adds another dimension to the reasons why many Adivasis here dislike the lorry-water now being provided to residents by the government. The ways in which their reliance on the lorry that brings potable water to the hamlets has disrupted their lives is obvious. Unlike the time when they could draw water from their wells whenever they needed it, they now have to wait for the lorry to arrive in the afternoons, and then collect enough water to last a couple of days. More often than not, it is women who are responsible for collecting water for their families, and therefore have to forgo work and wages. Since most residents are daily–wage workers, it is not difficult to imagine the hardship this inability to work every day causes. Moreover, now they also have to buy more pots to store the water. As mentioned before, since the pots have to be constantly carried back and forth from the place where the lorry stops, everyone in Plachimada and Vijaynagar now prefers the lighter plastic pots to the traditional clay ones that break easily and have to be replaced more often. Metal pots, the only other option, are heavier and unaffordable for most.

While these are significant reasons that explain why the Adivasis here dislike the lorry-water, they don't tell the whole story. As several Adivasis point out, they do not know where the lorry-water comes from. The source of that water is not in front of them to see, and that makes it hard for them to trust it. They worry about giving such water to their children. That is also the reason they will not use the canal-water for drinking or cooking. Their unease emerges in many ways – some say there might be dead animals or other such things in the water that comes from far away. It cannot be trusted for that reason. Some do not wish to give any reasons and simply say they will never take lorry-water.

The significance of this sense of disconnection from the source of water also offers a way to understand why Adivasis in the hamlets rejected the company-water, that is water that Coca-Cola brought in lorries for a while after the protests began. At one point during the proceedings in the Kerala High Court, the company had offered to supply drinking water in the hamlets. The High Court had also incorporated a direction to this effect in its order while allowing the company to continue to function.[116] Adivasis had, however, refused to take this company-water, which even though also brought in lorries, was not simply lorry-water. It was company-water. They preferred to walk longer distances to fetch well-water. Company-water evoked a different response than lorry- or canal-water. It appears to have been unacceptable because it was connected to the company, which they have learnt is selfish, unwilling, and incapable of living with others. Instead of becoming a part of their place, it turned their land into a "desert."

When the Adivasis say they need and want water, they do not want just *any* water. What they are saying is that they want the water in their wells. The well-water is significant because it is connected to, and connects them to, the land. As Kothandan, an Adivasi elder emphasized, they do not want lorry-water or water pumped from rivers and supplied through pipes. In his words: "That water, we don't want. Our water, the water in our compound [is what] we want to take and drink. That is what we want."[117] To make it easier for those of us who may still not understand, he has this to say: "We want water from this place. This water, don't take".[118] This is clearly not how Coca-Cola understands water as apparent from the fact that it continued to extract millions of liters of water from the place even as the wells around its plant were drying up.

Coca-Cola has all along denied any responsibility for the depletion of groundwater in the area. It has relied on scientific reports with data on rainfall, water tables, and so on to refute other reports and other data, which indicate that pollution and depletion of water were caused due to the company's operations. Something that none of these reports has determined is what Coca-Cola's presence in the place has done to the Adivasis' relationship with water. Perhaps, this is so because this cannot be determined only by testing the water but rather by listening to what people say and why. I was struck by how many of them repeated an expression over and over again – water was right there, but you could not drink it. It was

[116] See *Hindustan Coca-Cola Beverages Pvt. Ltd.* v. *Perumatty Grama Panchayat*, 2005(2) KLT 554, para. 54.
[117] Interview with Kothandan.
[118] Ibid.

perhaps something they had never imagined possible and could not relate to. Water that comes from another place (such as canal-water) can be suspect, but not water in your own well. This was clearly a new, unfamiliar, and discomforting way of being with or living with their wells. The water was there but not the same. Just as the land was there but not the same. In a place where everything is seen as connected with each element sustaining all the others, these were significant changes. They were unasked for and unwelcome changes.

What I want to draw attention to here is an experience of injustice that has not been articulated so far in any of the many stories told of the Adivasi protests in Plachimada. Coca-Cola's presence in the place has separated those who live in the place from all that was familiar to them. The land they have lived and worked on is there, but in significant ways it is not the same land anymore. Walls now enclose the only source of livelihood for many of them. Similarly, their water is also still there but they cannot drink it anymore. These separations from "this water in this place" are significant for people who see themselves as part of a whole, for people who have their own ways of relating to the place, and of living in the place.

Can this separation from a familiar way of life ever be compensated for? The answer to this question is often easy for most people who have never had to give up their homes to make way for a factory or other similar symbol of development.[119] Displacement, it is believed, is a cost that must be paid by some. Often this displacement is even perceived as a path to better lives for the displaced.[120] The answer to this question is not as easy for those who stand to lose the most and yet rarely get to voice their opinions. In Plachimada, the response to the issue of compensation is not only in what the Adivasis say about compensation but also in the pauses and the search for words that often precede their responses. It is in the stories they tell about themselves, others, and the place. The answer lies in acknowledging how local and global processes contribute to the injustices here.

[119] For critiques of development understood primarily as catching up with the developed West, see Wolfgang Sachs, ed., *The Development Dictionary: A Guide to Knowledge as Power* (New York and London: Zed Books, 1992). See also Arturo Escobar, "The Making and Unmaking of the Third World through Development," in *The Post-Development Reader*, eds. Majid Rehnema and Victoria Bawtree (London: Zed Books, 1997); Balakrishnan Rajagopal, "Counter-hegemonic International Law: Rethinking Human Rights and Development as a Third World Strategy," *Third World Quarterly* 27:5 (2006): 767; Pooja Parmar, "Undoing Historical Wrongs: Law and Indigeneity in India," *Osgoode Hall Law Journal* 49:3 (2012).

[120] See *Narmada Bachao Andolan* v. *Union of India*, 2000 INSC 518; AIR 2000 SC 3751.

2.6. PROTEST

As the residents of the area around the Coca-Cola plant struggled to understand the changes in their water and the rapidly increasing health problems, they also watched all the lorries carrying beverages out of the plant. They started talking about the number of bore wells on the "company land," and of their water being sent to other places. A consensus emerged in the community that the company was responsible for the changes they had all been noticing. Some of them approached the company. They had expected to resolve the issue as they resolve other matters within the community by sitting together and talking to each other.[121] Kannan, an Adivasi leader, recalls that the company's "manager" agreed that the scarcity of water was a result of the operations of the company. In fact, according to Kannan, the manager they spoke with even said that it was natural for such a company to affect the water within the radius of two to three kilometers around its premises. He also told them that the company usually provides employment to locals in order to compensate for this, but they were not bound to do that here. Most significantly, Kannan recalls the manager saying that "[t]here is no relation between public and the company" and that they must not go to it with their problems.[122]

By now, it was clear to them that contrary to what they had been told, the company was not there to live *with* them. They felt that something had to be done, but the decision to protest was not made easily. Maariamma remembers clearly the evening Kannan and some other young Adivasi men visited her home to seek her permission and support. She recalls the anxieties and the discussion at the time about taking on a big company with "land enclosed by walls."[123] In the end they decided to go ahead, mainly because they were by then convinced that Coca-Cola was responsible for both the depletion of water in their wells and for all the other unwelcome changes. As Amma explained, "a *nadu* cannot survive without water."[124] They felt that something had to be done before their land turned into a desert, and they were forced to move. They had to ensure that the company leaves, because, as many of them repeat, over and over again, they will not leave.

According to some Adivasi leaders, it was around this time that they asked Subramaniam, who self-identifies as a social activist and is from a nearby

[121] Interviews with Maariamma, Kothandan, and Kannan.

[122] Interview with Kannan.

[123] Interview with Maariamma.

[124] Interview with Amma. The word "*nadu*" is translated as territory, country, land, and also as a place including all that is connected to it and to each other.

village, to join them. He has lived and worked in the area for many years and knew about the water scarcity. He had accompanied many of them to the nearby medical clinics and to the hospital in Palakkad and was aware of the ill effects of the polluted water on their health. As it later turned out, he was also able to garner the support of non-Adivasis in the area.

Once a decision to do something was made, they first approached the Perumatty Grama Panchayat, which is the elected local village council of the area. It is the Panchayat that had granted Coca-Cola the license to operate in the area. At the time, the Panchayat refused to take any action against the company. A couple of local politicians intervened following a token one-day strike, after which the company agreed to provide drinking water to the residents of the hamlets. Some residents believed that only those who worked for the company could take the company-water. As mentioned before, the company-water was not acceptable to many Adivasis. Moreover, they were convinced by that time that the company had to leave. It could not stay in that place any longer because it had "made [their] land a desert."[125]

The Adivasi leaders decided to begin sustained protests against the company. An Adivasi Samara Samithi (translated as Adivasi Struggle/Strike/Protest Committee) was formed for this purpose.[126] Mylamma, a grandmother, and respected elder was chosen as the leader. Several Adivasis actively involved in a local Adivasi organization called *Adivasi Samrakshana Sangham* (Adivasi Protection Council), a group that according to one of its leaders came together to find answers, were in the forefront of the protests. Subramaniam, who was described as a patron of the organization at the time, was to provide advice and help in garnering support.

Initially many non-Adivasi residents of the hamlets were opposed to the Adivasi protests, even as everyone agreed that the depletion of water was a cause of concern for everyone. Most residents of the area do not wish to speak about the early reactions to Adivasi protests now. There appear to have been a range of reasons for the initial reluctance. Some, like the Adivasis themselves had earlier been, were not sure about taking on a big company. The few who were employed by the company must naturally have worried about losing their jobs. To some who had moved here recently from other places or

[125] Interview with Maariamma.

[126] The word *samara* or *samaram* is translated as struggle, protest, movement, and even strike. Sometimes, the word was translated differently in the same sentence by different people, indicating that both the context and the translator's understanding of the context play a role in the meaning that emerges.

were more familiar with the functioning of industrial units, the situation had not, however, appeared to be any different from many others.

Amma spoke about the insults hurled at them by some non-Adivasis in Plachimada and Vijaynagar as they went around asking for support. Others also mentioned that they had to initially face ridicule and contempt from their neighbors. This was, however, before the Adivasi protests turned into a *janakeeyam samaram* or a people's struggle. While not representative of how every non-Adivasi may have felt, an encounter on my first day in Plachimada offers some clues to the initial reactions to the Adivasi decision to protest. An elderly woman stopped to enquire if Shiny and I were from the census department. Upon learning about my research, she blamed the Adivasis for creating trouble. Even before I knew what she was talking about, I was taken aback by the look of contempt on her face. She mentioned that her community had been happy with the company. It even gave them water, she added.

Almost every one I spoke with in the hamlets, including members of the old woman's community, confirmed their support for the Plachimada Struggle. Many of them decided to join in once the *Adivasi Samara Samithi* was renamed as *Coca-Cola Viruddha Samara Samithi* or Anti–Coca-Cola Struggle Committee. This change was considered necessary because many did not wish to support an Adivasi struggle. In the words of Ramesh, owner of a small local business, who now supports the struggle: "If the struggle was done in the name of Adivasis we cannot join them."[127] He did not explain further, but his words become significant when seen in the context of the fact that the words "Adivasi struggle" are generally associated with the long-standing demands by Adivasis in Kerala for restoration of their lands that are currently occupied by non-Adivasi settlers.

The Adivasi struggle for alienated land in Kerala – narratives that are essential in order to understand the Adivasis' world of wrongs and rights – is discussed in detail in Chapter 7. Seen in the context of that struggle, it is easy to see that the opposition to Coca-Cola is inseparably connected to a longer story of dispossession. An "Adivasi struggle" would therefore understandably be a cause of concern for the settlers. Although not always articulated, the anxiety that mention of alienated Adivasi lands produces is visible in many ways. Almost always, the responses by non-Adivasis to my questions about Adivasi struggle for lands in Kerala were preceded by one or more of the following: frowns, narrowing of eyes, shifting in chairs, tightening of facial muscles,

[127] Interview with Ramesh.

or silence on the other end of a phone line. I was often asked why this issue was relevant for my research.

Opposition from the non-Adivasi residents was not the only challenge the early protestors had to face. Before the Panchayat came on board, the local administration and police too appeared to be on the company's side. Those who sit in the *samara pandal* often point to a picture that hangs there while speaking about the time when, from their perspective, the police had protected the company. The picture is a shot of a large posse of policemen in front of the Coca-Cola entrance. The policemen face the camera and the *samara pandal*, and appear to be protecting the company's premises behind them.

While speaking about the police, Adivasi men and women also describe how they were once beaten, rounded up, and taken to the police station in Chittur.[128] Women speak about their saris being pulled and blouses ripped as the police attempted to disperse the protestors gathered in front of the company premises. Although most of the men and women taken to the police station were allowed to leave after some time without being formally charged, a few were charged for obstructing traffic and other related offences. As these cases continue to drag on in the local court, every time the accused are required to attend proceedings, they have to lose work and wages for a day.

Despite all the challenges, the Adivasi protestors persisted. They continued to sit outside the plant demanding that Coca-Cola leave their place. As it began to get more and more difficult to ignore the depletion and other unwelcome changes to the water, other residents joined the protestors under the banner of the Plachimada Anti–Coca-Cola Struggle Committee. As the protests continued, the Perumatty Panchayat too stepped in and passed a unanimous resolution to not renew the company's license. Coca-Cola decided to temporarily suspend operations in early 2004. The facility has been closed since then, a fact widely celebrated as a significant success for the people's movement in Plachimada.

Today the Plachimada Struggle has the support of individuals from many parts of the world, as well as scores of local, national, and international organizations that subscribe to a range of ideologies. As set out in detail in the following chapter the dispute has brought together religious organizations, scientists, writers, nationalists, and anti-globalization activists, who have all found common cause in demanding the ouster of Coca-Cola. The basic issue

[128] See "Anti–Coca-Cola Agitators Arrested, Released Later," *The Hindu*, June 9, 2005, accessed September 20, 2010, http://www.thehindu.com/2005/06/09/stories/2005060903050700.htm, and "500 Arrested in Rally Against Coca-Cola in India," *India Resource Centre*, June 9, 2005, accessed November 30, 2005. http://www.indiaresource.org/.

as framed through social and political action is that of the violation of a community's right to its water by a powerful multinational corporation.

2.7. STATE RESPONSE TO THE RESISTANCE MOVEMENT

The sustained social action and relentless media coverage ultimately left the Government of Kerala no option but to take the protests seriously. Not only is it an active participant in the litigation related to the dispute today, in May 2009 it also constituted a High Power Committee headed by a senior officer of the state administration to investigate the nature and extent of damage caused by the Coca-Cola plant in Plachimada. On March 22, 2010, this committee submitted its report that indicates that the cola company had caused losses amounting to Rs. 216.26 crores [$48 million] and was liable to pay compensation to those affected.[129]

This report is based on the evaluation of various earlier reports, and consultations with scientists, lawyers, and others with expertise in environment, health, and water. The members of the Committee held a public hearing in the area that I attended. The Committee also asked for submissions of claims by those who had been affected. While I was in the village, volunteer students from a local college led by their teacher visited to help the villagers fill out the claim forms. The Committee acknowledges in its report that "no amount of money can be true compensation for the damages incurred" by those affected, but emphasizes that compensation could be seen as an acknowledgment that "people have been wronged".[130] The report also recommends the setting up of a separate tribunal or another statutory authority for adjudicating individual claims.[131]

Coca-Cola had at the very outset challenged the constitution, legality, and jurisdiction of this Committee,[132] and predictably, it has also repudiated its findings.[133] Despite some support for the company from the Commerce and Industries Department of Kerala,[134] the Kerala State Cabinet accepted the

[129] "Report of the High Power Committee" presented by Chairman K. Jayakumar to the Government of Kerala on March 22, 2010.

[130] Ibid., 5.

[131] Ibid.

[132] Ibid., 4.

[133] Narayan Laxman, "Coca-Cola's Response Disappoints Plachimada Activists," *The Hindu*, April 23, 2010, accessed August 5, 2014, http://www.thehindu.com/opinion/op-ed/article408788.ece; P. N. Venugopal, "End of Plachimada Battle. Or Is It?," *India Together*, April 30, 2010, accessed August 5, 2014, http://www.indiatogether.org/2010/apr/env-plachmada.htm.

[134] The principal secretary of the Industries Department in Kerala submitted a detailed note to the Cabinet raising questions about the findings of the High Power Committee's report. In his

report of the High Power Committee on June 30, 2010.[135] The state proposes to set up a special tribunal to determine individual claims for compensation, and to this end the state legislative assembly passed the Plachimada Coca Cola Victims Relief and Compensation Claims Tribunal Bill in February 2011. The Bill is currently awaiting the president's assent.

Despite these differences between departments of the government (partly a consequence of coalition politics in Kerala, and partly a reflection of the internal ideological dilemmas that have plagued the Communist Party of India), the position taken by the state suggests that the overall current environment in Kerala might make it harder for the unit to reopen. As one of the activists involved pointed out to me, unlike before when the state was considered to be supporting the company, now on "[o]ne side [is] the Coca-Cola Company, and [on] the other side, the state, community, Anti–Coca-Cola Struggle Committee, Plachimada Solidarity Committee, Pollution Control Board, Groundwater [authority], and other state apparatus, are together."[136]

2.8. THE LITIGATION

Coca-Cola has denied any wrongdoing or liability all along. When the Perumatty Panchayat refused to renew its license to operate in Plachimada, the company initiated legal proceedings against it. The many administrative and legal proceedings that followed are described in detail in Chapter 4. Briefly, in 2003 a judge of the Kerala High Court ruled in favor of the Panchayat. Coca-Cola successfully appealed this decision. The Panchayat, the Kerala State Pollution Control Board, and Coca-Cola have all gone in appeal against this decision to the Supreme Court of India where all the appeals are currently pending adjudication.

note he is reported to have recommended that the unit be allowed to reopen, and that any violation of specific laws by the company be dealt with by "initiating action under those laws." An adverse impact on the flow of private investment into the state, and the "overall prosperity" of the state, are some of the reasons he has cited against any attempts to hold the company liable for damages. C. Gauridasan Nair, "Industries Department Slams Plachimada Report," *The Hindu*, June 29, 2010, accessed August 5, 2014, http://www.thehindu.com/2010/06/29/stories/2010062954230400.htm. He has also publicly expressed regret over the fact that the "Coca-Cola unit could not be saved." The chief minister of Kerala, however, clarified later that those were not the views of the government. See "Chief Secretary to Look into Official's Controversial Statement on Coca-Cola," *The Hindu*, May 26, 2010, accessed August 5, 2014, http://www.thehindu.com/news/states/kerala/article438655.ece

135 "Tribunal to Adjudicate Compensation to People Affected by Coca-Cola Plant," *The Hindu*, June 30, 2010, accessed August 5, 2014, http://thehindu.com/news/cities/Thiruvananthapuram/article493750.ece.

136 Interview with Vasu.

The legal battle over the dispute in Plachimada is primarily between the Perumatty Grama Panchayat and Coca-Cola. This is often described as a battle of the small against the big: the story of a small village council with very few resources fighting a multinational giant that reports a net income of millions of dollars.[137] This story of a local body that did not have enough funds to meet the expense of litigation launched by Coca-Cola is a significant one. The litigation raises important issues related to rights and powers of a village *panchayat*, which is the foundation of the local self-governance model of the panchayat system in India. A decision from the Supreme Court on this matter is likely to have a significant impact on the future of decentralized system of governance in the country.

Many residents of the hamlets surrounding the Coca-Cola plant did not say much about the litigation. The straightening of backs and clearing of throats that followed any mention of "court" during my conversations with some men in the area indicated a discomfort and perhaps an unwillingness to comment on either this particular litigation or on courts generally. Those who offered a comment regard the litigation to be a matter between the Panchayat and the company. Kannan, a prominent leader, remarked that "there was no case now."[138] Given that concerns that are fundamental to why they want the company to leave have not been articulated in the litigation, it is not difficult to understand why an Adivasi would feel that there is now "no case." Some residents do believe that the Panchayat is fighting for them too. However, none of the Adivasis, some who are even named as respondents in some of the petitions, has ever been to the High Court of Kerala in Ernakulam or to the Supreme Court of India in New Delhi. The ways in which the courts, their proceedings, and their languages are far from the lives of the Adivasi protestors will become clear from the accounts presented in the following chapters.

2.9. THE *SAMARA PANDAL*

As described above, the *samara pandal* faces the large gate to the Coca-Cola premises from across the state highway. In English language reports it has also

[137] In the year 2010 the company reported a net income of USD 11,809 million. See, The Coca-Cola Company, "2010 Annual Review: Advancing Our Global Momentum," accessed August 2, 2011, http://www.thecoca-colacompany.com/investors/annual_review_2010.html. See also C. Surendranath, "Coca-Cola: Continuing Battle in Kerala," *India Resource Center*, July 10, 2003, accessed July 3, 2012, http://www.indiaresource.org/campaigns/coke/2003/continuingbattle.html, where the author notes that the "Coca Cola story in Plachimada is reminiscent of David versus the mighty Goliath."

[138] Interview with Kannan.

been described as the "vigil hut." As the word *pandal* suggests, the *samara pandal* was meant to be a temporary structure,[139] but it has now been standing in the same spot for more than ten years. During the numerous hours I spent in the *samara pandal*, I learned about the range of meanings the structure has acquired over the last several years both for those who built it and those who visit it. These meanings are connected to many stories: of Adivasi women who sit there everyday; of women and men who stop by the *samara pandal* as they go about their everyday lives; of other *pandals* that have been built and taken down; of those Adivasis who refuse to sit here anymore. Other meanings also emerge from stories that "outsiders" tell of the Plachimada Struggle. Many of these meanings will emerge more fully as the stories unfold in the following chapters.

Maariamma and Keyi are two elder women who sit in the *samara pandal* everyday. At times they are joined by other women – Adivasi and non-Adivasi – who stop by for anywhere between fifteen minutes and several hours during the day. Sometimes men too stop by to enquire about Maariamma's health or to chat for a few minutes. Keyi joins in the conversations occasionally, but on most days she prefers to listen to the conversations. Maariamma, on the other hand, never seems to tire of talking. She also loves to pose riddles, mostly short verses that are extremely difficult to figure out but almost always have simple answers connected to everyday lives of people here. To me these were constant reminders, as such things are, of my outsiderness. Maariamma believes, as she said on many occasions, that humor and laughter are signs of life – of being alive – a fact that her person represents more than her words. Of the many moods of Maariamma I witnessed, her wide smile and joyful, almost soundless, laughter are what comes to mind every time I think of her.

Maariamma has been sitting in the *pandal* from morning until late evening for more than six years. On days that she is sick or tired she lies down on the worn-out mat or the bare wooden cot. The rest of the time she just sits there, on the mud floor that is plastered every alternate day, sometimes looking out on to the road or at the Coca-Cola gate. At other times she sits with her back to the road and to the Coca-Cola plant. Sometimes she looks at the pictures hung on the walls, remembering, re-living those moments when famous people stopped by to lend their support.

[139] The word *pandal* usually refers to a temporary structure like a shed built for a specific purpose. It has been described as a "[t]hatched shed put up for temporary purposes" in T.K. Velu Pillai, *The Travancore State Manual*, vol. 4 (Travancore: Government of Travancore, 1940), 810. Temporary canvas sheds erected by protestors or those "on strike" are a common sight throughout Kerala.

The *samara pandal* is where all the people with questions about the famous Plachimada Struggle stop by. She tells them stories she has repeated more times than she can remember. Many visitors in the past, she recalls, brought their cameras. Some asked her to walk in front of the company's gates, while others asked her to pose with one arm raised. It was awkward in the beginning, before she got used to, and then tired of, all the cameras and all the questions about the company.

On quiet days when not many people stop by the *pandal*, Maariamma admits she is fed up of sitting here and tired of re-telling the story. Tired also, she says, of waiting for the company to leave. But she is proud of her role as a leader of the community and takes her responsibilities very seriously. The pride shows on her face when she talks about the evening when Kannan and other Adivasi young men approached her to talk about the protests. Even today she remains committed to their demands for removal of the Coca-Cola plant from their place. It is not easy for her to sit in the *pandal* all day everyday. This eighty-six-year-old woman would rather work in the fields than rely on others for food and her other few requirements. But despite all this, she remains committed because, she says, once they decided to take action, they have to stay together in this fight. This is why she wishes for the return of those who left the *pandal*.

2.10. A SEPARATION

In August 2006, four years after the protests against extraction of water by Coca-Cola were formally launched, some Adivasi leaders decided to part ways or, as it is often described, separated. All the Adivasis who "left" the *samara pandal* had been at the forefront of the protests against the company. They were the ones who had been strongly in favor of initiating action against the company, when many were worried about the consequences of taking on the big company that had "enclosed land with walls." Mylamma, the woman who had spearheaded the agitations, helped build the *pandal*, and traveled across the state and beyond to speak about issues that mattered to her community and to garner "outsider" support, was also the one who led those who eventually left.

Every Adivasi in the area today remains committed to the expulsion of Coca-Cola from the place, but those who separated refuse to sit in the *samara pandal*. In this close-knit community, this separation, as many Adivasis refer to it, has caused immense pain. This pain showed in the eyes of Maariamma and other elders much before any of them decided to speak about the separation. It was in the silence or the tears that often followed the mention of some names. Sometimes it was in the worried expression on Maariamma's face as she looked in a certain direction, the significance of which I was unaware of at the time.

The story of the separation, set out more fully in Chapter 5, is a complicated one. Defying a neat narrative, it is not a story with a well-defined beginning, middle, and end. It is instead an assortment of events that shed light on an unrecognized violence by offering a deeper understanding of the Adivasi protests. It is an illustration of the extent to which Coca-Cola's presence in Plachimada has disrupted the lives of its residents, and of the fact that not everything that has been destroyed in Plachimada can be made whole again; that it would require more than monetary compensation to put together all that appears to have fallen apart in the place.

The events and narratives surrounding the separation have been the hardest for me to write about, but it is through my struggles with them that I have begun to understand the motives of many who have chosen to exclude the separation stories while speaking or writing about Plachimada. I have chosen to include them because I gave my word to several Adivasis who shared so much about their lives with me and asked for nothing other than that I write their stories. I promised to write them as best as I understood them. The accounts of separation are an inseparable part of the other stories unfolding in and around Plachimada, and necessary for a fuller understanding of the dispute.

2.11. WATER, PROTESTS, MEANINGS

What the protests in Plachimada mean to those who started them is what I had set out to discover through this project. Meanings of the protests against Coca-Cola for Adivasis and their many supporters emerged over long conversations with many of them. They emerged not only from what the respondents said about water or about Coca-Cola but also from all the other things they spoke about or were hesitant to speak about. One thing that I hope the multiple accounts presented here will show is that such disputes over water are misconstrued if they are understood as events in themselves, unconnected with past struggles and events.[140]

[140] See Amita Baviskar, ed., *Waterscapes: The Cultural Politics of a Natural Resource* (New Delhi: Permanent Black, 2007). This is a collection of studies that indicate that such struggles are "simultaneously struggles for power over symbolic representations and material resources" (Baviskar, *Waterscapes*, 1). In this volume, see especially David Mosse, "Ecology, Uncertainty and Memory: Imagining a Pre-colonial Irrigated Landscape in South India," in which Mosse uses "oral histories of water and rule" to note the symbolic or representational nature of such struggles, and Lyla Mehta and Anand Punja, "Water and Well-being: Explaining the

The Adivasi protests are not only for water but also for land, education, jobs, respect, and inclusion in decision making. All of this they desire to find "here," in the place they have lived and worked since the time when there was no one else here. The protests are therefore also about not having to leave. That, however, is not possible unless the company leaves. As Kothandan, the elder from Madhavan Nair Pathy said after a long conversation, as if to ensure I did not miss what was most important:

> We are here. We are not going to go anywhere. The company should be taken away. The company should be taken away. That is all about the *samaram*.

Gap in Understandings of Water," where experiences of displacement of Adivasi groups in Gujarat are presented to suggest that struggles over water are not just about access but are also struggles of meaning (Baviskar, *Waterscapes*, 209). The position that struggles have situated meanings that are at times lost in legal accounts has also been convincingly illustrated in E. P. Thompson, *Customs in Common: Studies in Traditional Popular Culture* (New York: The New Press, 1993).

3

A People's Movement

3.1. PLACHIMADA: A PEOPLE'S RESISTANCE MOVEMENT

In this chapter I present the popular accounts of what has come to be known as the Plachimada Movement or Plachimada Struggle. In drawing attention to these accounts, my purpose is two-fold: to highlight the concerns and commitments that underlie the immense support received by the protestors in Plachimada over the years, and to indicate how the commitments and strategies of various translators have shaped the popular understanding of the dispute.[1] These are critical to understanding what is missing from the popular accounts and why.

The fact that not only the initially reluctant, and some even hostile, non-Adivasis in the area but also the numerous organizations at the district, state, national, and international level support the demand to oust Coca-Cola from Plachimada today is an indication of the success of the committed people who self-identify as social activists, human rights activists, antiglobalization activists, health activists, environmental rights activists, and peace activists. Like the Adivasis who began the protests, they too want Coca-Cola to leave, and many of them continue to work tirelessly toward that end. It is difficult to say at this stage – more than a decade after the fact – what course the Adivasi protests against Coca-Cola in Plachimada would have taken without this support and advocacy. What can be said is that the commitment of these self-identified activists and other supporters to what they generally refer to as the Plachimada Struggle or the Plachimada Resistance Movement is impressive, important, and inspiring.

[1] For the role of activists as translators who reinterpret global ideas into local terms as well as render local stories into more politically persuasive terms, see Sally Engle Merry and Rachel E. Stern, "The Female Inheritance Movement in Hong Kong: Theorizing the Local/Global Interface," *Current Anthropology* 46:3 (June 2005): 387–410.

The individuals and organizations I mention here have been instrumental in drawing attention to the issues in Plachimada, garnering national and international support, and ensuring a response from the Government of Kerala.[2] While doing so, they have also played a crucial role in shaping the popular conception of the meaning and significance of the dispute in Plachimada. In looking more closely at this material my purpose is to shed light on the processes and practices of translation to gain a better understanding of why and how meanings change as many concerned individuals translate local events and issues into a language of rights and resistance. These stories are therefore an important constituent of the larger theme of loss and gains of meanings as complex issues are shaped into abstract claims that appeal to a wider audience.

The stories in this chapter, like all others in this book, are framed by fundamental ideas about right and wrong, which inhabit the normative universe of their principal actors and are presented in languages that they often share with their audiences. These stories represent the personal, professional, individual, and collective commitments of many people who have supported the protests against Coca-Cola over the last decade. Unlike the Adivasi stories presented later, the ones in this chapter are the well-recognized popular accounts of the dispute in Plachimada. But this is not the only crucial difference. Unlike the Adivasi stories that are mainly of people in search of answers, the ones in this chapter are essentially of those who believe they have the answers. Many of them are about *rights over* and *to* water, an idea that frames the beliefs, responses, choices, and actions of many activists, politicians, authors, religious leaders, and reporters. These are stories about *rights of* local people, local communities, citizens, and local bodies, and about *rights to* water, life, environment, common property resources, local self-governance, and regulation and management of resources. They are also stories about the range of, at times overlapping legal rights available today – democratic rights, constitutional rights, statutory rights, international human rights – revealing in their invocation the sources that endow these rights with authority and legitimacy. Other ideas that feature prominently in these popular stories are those of resistance, capitalism, globalization, and growing corporate control over water and resources. Being central to the normative universe of the many supporters of the Adivasi protestors, these words and concepts represent the dispute in specific important ways.

Conspicuous by their absence are the more complex themes that recur in Adivasi stories presented in Chapters 6 and 7: relationships of belonging, the

[2] See K. Ravi Raman, "Transverse Solidarity: Water, Power, and Resistance," *Review of Radical Political Economics* 42:2 (2010): 251–268.

injustice of past displacements, fear of losing homes, familiar ways of life and livelihood, fear of losing children and families, and of continuing social, economic, and political exclusion. It is these elements, central to the Adivasi accounts of the dispute, that have been eclipsed in the popular, well-documented, and well-meaning accounts by their translators. This reframing of their concerns, and denial of opportunity to present their stories in their own terms, has contributed to the sense of betrayal experienced by Adivasis who left the *samara pandal*.

In the following section, I begin with stories of those who have led and actively supported the protests in Plachimada within and outside Kerala. These are individuals and organizations that got involved at the time of or soon after the decision to commence sit-in protests outside the Coca-Cola premises was made, and they continue to extend their support for many reasons and in many ways. The third section offers an account of the wider support received by the protestors and the global ideas that are connected to Plachimada. I then present accounts of the dispute that emerge from what has been written about it. Here I take a closer look at the manner and extent to which the protests have been reported locally, nationally, and internationally, often by groups and individuals sympathetic to demands of closure of the Coca-Cola plant. In the fifth section of this chapter I draw attention to some practices of translation before offering some concluding thoughts in the last section.

The accounts presented in this chapter are based mainly on interviews and a study of various published texts. Of the six interviews with those who identified as activists, three were conducted in English, two in Malayalam, and one in both Malayalam and English. Of the two interviews with local politicians, one was conducted in English, and the other in Malayalam. A large proportion of the media reports and other activist literature are available in the English language. In addition to these, I also collected and read translations of many articles, news reports, campaign posters, and notices published in Malayalam.

3.2. ACTIVISTS AND ORGANIZATIONS IN KERALA

A large number of organizations have supported the Plachimada Struggle over the last decade. The *Plachimada Coca-Cola Viruddha Janakeeya Samara Samithi* (Plachimada Anti–Coca-Cola Peoples Struggle Committee), also often referred to as the *Coca-Cola Viruddha Samara Samithi* (Anti–Coca-Cola Struggle Committee), has been at the forefront of the agitations ever since it was formed in May 2002.[3] This committee comprises a group of people who

[3] Haritha Bhumi, "Anti Coca-Cola Agitation – Plachimada: 1000 Historical Days," trans. Praveen Hariharan, *Keraleeyam* 1:7 (January 2005): 29–40.

live in the area, mostly Adivasis, but also others, who came together to do something about the hardships caused by the Coca-Cola plant in Plachimada and have been actively involved in the agitations against the company. Although earlier reports mention Kannan, an Adivasi leader, as the convener of this committee, it is Subramaniam, a non-Adivasi activist, described as the patron of this committee, who is considered by most as the one involved in all the decision making.

Another name that often appears in the media, public notices, and court records is that of the Plachimada Solidarity Committee. Its convener Vasu described it as a support group. It is an informal coalition of "many mass organizations, people's movements, civil society movements, youth organizations, [and] political parties" that work together, in a "democratic" manner, in support of the agitators under the "umbrella" of Plachimada Solidarity Committee.[4] This group has indeed played a very significant role in keeping the issue alive outside Palakkad, especially in the state's capital.

By some accounts there are a hundred or more large and small organizations that have supported the agitations in many ways over the years. A remarkable aspect of the anti–Coca-Cola struggle is in fact that organizations and individuals ascribing to many different, at times even conflicting, ideologies and faiths have sustained the protests for several years without an organizational/institutional base, or any regular funding arrangements. Water, more specifically strong reactions to denial of water – described by many involved as the source of life – seems to have played a significant role in bringing all these people together.

Many of these organizations continue to actively participate in the agitation, while a few have parted ways. The Plachimada Solidarity Committee and Plachimada Anti–Coca-Cola Agitation Committee continue to coordinate the support of several of these organizations. But there are many that have come forward on their own to express solidarity by either visiting the *samara pandal* or through independent press statements or actions. Some names I came across during my research (listed in alphabetical order) are: *Adivasi Gothra Mahasabha* [Adivasi Grand Assembly], All India *Kisan Sabha* [All India Farmers Assembly], All India Peoples Resistance Forum, All India Youth Federation, All India Bank Officers Association, Centre for Folklore Studies, Democratic Youth Federation of India, Farmers Protection Committee, Gandhi *Yuva Mandalam* [Youth organization] State Committee, Greenpeace, Jamaat-e-Islami Hind (JIH) Kerala, *Jananeethi:* Peoples' Initiative for Human

4 Interview with Vasu.

Rights, Kerala Anti-Liquor Committee, Kerala Council of Churches, Kerala *Sasthra Sahitya Parishad* [Kerala Forum for Science and Literature], National Alliance of People's Movements, National Peoples' Rights Committee, People's Union for Civil Liberties, Revolutionary Youth Front, Solidarity, Vanditavalam Developmental Youth Society, *Vikas Adhyayan Kendra*, Youth Congress Working Committee, *Viplava Streevadi Prasthanam* [Revolutionary Feminist Movement], *Yuvajana Vedi* – the youth wing of the Communist Party of India (Marxist-Leninist). Although this is not an exhaustive list, it is representative of the range of organizations involved.

As the names suggest, some are religious organizations, whereas others are affiliated to a national or local political party. Several are nongovernmental organizations (NGOs) committed to human rights generally or to particular social causes or political ideologies. The nature and extent of the involvement of these organizations varies greatly. Some have issued statements in solidarity with the protestors, or provided logistic support, whereas others have visited Plachimada and organized protest marches. Some groups have chosen their own independent ways of expressing their support. For example, organizations and institutions involved in research have conducted studies and published reports, whereas literary societies have staged street plays and other events to raise public awareness and garner support for the agitation.

There are also many individuals who are not associated with any specific organization but have volunteered, helped raise funds, or participated in protest marches and sit-ins in Plachimada. Several others have spoken and written about it, working tirelessly to raise awareness about the issue, and garner public support. Some activists have organized events, such as those held on each anniversary of the day the agitation was officially launched. They have spent time meeting with public authorities and lawyers. They have questioned decisions taken by the state government and have demanded that it take action. A few have contributed their personal savings as and when required to support protest marches or other events. During the early phase of the agitations, some activists were also arrested along with Adivasi protestors.

Some activists have supported the Plachimada Struggle even in the face of threats to their personal safety. Subramaniam is one of them. He describes himself as a "human rights activist" who has been participating in "the struggles of the people" in Kerala for over three decades both independently and through his association with a civil liberties association.[5] His tireless efforts in local environment protection and anti-liquor movements are recognized and

5 Interview with Subramaniam.

commended at events that he is regularly invited to speak at. He also supports local agitations against what he describes as "cultural deterioration."[6] But his commitment to social justice runs much deeper than supporting public protests. It shows in the things he does everyday.

For the past several years, Subramaniam has been helping residents of the hamlets in the area deal with crises of various kinds, and it is therefore hardly surprising that he was with them when the water crisis began. His work in the area involves such things like accompanying a farm laborer's family to the police station to ensure their complaint against those who abducted their nine-year-old daughter is registered; helping to get a sick Adivasi man to a hospital in the nearest town and making sure that the man gets treated; arranging a vehicle to take an old woman to the land records office; helping those who do not read or write to fill out forms so they can apply for pensions and other things; and submitting those forms to appropriate authorities. The significance of such service for those who seem to have been forgotten in a nation's pursuit of a stronger global presence should be obvious to anyone who spends even a few days in the area. And it is this service that has endeared Subramaniam to the Adivasis and many other communities in this and neighboring areas. Many address him as "elder brother," and regard him as family.

Subramaniam is a prominent leader of the Plachimada Struggle Committee. Other activists, media reports, and legal documents describe him as the patron of the *Coca-Cola Viruddha Samara Samithi* (Anti–Coca-Cola Struggle Committee). He has been in the forefront of many protests and events organized in Plachimada, and he continues to work tirelessly to garner support for the struggle. In fact some other non-Adivasi activists I met had decided to join in the early days of the protests only because of their faith in Subramaniam's long commitment to various causes in the area. It is not surprising therefore that many believe that he started it all. Several Adivasis also regard his early and continuing support as invaluable.

After decades of working and living among the most marginalized communities, it is perhaps not surprising that Subramaniam does not have too many expectations of the political parties or the state administration. He is also not sure about what to expect from the formal legal processes. Judges, according to him, "don't know anything about the local people."[7] But he has tremendous faith in what he refers to as the "people's power".[8] He sees this as

6 Ibid.
7 Ibid.
8 Ibid.

a "democratic struggle" that, despite the "illiteracy and backwardness of the area," will win against an influential "multinational corporate giant."[9] People's power, he feels, will ensure that Coca-Cola leaves not only the village but also "the nation."[10]

Subramaniam was not among those who celebrated the setting up of the Coca-Cola plant in the area as a sign of "development." Given his ongoing everyday battles with inequalities that continue to be overlooked, his distrust of such efforts is not surprising. He had doubts about the promise of jobs, elimination of poverty, and the general prosperity for the area that Coca-Cola held for many. The company, as it turned out, proved him right. He always had reservations about the promise of prosperity, but he did not know that the wells would also dry up. According to him, it was only after the water around the factory became unfit for drinking and began to cause "different diseases" that the "local peoples" realized that he had been right.[11] He recalls that they first formed an "action committee."[12] Initially they petitioned "related authorities" in the area, but since no results were forthcoming, he says: "we decided to start the struggle in 2002."[13]

Subramaniam did not specify who constituted "we" at the time. He did not mention the role of the members of the *Adivasi Samrakshana Sangham* during this early stage, the formation of the *Adivasi Samara Samithi* by Adivasi leaders, or the subsequent decision to change its name to Coca-Cola Viruddha Janakeeya Samara Samithi (Anti–Coca-Cola Peoples Struggle Committee). He did not even mention Mylamma, the respected Adivasi leader, or speak about any of the other Adivasis who spearheaded the initial protests, until specifically asked to. In fact, most non-Adivasis I interviewed or spoke with informally did not talk about the Adivasis' role until specifically asked to. Almost every such account of the beginning of protests repeatedly referred to "the people." During several of these conversations, I sensed what seems to be a desire that this be understood as a broader people's movement. The response of a local politician, Easwaran, who belongs to the political party that has a significant presence in the area and in the Panchayat and has been supporting the action against Coca-Cola, is illustrative. When

[9] "Peoples Fight for Justice," trans. Jiss Verkey. This interview was published in Malayalam. I have not included the complete reference to the source in order to protect his identity.

[10] Interview with Subramaniam.

[11] Ibid.

[12] Ibid.

[13] Ibid.

asked what, if any, issues the Adivasis might be generally facing in the area, his response was:

> It is not about Adivasis alone, but all the people in this area are affected. There are some Adivasis who are living near the factory, and it just started there. That's it. Not only them, all the people were affected.[14]

In the more than ten years since the decision to commence protests outside the Coca-Cola plant, the Plachimada Struggle has become the most recognizable contemporary people's movement in Kerala. It is clear from my numerous formal and informal conversations with several supporters, subscribing to a range of religious, social, and political ideologies, that the Plachimada Struggle offers much to each of them. Although each emphasizes a particular ideology or cause, there are several overlaps.

To many involved it offers hope in what they see as a time of disillusionment. To some it offers inspiration and provides a sense of purpose. One such person is a twenty-year-old student, who feels trapped in an education system that he perceives as nothing more than a pointless pursuit of coursework he has trouble coping with. This student, who self-identified as a member of the *Rashtriya Swayamsevak Sangh*, a right-wing Hindu nationalist organization, believes his work for the Plachimada Struggle is one of the best things he has ever done.[15]

Members of the Solidarity Youth Movement,[16] who according to Feroze, one of its leaders, believe in Islam "as a way of life," support the struggle because "water is not a commodity."[17] It is a "gift from god."[18] The organization is against Coca-Cola because it represents commodification of this gift. As he further pointed out, their primary goals in supporting the struggle are to help the "most poor and marginalized people," and prevent the corporate ownership of water.[19] Natural resources are gifts from god, and must be shared by all, he added. This same understanding of water, and a commitment to

[14] Interview with Easwaran.
[15] According to its web site the *Rashtriya Swayamsevak Sangh* was founded in 1925 and its membership is open to "[a]ny Hindu male." For more see the organization's web site http://www.rss.org/. Last accessed February 2, 2015.
[16] Solidarity Youth Movement (SYM) is the youth wing of JIH in Kerala. Its objective as stated on its web site is "to liberate the generation of youths from moral bankruptcy and debauchery and to transform them in to a radical vanguard fighting for the betterment of society." For more on SYM and JIH see www.solidarityym.org and www.jihkerala.org, respectively. Last accessed February 2, 2015
[17] Interview with Feroze.
[18] Ibid.
[19] Ibid.

empowerment of women also appears to be the motivation for the Women's Wing of the JIH Kerala, whose banner from a recently organized rally in support of the Plachimada Struggle lies in the *samara pandal*.

A few members of the *Swadeshi Jagaran Manch*,[20] the economic wing of the above-mentioned *Rashtriya Swayamsevak Sangh*, have also supported the struggle. At least one of them has been actively supporting the Plachimada Struggle Committee from the very beginning. Activists like him are committed to opposing multinational corporations in India, be it Wal-Mart in Punjab or Coca-Cola in Kerala. As the organization's web site explains, its members are not against "creation of wealth," but are rather opposed to "unlimited consumption".[21] Although the organization itself claims to not being averse to assimilation of "wholesome and beneficial elements from the outside,"[22] some of its members, like the one who declined my request for an interview because of my affiliation, are against all things he considers foreign, including universities. This is what also, of course, strengthens and sustains his commitment to the Plachimada Struggle.

Some like Gopal, a dedicated "Gandhian peace activist," and a member of the *Kerala Sarvodaya Mandalam*, support the struggle because it began as, and continues to be, a nonviolent struggle. He recounted that at times during meetings, some had wanted to respond to violence with violence. This was during early days of the protests, when the police, understood by the residents to be acting variously on behalf of the company and the government at the time, began to arrest protesters outside the factory. Those who resisted arrests were also pushed around and beaten up. Adivasi women, on more than one occasion, talked about being hit by batons, dragged by their saris, and of their blouses being ripped during scuffles with the police.

Some organizations in other parts of the state had in fact at the time engaged in activities like forcibly entering Coca-Cola's distribution center or other premises, and had destroyed bottles in protest.[23] But as Gopal recalls, protestors in Plachimada were always in favor of a nonviolent struggle. It is this commitment to nonviolence, he feels, that provides the "people" involved

[20] *Swadeshi Jagaran Manch* opposes "economic imperialism" and is committed to the cause of building a self-reliant nation by ensuring "security, unity and integrity," "nourishment of Bharatiya [Indian] cultural values," "preservation of natural wealth," and a "balanced development of all regions and the society as a whole." For more on its philosophy, stand on various issues, and affiliations, see the organization's web site: http://www.swadeshionline.in/. Last accessed February 2, 2015

[21] Ibid.

[22] Ibid.

[23] Bhumi, "Anti Coca-Cola Agitation," 225.

in the struggle with the "spiritual power" that has sustained this "movement for the truth" for this long.[24] And that for him is where the significance of Plachimada Struggle lies. He emphasized that the struggle would have been crushed had it turned to violence at any point.

It is this power of nonviolent resistance that also connects, for Gopal and several others involved, the protests against Coca-Cola to the Indian freedom movement. In the support for the Plachimada Struggle from around the world, they see a reenactment of the manner in which Gandhi's emphasis on nonviolence brought the world's attention to India's struggle against the British. Gopal mentioned all the well-known activists from India and elsewhere who have visited the "small hut" in Plachimada in solidarity.[25] He believes all these people have lent their support, "because this is a struggle for truth, for *dharma*."[26] Gopal's conviction shines bright in his eyes when he says:

> We have a strong belief that the Plachimada Adivasis will win. As long as truth and *dharma* prevail in the world, they cannot fail.[27]

Many women, men, organizations, and communities in Kerala support the struggle because of what the Coca-Cola Company represents to each of them. To those who self-identify as the true socialists, Coca-Cola represents global capitalism, and it is that which they are resisting. Some are defending the nation against foreign corporate invasion. Some draw parallels with the East India Company and centuries of British colonial rule that followed its arrival in India. Others see it as a corrupting Western influence on Indian culture. When asked to elaborate, many pointed out how much better tender coconut water (traditionally the most popular thirst-quencher in Kerala) is as compared with Coke and Pepsi: not only is the former healthier, and does not require extraction of millions of liters of water, it is also indigenous.

Coca-Cola's association to the West also became significant in a different context for some supporters of the Plachimada Struggle. In a clear illustration of the many ways in which the local and the global are connected, Coca-Cola's ties to the United States played a significant role for some who joined the movement to oust Coca-Cola soon after the U.S. invasion of Iraq in 2003. They felt that like the country it comes from, Coca-Cola must leave places where it is not wanted. The company's insistence on continuing operations

24 Interview with Gopal.

25 Ibid.

26 Ibid. The word *dharma* is often loosely translated as religion, but here it refers to righteousness as understood within the traditional Hindu principles of order.

27 Interview with Gopal.

contrary to the wishes of the residents seemed to them to be yet another manifestation of the American empire at the time.

In many corporate–global–foreign invasion accounts, the predominant theme is that of resistance. The commitments of individuals and organizations involved are to resist various forces of oppression: imperialism, colonialism, foreign capital, and Western culture. Within this narrative, Plachimada's victory would also be a win for resistance movements everywhere. It would offer hope to all those who are committed to resisting globalization, hegemony of global capital, and corporate control of nature around the world.

In a country that ousted its colonial rulers over six decades ago, resistance to invasion and struggles for freedom have deep and powerful resonance. As stated above, parallels with the East India Company were often drawn in speaking about Coca-Cola. In the same spirit, prominent freedom fighters (the men and women who were born in British India and participated in the Indian freedom struggle) in Kerala have in the past been invited to speak at events organized in Plachimada on more than one occasion.

3.3. SUPPORT FROM A WIDER COMMUNITY

The Plachimada Struggle has also received immense invaluable support from a range of environmental and water rights activists and organizations. Corporate theft of a community's water is an issue raised by many supporters of Plachimada. As Subramaniam emphasized, the main issue for many like him is "control over water."[28] The reasons are obvious. The depletion and pollution of groundwater has made life more difficult for the people who live around the Coca-Cola plant. A community whose water is drying up or has been made unsafe for use has a right to demand that further extraction of groundwater be stopped. It is the recognition of this right that many supporters of the struggle are demanding. It is the same right that many social and human rights activists advocate worldwide through campaigns for recognition of a human right to water in international law.

The water crisis in Plachimada received considerable national and international attention and media coverage when several activists attending the World Social Forum organized in Mumbai traveled to Plachimada to speak at the World Water Conference held there on January 21 and 22, 2004. Almost everyone I spoke with in the village remembers the time (although often not the exact dates or names) when Canadian author and activist Maude Barlow,

[28] Interview with Subramaniam.

French farmer and antiglobalization activist José Bové, and Indian author and environmental activist Vandana Shiva spoke in support of the people in Plachimada. Among several others present were environmentalists from Sweden, Canada, and the United States, as well as activists, writers, and politicians from Kerala and elsewhere in the country.

This event drew considerable interest and inspired many non-Adivasis to join the movement. At the event, the distinguished visitors spoke about the need to "resist globalization" and "globalize resistance."[29] They spoke about "American culture," privatization and commodification of water, and the global struggles against "monopolistic corporations."[30] Most significantly for those engaged in protests in a small village, they spoke about the support of "anti-globalization resistance movements" around the world.[31] At the conclusion of the conference, the participants adopted the Plachimada Declaration.

The Plachimada Declaration recognizes that "water is the fundamental right of all people."[32] It further declares that water is a "gift of nature" that "belongs to all living beings."[33] Water, it states, is "not a commodity," and the right of local communities to "conserve, use and manage water" is the "very basis of water democracy."[34] The declaration concludes with an expression of "full solidarity with the Adivasis who have put up resistance against the tortures of the horrid commercial forces in Plachimada."[35] Maude Barlow and Dr. Sukumar Azhikode, the Chairman of the Convening Committee of the conference in Plachimada, read out the declaration.

To those who understood what was said at the conference, this was an opportunity to see how their protests in a small village were connected to other struggles worldwide. Some Adivasis who did not understand all the words that were spoken cherish the memories of seeing members of their community sharing space on the stage with important visitors. They remember the kind manner in which the visitors spoke to them and recall with affection the joining of hands in solidarity. They bring out the pictures taken at the time to point to the woman who touched her forehead to an Adivasi woman's

29 C. Surendranath, "What the World Water Conference Reminds," in *Plachimada: Water Exploitation and Peoples Resistance*, ed. A. Vasudevan, trans. Praveen Hariharan (Kozhikode: Mathrubhoomi Books, 2005), 54.

30 Ibid.

31 "World Water Conference Plachimada: An Evaluation" in A. Vasudevan, *Plachimada: Water Exploitation and Peoples Resistance*, 59.

32 Vasudevan, *Plachimada: Water Exploitation and Peoples Resistance*, 61.

33 Ibid.

34 Ibid.

35 Ibid.

forehead, a gesture that conveyed to them, more than perhaps words could, that this outsider believed them. Unlike many others, these outsiders believed that water in this place had been affected. They believed that the protestors were telling the truth.

Another event that inspired many more to support the agitations was the launch of the *Desh Bachao Desh Banao Abhiyan* (Save the Nation Build the Nation Campaign) in Plachimada by Medha Patkar, a committed social activist known for her leadership in the *Narmada Bachao Andolan*[36] On January 26, 2003, she joined other activists, representatives of several local organizations, freedom fighters, and some others associated with the National Alliance of Peoples' Movements to launch the campaign that was aimed at promoting collective action on several issues, including the rights of local communities to natural resources. The campaign began with a "protest against the Coca-Cola factory as a symbol of the struggle against Globalisation" in Plachimada.[37] For many residents, this was simply the important day that "Medha" visited to support them. An Adivasi man described her as "very wise."[38] An Adivasi woman remembers that their traditional bow and arrow were presented to her. Her support, as of many other visitors to the place, appears to mean a lot to all the residents of the hamlets.

The struggle also gained credibility and supporters after reports began to be published about the presence of pesticides in soft drinks, including the ones produced by Coca-Cola.[39] Events were organized across the state to raise public awareness about this and the difficulties faced by those who live near the Coca-Cola factory. Activists like Gopal spoke about Plachimada when they traveled to other parts of the country. He also initiated e-mail campaigns. Some committed individuals like the coordinator of India Resource Centre (IRC), an initiative that "works to support movements against corporate globalization in India,"[40] have provided regular updates through its web site in an effort to build "global links for justice."[41] The organization's web site has

[36] The *Narmada Bachao Andolan* is a movement that has long opposed the construction of large dams on the river Narmada and the resultant displacement of millions living in the valley.

[37] National Alliance of People's Movement (NAPM) Press Release, accessed October 1, 2010, http://www.napm-india.org/node/14. See also NAPM Press Release, "Desh Bachao Desh Banao Abhiyan: Save the Nation, Build the Nation Campaign (National tour programme)," January 25, 2003, http://www.narmada.org/nba-press-releases/january-2003/invitedbdb.html.

[38] Interview with Ottukan.

[39] See Sujith Koonan, "Groundwater: Legal Aspects of the Plachimada Dispute," in *Water Governance in Motion: Towards Socially & Environmentally Sustainable Water Law*, eds. P. Cullet et al. (New Delhi: Cambridge University Press, 2010), 159.

[40] See the IRC web site, http://www.indiaresource.org/about/index.html. Last accessed February 2, 2015.

[41] Ibid.

also been reporting the demands for transparency and accountability over Plachimada at Coca-Cola's shareholder meetings in the United States on a regular basis.[42]

Vasu, an activist involved in coordinating support of many organizations that have pledged solidarity with the groups working in Plachimada, has also been reaching out to a wider audience through the Internet. Like many, he too sees the closure of Coca-Cola plant as a "major victory" in the "ongoing struggles against neoliberalism [and] globalization."[43] Like him, there are others who see Plachimada as a local component of global movements of the people against the corporation–state alliances. Just like the large corporations in India and other places in the world, Coca-Cola is seen as trampling over the rights of a small community in connivance with the state. Closure of Coca-Cola would be the victory of people all over the world who believe water, like all natural resources, belongs to all, a victory for those who dedicate their lives to fighting inequality, those who question the imbalances of power everywhere.

The victories of Plachimada are therefore understood as the victories of all other similarly situated "small people," an expression I heard several times in the area. They offer hope and glimpses of a different, more just future. This sentiment is perhaps best illustrated by a sculpture installed next to the *samara pandal* on October 12, 2007 to mark the completion of two thousand days of the agitation. It stands there today, its weather worn edges indicating the passage of time. This sculpture, described as "depicting the suffering and resistance of the agitating people" in a news report, was created by a local artist Mohanan and installed by T. Shobhendran, an environmentalist.[44] The report further presents the description of that sculpture by an art critic in the following words:

> Two granite stupas,[45] cube-like blocks placed one upon another, have a grave yet graceful quality to them. Around these stupas are grave faces, weary with misery and suffering, yet beaming with compassion and transcendence.

[42] See, for example, "Coca-Cola Not Disclosing Full Liabilities in India, Misleading Shareholders: Company Challenged at Shareholders Meeting," April 19, 2006, http://www.indiaresource.org/news/2006/1055.html. Last accessed February 2, 2015.

[43] Interview with Vasu.

[44] "Plachimada Stir Completes 2000 Days," *The Hindu*, October 13, 2007, accessed June 23, 2008, http://www.thehindu.com/2007/10/13/stories/2007101362600600.htm. On the same day a seminar on "Globalisation and corporatisation and the experience from Plachimada" was also organized. Subramaniam, the chairperson of the Plachimada Anti–Coca-Cola Agitation Committee, inaugurated the seminar.

[45] *Stupa* generally refers to a Buddhist reliquary or a mound-like structure.

> They brim with pain, yet pulsate with the spirit of resistance. These figures entwine themselves, as if spiralling upward in a prayer to the beyond, as if leaping towards states more human and just.[46]

Like "freedom," "rights," and "resistance," "democracy" too is a word that came up often during conversations with various supporters of Plachimada protests. For Gopal, the struggle is also for the protection of the "democratic system of the world."[47] The ideals of democracy are what he and some others believe will ultimately lead to justice and the victory of a people's right to water over that of a corporation.

In addition to garnering support for the Plachimada Struggle, some activists are also participating in the legal dispute that is basically between Coca-Cola and the Perumatty Grama Panchayat. Their hope is that recognition of the people's right to water by the Supreme Court will ensure that justice is done to those whose water is being taken away. Once upheld by the Supreme Court, a people's right to water and a *panchayat's* right to make decisions regarding use of natural resources at the village level will pave the way for a better and stronger legal framework in the country for protection of the environment in general and water in particular.[48] It would also, as noted in the next chapter, have a significant bearing on the future of a decentralized and participatory system of governance envisaged under the *panchayat* system in India.

Some activists hope that a decision from the Supreme Court in favor of the people's right will throw light on the new realities of pollution that antiquated laws cannot address. In fact, as Sreejith, an activist, suggested, as a "legal person" I should use this opportunity to identify the "legal lacunae persisting in the laws related to water, especially laws related to groundwater" based on the "Plachimada experience."[49] Another activist suggested that I focus my research on framing a "legal basis" for holding Coca-Cola accountable, even as he referenced Bhopal and the continuing struggles of the victims of the gas leak for justice.[50]

46 "Plachimada Stir Completes 2000 Days."

47 Interview with Gopal.

48 For a discussion of the common law rules and statutory provisions related to the dispute in Plachimada, see Sujith Koonan, "Legal Implications of Plachimada: A Case Study," (working paper number 5 International Environmental Law Research Centre, 2007) (2007): http://www.ielrc.org/content/w0705.pdf.

49 Interview with Sreejith.

50 Interview with Vasu. Similar sentiments had perhaps prompted a retired judge of the Kerala High Court advise me to focus my energies on what was important and not spend so much time in the hamlets.

3.4. MEDIA

The water crisis and the plight of residents (often described in news reports as tribals, *dalits*, and poor farmers) in Plachimada have been widely reported in the local, national, and international mass media.[51] The significant role of the media coverage of the events in Plachimada has also been noted by the High Court of Kerala in an important judgment handed down in December 2004.[52] Newspapers continue to offer regular updates on developments in Plachimada as well as on decisions taken by the state government from time to time.[53] It is unlikely that the events in Plachimada would have reached so many worldwide without the continued coverage of the agitation on television and in newspapers and magazines. In addition to reporting on the events, these media have carried the messages, opinions, and stories of many participants and supporters of the protests against the company. They have also regularly published the company's response to the various allegations and agitations. Most significantly, perhaps, they have helped in maintaining a continuous pressure on the state government to respond and act.

Early reports by John Waite, a BBC Radio 4 presenter, broadcast on the "Face the Facts" feature, played a particularly important role in bringing the seriousness of the issue to a wider international audience. The BBC team first visited Plachimada in October 2002. They spoke with the residents of the hamlets around the Coca-Cola plant and recorded their statements about the changes in the water. A transcript of the feature indicates that the team inspected the well in the "crowded settlement of Plachimada," and noted the various ways in which the polluted water was affecting the lives of everyone in the area.[54] They even followed a "tractor and trailer" which carried waste from the Coca-Cola plant and dumped it on a riverbed.[55] A report in *Keraleeyam*, a local Malayalam language news and feature periodical, indicates that this was

51 Reports published beginning in 2002 are too numerous to cite here. Several of them are listed in the bibliography.

52 The judge who wrote the decision in fact devoted two pages to the need for a court to be impervious to the pressures that such coverage of issues creates. See *Perumatty Grama Panchayat* v. *State of Kerala*, 2004 (1) KLT 731 para. 11.

53 *The Hindu*, published in English and available online, is a national daily that continues to provide updates. Among the local dailies published in Malayalam, *Madhyamam* and *Mathrubhoomi* are the two that reported regularly on the matter and related events at least during the time I was in Kerala in 2009.

54 John Waite, "Face the Facts: Coca-Cola Update 02.01.04," (transcript), 2, *BBC Radio 4*, http://www.bbc.co.uk/radio4/youandyours/yy_20040102.shtml.

55 Ibid.

the nearby Chittur River.[56] The representative of Coca-Cola, when asked by John Waite, denied that the company was causing any pollution.[57]

The BBC team collected samples of water from wells next to the plant as well as samples of the sludge that the company had distributed to some farmers for use as fertilizers.[58] These samples were analyzed at the Greenpeace research laboratories at the University of Exeter. Dr. David Santillo, a senior scientist at the university, while explaining the results to BBC, stated that the water was in fact "unsuitable for drinking."[59] Even more disturbingly, he reported that the sludge from the factory contained "very high levels of toxic heavy metals, namely cadmium and lead".[60] Cadmium, he further explained, affects the kidneys and liver and is also known to be a human carcinogen. The other metal, lead, according to him, "can be a very potent developmental toxin and it's particularly toxic to the developing nervous system in children."[61] This is the same sludge that the company had been promoting as a fertilizer, and which had been "leeching down into the groundwater."[62] It was the same sludge that the president of the Coca-Cola Company in India had earlier assured the BBC presenter was "absolutely safe."[63]

After the BBC report was broadcast the issue that was up until then mainly being covered by the local media in Kerala, reached a wider audience. Anti–Coca-Cola demonstrations were staged across Kerala. Public authorities that had either been unaware of, or preferred to ignore the findings of a previous study conducted in Plachimada,[64] sat up and took note of the agitation against the company. The issue was even raised in Rajya Sabha (the Council of States that is the federal chamber of the Indian parliament) on the basis of the BBC report.[65]

Pursuant to the report, pollution control boards in Kerala and elsewhere in the country conducted their own investigations. Tests conducted by the

56 "The Problem of Solid Waste at Plachimada: An Evaluation," *Keraleeyam* 4–24 (August 2005): 5.
57 Waite, "Face the Facts," 4.
58 A few residents mentioned that a "BBC reporter" had also been detained by the local police during one of his visits to the area. Elsewhere, it is recorded that a "BBC reporter" and an activist were arrested in December 2002. See Bhumi, "Anti–Coca-Cola Agitation", 101.
59 Waite, "Face the Facts," 4.
60 Ibid.
61 Ibid.
62 Ibid.
63 Ibid.
64 "Jananeethi Report on the Amplitude of Environmental and Human Rights Ramifications," July 2002, accessed October 6, 2010, http://www.jananeethi.org/jananeethi/majorevents.htm.
65 Bhumi, "Anti Coca-Cola Agitation".

Kerala State Pollution Control Board confirmed the findings of the BBC report.[66] The president of the company, when confronted with the findings of the University of Exeter by the BBC presenter, once again denied any bad faith on the part of the company. He did, however, try to steer the conversation toward a discussion about whose "science and facts" may be right.[67]

Ever since Plachimada came to the attention of a wider audience outside Kerala, the issue and developments have been followed and reported extensively. It is the local newspapers, however, that have made a considerable contribution in keeping the issue alive and in exerting pressure on the state government. No event, big or small, goes unreported by a few newspapers and periodicals published in the state. The two Malayalam language dailies generally believed to have the most circulation in Kerala – *Mathrubhoomi* and *Madhyamam* – continue to publish regular reports of events in Plachimada. It is not surprising, then, that everyone I met in Kerala knew something about the protests over groundwater in Plachimada.

The publishers of *Mathrubhoomi* have also published a compilation of reports and essays titled *Plachimada: Jalachooshanavum Janakeeyaprathirodhavum* (Plachimada: Water Exploitation and People's Resistance) in an effort to create a "historical record".[68] This 120-page Malayalam publication documents the events and views of many of those who have been involved in the struggle, as well as others who have extended their support to it. It also contains the text of the Plachimada Declaration and a few articles in the English language.

According to Easwaran, who holds a senior position in the management of *Mathrubhoomi*, the publication decided to forgo the revenue from its business with Coca-Cola after it began reporting on the dispute. Their decision to stop publishing the company's advertisements was understandably a "big decision."[69] This attention to the dispute by *Mathrubhoomi* is partly due to the personal commitment of Easwaran, a man with a long association with Press Trust of India and the Indian Newspaper Society. Easwaran is also an author committed to conservation of nature. His interest in the Himalayan glaciers, and the disappearing rivers and forests, are some of the environmental concerns that he specifically mentioned during our conversation. According to him, corporate control of rivers, lakes, and ponds is the "biggest danger of the century."[70] He has been supporting the agitators in Plachimada for a long

66 Waite, "Face the Facts," 8.

67 Ibid., 9.

68 Vasudevan, *Plachimada: Water Exploitation and Peoples Resistance*, 3.

69 Interview with Easwaran.

70 Ibid.

time. He has attended and has been involved in organizing events such as the World Water Conference in Plachimada. He talks passionately about what he refers to as the "symbolic battle" in Plachimada.[71] He describes it as a "pilgrimage" for "environmentalists," "an epicenter" for all those who believe that natural resources like water should not be privatized and for those who are opposed to corporate control of natural resources.[72]

A less known Malayalam language publication that has devoted considerable space and resources to Plachimada is *Keraleeyam*. In this case too the editor's commitment to social justice appears to have played a major role. This periodical has published special issues to highlight the dispute and events in Plachimada. It has regularly published reports, opinions, and interviews. Given the interest in the issue, the publishers have even compiled the material published by them and other publications in binders for anyone interested in a detailed study of the dispute. It is in the small office of *Keraleeyam* located in a not-easy-to-find lane that I discovered a significant archive. Those binders contain records that are not available elsewhere – interviews and statements of Adivasis who started the protests. It has also published pieces that document their central role in the agitation. Most significantly, this is the only publication that considers the differences among those who are involved in the protests as part of the story, albeit a small one. I will return to this material in Chapter 5.

Before I went to Kerala, much of my own understanding of the dispute in Plachimada was based mainly on reports published in English language national newspapers and other periodical publications available online. Locating and translating the material published in Malayalam in local journals, newsletters, newspapers, and special publications on the Plachimada required more time, effort, and resources. It was, however, a worthwhile effort.

The Malayalam language material is not only more detailed, it also offers information and insights that are missing from the coverage and reflections in most English media. One of the reasons for this difference appears to be distance – not only are the offices of English publications located farther away from Plachimada, the concerns and interests of their readers are also far removed from the lives of those involved in the agitations in Plachimada. What matters most to the former are the concepts and ideologies that the different groups involved in the dispute represent. The tale of the dispute resonates when presented in words that are familiar to these readers. Pollution and global capital are familiar concepts and urban readers are able to relate

71 Ibid.
72 Ibid.

to a story that contains these words. An Adivasi's refusal to leave, on the other hand, is unfamiliar. For many it is in fact an unreasonable assertion since it does not fit into the popular belief that everyone *must* want to leave what is seen as the most backward part of the state. Although these distances in locations, interests, and worldviews must surely exist to an extent in the case of readers of Malayalam publications as well, they appear to be less than in the case of English language publications.

There is also the issue of translation. For example, the Malayalam word *samaram* or *samara* is almost always translated as "struggle" in the context of Plachimada, but as I learnt in Kerala, that is only one way the word "*samaram*" can be translated. Depending on the context, it is also used to refer to a "strike," "protest," or "agitation." In fact the three people who translated much of the printed Malayalam material for me have used all these words, because as one of them explained, each of these English words "feels right" in a particular sentence and context. In some instances one could replace the other, but not always.

In pointing to the issues of distance and translation, my purpose is not to undermine the role played by the English language media in spreading the word about Plachimada. In fact I may never have learnt of the place in the absence of these reports. What I want to indicate, therefore, is that there is a need to be aware of the accounts and meanings that get left out due to such distances and translations of stories of those whose lives and views are unfamiliar to us. When events are re-presented in abstract universal terms, they become accessible to a wider audience, but they also lose some of their situated meanings.

3.5. TRANSLATING FOR THE "OUTSIDE"

As I began to notice the stark differences in the Adivasi and other accounts of the agitation, I was troubled by the absence of the role of Adivasis in most of the non-Adivasi activist and media accounts of the protests. What bothered me most was that some of those who are or have been actively working with Adivasi communities at the grassroots level could not possibly be unaware of the stories Adivasis share with those who are prepared to listen. How did they not see the significance of the larger context and histories of Adivasi dispossession in Kerala to the expression "we will not leave" that Adivasis repeat all the time when talking about Coca-Cola? These activists and reporters, like most people in Kerala, must know the long and troubled history of the Adivasis' struggle to reclaim lands traditionally occupied by them. These demands have made headlines from time to time, as in 2003 when Adivasi groups entered a forest reserve in Muthanga in northern Kerala to protest against the failure of successive state governments to honor promises of restoration of alienated lands to Adivasis.[73] I found some answers to my questions during my conversations with an activist who has been advising many involved in the agitation in Plachimada from the time when the protests began.

Madhavan has been working for decades with "mass organizations and movements" primarily around "issues related to Adivasis" in various parts of the country.[74] Most notably, he was involved with campaigns that were instrumental in the enactment of the *Scheduled Tribes and Other Traditional Forest Dwellers (Recognition of Forest Rights) Act* in 2006, and continues to work with others to ensure that this law is effectively implemented. He is well versed with the legacies of colonial policies and the economic interests that lay behind them, and the ways in which they continue to have a profound impact on the lives of Adivasis in the country today. He speaks with passion about the "systematic invasion of tribal lands" during the colonial period and about the stubborn resistance to such invasions by Adivasi communities.[75] During our conversation he also pointed to the persistent questions of Adivasi autonomy and its connections to traditionally occupied territories.

Madhavan has also been associated with the Adivasi land struggle in Kerala for many years. His familiarity with the history of their dispossession in Kerala and elsewhere, the insights he has gained about their lives over years of association with issues related to their lives, his commitment, and his advocacy skills make him an invaluable asset for many movements for justice he is associated with, including the agitation in Plachimada. These are also the reasons why his understanding of Plachimada, or what he shared with me, offers valuable insights into the complicated reasons for the silence about what matters most to the Adivasi protestors on the part of some of their supporters.

Madhavan admitted at the outset that his involvement with the agitation in Plachimada was limited to offering advice on strategy and planning. He has, however, visited the place and spoken with Adivasi protestors. During our conversation, after speaking about Coca-Cola and pollution, he said that "at one level" the issue was that the decision about setting up the Coca-Cola plant had been made without any consultations. But this, he admitted, "is not strongly projected outside."[76] The primary reason for this according to him is that "the

[73] For a detailed account of this event and Adivasi struggle for lands in Kerala see Chapter 6.
[74] Interview with Madhavan.
[75] Ibid.
[76] Ibid.

outside," which he noted includes the "non-tribal," the "Panchayat," and the "political parties," will not understand the protestors' position.[77]

The "outside world," according to Madhavan, will also not allow any questioning of its wisdom in making decisions like the one about Coca-Cola. In his words:

> So naturally, whenever these people communicated to the outside world, they would always try to tell you and show you – start the whole dialogue with something which you can understand. OK? So, you can understand that there is water pollution. You can understand that the water is being sucked out. So, that is what they would primarily put forward. Which is not their primary [pause] the underlying core. Their underlying core is that, you know, we have been, I mean, our fate – whatever it was, you know, we're still being pushed out. We are trampled upon. And the trampling upon is not just by the Coke alone. It is a collaborative thing between the government, the Coke, all the political parties, the Panchayat, – everybody is involved. Media – everybody is involved.[78]

Madhavan conflates the local activists who are communicating with the "outside world" and those who are "still being pushed out."[79] To the extent that I can understand them, the reasons for his reluctance to name these two groups in this instance is that, like others, he wanted to emphasize that despite the differences that have arisen, the two are united in their opposition to Coca-Cola.

Madhavan has been involved with "Adivasi issues" long enough to know what the "outside" will and will not accept. He pointed out that "[u]p to the point that Coke is a problem, it is fine," because these are the kinds of issues that the "middle class, and donors and NGOs," among others, are interested in.[80] But as his words indicate, and I suspect, many other local supporters of Plachimada Struggle know too, Coca-Cola is only part of the problem from the Adivasis' perspective. What Coca-Cola triggered through its careless extraction of groundwater was a fear of further dispossession, of being forced to leave, which is rooted in a longer, more complex history than a story of corporate greed can convey. This complicated story, however, is not a story that moves the middle class, the donors, and the NGOs in the same way, if at all.[81]

77 Ibid.

78 Ibid.

79 Ibid.

80 Ibid.

81 See Rob Nixon, *Slow Violence and the Environmentalism of the Poor* (Cambridge: Harvard University Press, 2011), 3, where Nixon describes certain kinds of violence as "disasters that

Despite his forthright opinions on Adivasi struggles more generally in India, and his insightful comments about the expectations of the "outside" vis-à-vis Plachimada, Madhavan seemed hesitant to name land or fear of separation from home as a central issue in the context of Plachimada. After speaking about these larger struggles, he returned to the "rights of the local community to decide on water," and to its "right to safe water."[82] Even while speaking about an early decision for the protests to be "centered around the land" instead of outside the state secretariat in Thiruvananthapuram or the district administration headquarter (as is the regular practice of protestors in the state), Madhavan stated only that this was a "good" and "convenient" decision because the "community and the plant [were] at the same place."[83]

There appear to be several reasons for Madhavan's reluctance to say anything more than he did during our conversation. To begin with, centering of Adivasi struggles over land in what has resonated with many as a people's movement runs the risk of alienating many non-Adivasi supporters who were initially reluctant to associate with an Adivasi struggle. Part of Madhavan's reluctance to say more than he did is also due to the opinion he holds of academic researchers, their ability to understand, and their motivations. He believes researchers "like to research about Plachimada, because it is about Coke," which according to him is a "soft" issue.[84] Like other "international agencies" and researchers, I would not be interested, he had declared, in writing about struggles that according to him "challenge power."[85] I thought this was an unfair assumption, but one that, by that time, did not surprise me. Several lawyers, activists, politicians, and government officials I met had strong (albeit varied) opinions both about my research and my reasons for undertaking it. Some, as mentioned above, also expressed their views on what I should be writing about instead.

Madhavan's long involvement and advocacy of Adivasi rights also makes him cautious about trusting strangers. That much was obvious even in the manner in which our meeting was arranged. There are dangers involved in raising questions of land and Adivasi dispossession in India today. As Madhavan himself pointed out while reflecting on Coca-Cola's initial reaction to the Adivasi protests, the standard response increasingly is that of labeling any

are slow moving and long in the making" as against stories that are "dramatic enough to rouse public sentiment and warrant political intervention."

82 Interview with Madhavan.

83 Ibid.

84 Ibid.

85 Ibid.

dissent as "Naxalite/Maoist instigated."[86] Once labeled as such, issues of serious injustices can be easily diverted or disregarded. Naxalism has been identified as the biggest internal security threat to the country.[87] The loss of lives and immense human suffering due to the continuing violent conflict in parts of central India between those driven by a revolutionary ideology and the Indian State is indeed a serious issue. This is particularly so for the impoverished Adivasi communities in central India in whose homes this conflict is being played out. Repeated invocation of words like "threat," "security," and "terror" have conjured a reality that disables critical engagement with past and current State policies that have led to displacement and impoverishment of Adivasis in these areas.[88]

Although these are all significant reasons that appear to lie behind Madhavan's reluctance to name the centrality of a fear of dispossession in the Adivasi agitation against Coca-Cola, there is something else that points to a much more significant loss in translation than the one acknowledged by him. My long conversation with him indicated that his hesitation is also connected to ambivalence toward the very nature of Adivasi claims in India today. This ambivalence relates both to the question of who can make a valid claim to being an original inhabitant of the subcontinent, as well as to the search for an authentic identity as a response to this question.

According to Madhavan, Adivasis in Plachimada and neighboring areas do not "have a living memory of having owned any territory."[89] As will be revealed in Chapter 6, the living memories of Adivasis in Plachimada complicate and challenge this assumption in many ways. This is nevertheless an interesting observation that I want to unravel in light of a few other things Madhavan said during our conversation. I have mentioned before that Madhavan had confessed at the outset that he has been supporting the protestors in Plachimada from a distance. By his own admission, he is also not familiar with the particular history of the place. His crucial observation about the absent "living memory" is therefore based on a general perception of the difference between tribes that either continue to live on land they traditionally occupied or have been recently displaced on the one hand, and those who are regarded as assimilated in the non-Adivasi mainstream on the other. The claims of the latter group are suspect primarily because they were displaced or dispossessed so long ago

86 Ibid.

87 *The Hindu*, "Naxalism Biggest Threat to Internal Security: Manmohan," May 24, 2010, http://www.thehindu.com/news/national/article436781.ece.

88 See for example, Ramachandra Guha, "Adivasis, Naxalites and Indian Democracy," *Economic and Political Weekly* 42:32 (2007): 3304–3312.

89 Interview with Madhavan.

(and perhaps more than once) that they could not possibly make a valid or tenable claim as an original inhabitant of a place where they currently live, even if they have lived there for centuries. Within this logic, the "assimilated" Adivasis, who often and inevitably adopt non-Adivasi practices, are unlikely to be able to prove a living connection to a certain specific territory that is required to make a valid claim within the current global discourse of indigeneity. This, as the stories in Chapters 5 and 6 indicate, is a misunderstanding of the Adivasi conception of territoriality and belonging in Plachimada.

At the heart of this sometimes articulated, sometimes implied difference between Adivasi communities that continue to live on the same lands and thereby maintain a continuous relationship to traditional territories, and those who are assumed to have "no living memory" of a similar connection lies the ambivalence toward and anxiety about Adivasi identity in India. Who is an authentic Adivasi or original inhabitant in a place where there are many claimants? What should be the markers of such an authentic identity? The increasing demands for inclusion in the recognized list of Scheduled Tribes in India by specific communities has also led to a sharper focus on distinguishing the "real" Adivasis from others with suspect claims. As a lawyer in Delhi wanted to know: "Are these Adivasis [in Plachimada] real Adivasis?"[90] Not being sure how to define "real," he began by offering descriptions of "short" and "dark," before stopping mid-sentence in what I hope was embarrassment.[91]

Several people, including the activist Madhavan, believe that Adivasis in Plachimada and surrounding hamlets were brought by local landowners to this area as slaves from nearby hills and forests at some point in the past. According to Madhavan, their long contact with non-Adivasis, and more specifically the "heavy landlordism [and] feudal stranglehold" in this area explains "the significant absence of many of the traditions, many of the traditional forms of governance [...] in Plachimada."[92] This "interact[ion] with outside world" is also what according to him accounts for the loss of confidence among Adivasi men as compared with women, who he believes are "more inside the community," or less in contact with non-Adivasis.[93] He contrasts this with Adivasi communities that continue to live in forests and on lands occupied by them for centuries in the Wayanad district of Kerala, where both men and women are equally "articulate" and more politically active.[94] Adivasis in Plachimada, he believes, are "basically ghettoized" as they have "continued to be under

90 Interview with Rohan.
91 Ibid.
92 Interview with Madhavan.
93 Ibid.
94 Ibid.

the sway of upper caste landlords."[95] In fact, they were "invisible" according to him "until the Coca-Cola struggle came [along]."[96]

The search for an authentic Adivasi identity is evident in Madhavan's observations. What I also want to point to here is the significance of his comment about the invisibility of the Adivasis in Plachimada before they began protesting against Coca-Cola. As people who have lived and worked on the land in the area for centuries, the Adivasis were certainly not invisible to their many neighbors who refer to them as Adivasis. They could not have been contributing to the local economy as invisibles. They are also a visible part of the local social hierarchy. They can certainly not be invisible to those who have or continue to defraud them of their lands. The Adivasis are also not invisible to the local administration, which continues to express its inability to address their claims for restoration of alienated land. They are certainly not invisible to the state, which records their presence in the census and formulates policies for their "welfare." Many of these groups do seem to look away from the realities of Adivasis, perhaps even pretend from time to time that their difficulties do not exist, but this does not mean that they are in fact invisible. They have always been visible as Eravalans, Malasars, Adivasis, or Scheduled Tribes in the place.

3.6. CONCLUSION

A range of actors have offered support to the protestors in Plachimada either through active participation in the protests or by offering advice or by writing about them. The stories that these individuals tell comprise the popular accounts of the Plachimada Resistance Movement. In most of these accounts, the Plachimada Struggle emerges as the fight of the small and the poor against the very big and powerful. There are repeated references to the "small community," a "small *panchayat*," or "local peoples" and "illiterate people" that have taken on a powerful multinational corporation.[97] Adivasis who started the protests are either absent from these accounts or remain marginal to them, emerging occasionally as symbolic bearers of bows and arrows.

The fact that the protests have continued despite all efforts by Coca-Cola and in the face of opposition and even violence; the fact that it is the company that has been forced to suspend operations in the face of what was described as "peoples power"; the fact that initially hostile and at times apathetic local

95 Ibid.
96 Ibid.
97 Interviews with Gopal and Subramaniam.

and state administrations are now with "the people"; and the fact that commitments to save the planet and its resources for all can prevail (to the extent that they have in Plachimada) over pursuit of profits by some are all facts that make for a very powerful narrative.

This popular story of the Plachimada Struggle is an important one for several reasons. To begin with, it has drawn the attention of people within the country as well as around the world to the hardships faced by communities in a place that was previously unknown outside of the region. The issues of pollution, access to scarce resources, consumption, development, and corporate behavior in places like Plachimada, which have been raised by many involved, need to be addressed not only in Kerala or India, but everywhere.

Most significantly, it is the insistence of Plachimada's supporters upon these issues that have forced the government to take the dispute seriously. It continues to pledge its support for protestors even as it attempts to find ways to ensure such a situation does not recur by examining the gaps in the legal and regulatory frameworks in the state. The *Kerala Groundwater (Control and Regulation) Act of 2002* came into effect in the area as a direct consequence of the Plachimada Struggle.[98] The state assembly recently passed a bill to enact a special law to address the issue of compensating residents for the various losses suffered by them after the plant was set up. Even at the national level, there is an increased focus on the regulation of groundwater usage and related issues that have most famously been highlighted by the dispute in Plachimada.[99] This popular story therefore needs to be told and remembered for all that has been achieved through its iteration.

It is also important to note that the support and advocacy of many involved in the struggle stems from the different ways in which they identify with this agitation against Coca-Cola. Many see in it an actualization of their own religious, social, and political beliefs. The very nature of water – that it supports life everywhere, and the material and affective ways in which human beings relate to it – has also made it possible for people of diverse leanings to connect to the struggle. The strength of their support, however, lies in their commitments to the various causes they believe in. Some are helping the "innocent" and the "marginalized" Adivasis, some are supporting the poor

98 Although the legislation was enacted in 2002, the Plachimada area was not brought within its purview until 2005. See Koonan, "Legal Implications," 15.

99 There is now a move to enact a new law for management and regulation of groundwater use. Aditi Nigam, "Model Bill for Permit System, Stiff Fines to Regulate Groundwater Use," (n.d.), http://www.thehindubusinessline.com/industry-and-economy/government-and-policy/article2313846.ece

and the illiterate in their fight against a multinational corporation, whereas others are protecting nature for the future generations. Some oppose "global capitalism" and "America"; others are defending traditional practices, freedom, and democracy. Some are against globalization, and neoliberalism, others are resisting "Western culture." All of these concepts are interpreted by each in ways that can be connected to their individual commitments. Just as the struggle reaffirms their beliefs, the desired outcome – permanent closure of the Coca-Cola plant – holds the potential of realizing their visions for a different, more just future.

For this to happen, at least some supporters believe the story must be told in the manner that the "outside" can relate to. Pollution, protection of environment, globalization are all words that evoke familiar responses among concerned people everywhere. These popular narratives do not, however, tell the whole story. These accounts have eclipsed other accounts that hold more significant meanings for the ones who started these protests. Although I will turn to those stories later, what I have highlighted in this chapter is that the eclipsing of the Adivasi accounts is not necessarily a result of conscious intentions to hide these stories but rather arises from a desire to tell what is regarded as a more credible, stronger story that puts forward a claim that the desired audiences can comprehend and respond to. The recasting of stories of violation is therefore often an outcome of the processes of translation. Many translators who seek to present Adivasi claims are committed to justice for the "local people" whose water was damaged and depleted by Coca-Cola. Like the Adivasis who began the protests, they too want the company to leave. Missing from these accounts, however, are the more complex and broader questions about the place that Adivasi accounts raise. What this draws attention to is the injustice that results from the very process of translation when issues that matter most to Adivasi protestors are eclipsed by translators due to ignorance, unexamined assumptions, and at times, strategic decision making in pursuit of what are perceived as better stories and claims told in stronger language.

4

Litigants, Lawyers, and the Questions of Law

This chapter offers a close look at the litigation that has arisen from the dispute between Coca-Cola and its Adivasi neighbors and offers an opportunity to examine the processes and practices of legal translation as the specific and situated is re-presented and reorganized in accordance with the language, logic, concerns and demands of a formal legal system.[1] As situated experiences of having been wronged are transformed into "a matrix of abstract legality,"[2] some meanings are added whereas others are lost, some truths are crystallized whereas others disappear. Recognizing these processes of translation is critical in order to understand ways in which the law and legal institutions fail to respond to certain claims.

The detailed account of the legal battles presented here shows how violations are transformed as they are received into the formal legal processes.[3] As the concerns of those who began the protests against Coca-Cola are translated into the "normative language of state" by lawyers and judges who frame the "legal" issues for determination, meanings are gained and lost.[4] The abstraction and decontextualization involved in this process of translating complex issues into a "legal problem" lead to a loss of critical situated meanings that limits the possibility of justice for those on whose behalf demands for justice

1 For a compelling illustrative account of the reordering of "many-sided and complex" human dilemmas into a "case" in a court of law, see Guha, "Chandra's Death," 135–165. For translation of complex issues into legal problems, see Bankowski and Mungham, *Images of Law*. See also James Boyd White, "Law as Language: Reading Law and Reading Literature," *Texas Law Review* 60 (1981–1982): 415. White argues that law is a language and its particular way of reading, writing, and speaking is a way of "maintaining a culture" of its own.

2 Guha, "Chandra's Death," 141.

3 For the significance of studying transformations of disputes before and as they enter formal legal institutions, see Felstiner, Abel, and Sarat, "The Emergence and Transformation of Disputes," 631–654.

4 Cain, "The General Practice Lawyer and the Client," 331, 335.

are being made. In focusing on the practices and processes of legal translation in this chapter, I wish to draw attention to the violence of this particular eclipsing of "subaltern voices" that is in fact necessitated by the very processes that are meant to create spaces for them to speak.[5]

The first part of this chapter offers an account of the litigation, the parties involved, and the number of petitions, appeals, and interlocutory applications filed since 2003 when Coca-Cola initiated litigation in this matter. Since then there have been claims and counterclaims in administrative proceedings and a number of petitions, reviews, and appeals in the High Court of Kerala, all finally culminating in appeals to the Supreme Court of India that are yet to be decided.[6] The litigation between Coca-Cola and the village council now involves many more: the Local Self-Government Department of Kerala, the Kerala State Pollution Control Board, the state's Ground Water Department, interveners that include leaders of groups involved in the struggle in Plachimada, concerned activists elsewhere, social groups, research organizations, an employee association, and a farmers' association.

This detailed account of the litigation, as the dispute in Plachimada traveled from a "ST colony" to the Supreme Court of India in New Delhi, with stopovers at the office of the Perumatty Panchayat, the office of the Local Self-Government Department of Kerala, and the High Court in Ernakulam, illustrates the advantages held by the "haves" over others in

5 Mark Harris, "Mythologising 'Recollections of Squatting in Victoria': Law's Intersection with Colonial Memory," *Law, Social Justice and Global Development Journal* 1–14 (2003): 6, where, while discussing the court's inability to understand the Yorta Yorta peoples' claim to land and water, Harris suggests that it "exemplifies the practice of courts" to allow "the subaltern voices to speak, but not hearing their voices." He suggests that processes of courts and formal legal discourse "necessitates the diminishment of the narrative of belonging to the land" that is presented to the courts. See also Spivak, "Politics of Translation"; Bhabha, "The Voice of the Dom," 16.

6 High Courts are the highest courts of appeal in each province/state in India and appeals from High Courts lie to the Supreme Court of India. For jurisdiction and powers of High Courts generally see *Constitution of India*, Chapter V. Under Article 226 High Courts are also authorized to issue writs in the nature of *habeas corpus*, *mandamus*, prohibition, *quo warranto*, and *certiorari* for the enforcement of fundamental rights guaranteed under Part III of the Constitution. Both Coca-Cola and Perumatty Panchayat originally applied to the High Court of Kerala in Ernakulum (hereafter "High Court") for remedies under this provision. The Supreme Court of India is the highest judicial forum and the final court of appeal in India. As the highest judicial court in the formal legal system of the country, the Supreme Court replaced both the Federal Court of India and the Privy Council when it came into being in 1950. Currently it comprises of the Chief Justice and thirty other judges. See *Constitution of India*, Chapter IV: The Union Judiciary of the Constitution of India. See also *Constitution of India*, Article 32 for the Supreme Court's power to enforce fundamental rights guaranteed to citizens under Part III of the Constitution of India.

such proceedings.[7] It also helps to look closely at the processes and procedures that transform specific situated claims into abstract questions of law. In part two I examine the significant role lawyers have played in this transformation of the specific into the abstract. A close look at such translations offers crucial insights into the ways in which the attitudes, training, and "concrete practices" of lawyers reconstitute violations into a language of "trans-situational applicability."[8]

4.1. LITIGATION

4.1.1. *Perumatty Grama Panchayat*

The Perumatty Grama Panchayat[9] or the village council is one of the central actors in the litigation related to the dispute in Plachimada. The Coca-Cola plant, as already mentioned, is located within the Panchayat area. In January 2000, the Panchayat had approved Coca-Cola's application for installation of an electric pump on the site of the beverage plant, and thereafter, as per its practice, granted the company a license to operate for one year. The license was subsequently renewed for another year in 2001.

Mohan, who was the president of the Panchayat at the time, recalls that about one year after Coca-Cola began operations, the "Adivasis in the area" marched in a procession to the Panchayat office over the issue of water shortage.[10] Some activists and Adivasi protestors recall that this protest march took place soon after the decision to launch an agitation outside the Coca-Cola premises was taken in April 2002. According to Mohan, between 200 and 250 people were in the procession that included some activists and other residents of the area as well. The protestors presented a petition to the Panchayat, and asked that it cancel the license of the company. The reasons for this demand, Mohan recounts, were depletion of water, changes in the water and in food cooked in the water, and skin allergies. He recalls:

> According to them, before the company came the water was so pure and now when the company started working, these were the problems faced by them and they wanted the Panchayat to intervene and cancel the license

7 Marc Galanter, "Why the "Haves" Come Out Ahead: Speculations on the Limits of Legal Change," *Law and Society Review* 9:1 (1974): 95–160.

8 Cain, "The General Practice Lawyer and the Client," 335.

9 See *supra* note 2 in Chapter 2. The Perumatty Grama Panchayat is hereafter referred to as the "Perumatty Panchayat" or the "Panchayat."

10 Interview with Mohan.

> of the company and ask the company to stop its operation. They asked the Panchayat to look into the matter and help the people.[11]

Most people involved in the early protests say that the Panchayat was initially reluctant to intervene. Mohan explained why, despite the fact that the members of the Panchayat held a meeting to discuss the issue on the day of the protest march, it was impossible for them to take any immediate action. The Panchayat felt that as "part of the government machinery," they could not "criticize the company outright."[12] Since the plant had been set up with the approval of the state government, an intervention by the Panchayat would amount to "talk[ing] against the government."[13] But after repeated complaints from the residents, increasing water and health problems, and increasing pressure from "political and social organizations," the Panchayat felt compelled to take action.[14] The local unit of the Janata Dal (S), the political party that has a very strong presence in the area, also supported the Panchayat's decision.

Eventually, the Panchayat constituted a subcommittee to study the matter, which found that the water had in fact been affected. Mohan says that they found that "almost fifteen open wells" in the area had "dried up, and there was shortage of water in the other wells."[15] They also noticed that the water was "not good for consumption."[16] In January 2003 the Medical Officer at Perumatty also prepared a report stating that the water in the area was affected and unfit for use. Despite all this, the Panchayat still did not take immediate action, as the company was a major source of revenue for the Panchayat. But ultimately, despite the "financial crisis" it was likely to face, the Panchayat felt compelled to do something, given that, says Mohan, "the complaints of the public were genuine."[17] It decided to cancel Coca-Cola's license. The legality of that decision, challenged by Coca-Cola, has been examined by various courts and will be considered again by the Supreme Court of India.

According to Mohan, the Panchayat is fighting for justice.[18] It is committed to preventing excessive extraction of groundwater and pollution within its area. As a body of elected representatives of the residents of the Perumatty Panchayat area, the members feel it is the Panchayat's responsibility to address

[11] Ibid.
[12] Ibid.
[13] Ibid.
[14] Ibid.
[15] Ibid.
[16] Ibid.
[17] Ibid.
[18] Ibid.

the grievances of the people. It also has a statutory duty to ensure access to safe water for residents of the area and to protect their traditional water sources.[19] Incidentally, archival records indicate that construction and maintenance of wells and ensuring adequate water supply have, in fact, been important responsibilities of the local administrations including that of village *panchayats* in Cochin since at least the beginning of the last century.[20] Whether, and to what extent, this history and understanding of a *panchayat's* responsibilities influenced the manner in which the members of the Perumatty Panchayat perceive the dispute and the litigation requires further investigation, but this is beyond the scope of this project.

One thing that has influenced the actions of the Panchayat is that its members belong to the same community of residents of the area. In the words used by Mohan, they are "face-to-face" with everyone else on a daily basis.[21] This meant that they felt compelled to respond to the situation. Moreover, according to Mohan, even though the members of the Panchayat did not live in the vicinity of the Coca-Cola facility, as residents of the area they could see how the effects of pollution and depletion of water continued to spread, if left unchecked.

During our conversation Mohan also spoke at length about the company's attempts to influence the Panchayat's decision making. According to him, at first the company's attempts were focused on resolving its issues with the Panchayat. He also alleged that representatives of the company had offered him money at one point. Some other supporters of the protests also mentioned this. An article published in 2004 also asserts that "Coca-Cola tried to bribe the Panchayat President [...] with Rs. 300 million, but he refused to be corrupted and coopted."[22]

According to Mohan, once the company realized that personal bribes would not work, they "changed their strategy and said they will contribute to

[19] See especially *Kerala Panchayat Raj Act* (1994), section 166 and Schedule III A for the mandatory functions of a village panchayat. See also sections 218, 234A, and 234C.

[20] *The Cochin Village Panchayat Regulation*, Regulation V of 1089 M.E. (1914 C.E.) Kerala State Archives, Ernakulam, page 1 where in addition to rendering the "principal and more intelligent subjects of His Highness the Raja useful by employing them in administering justice to their neighbours," the Regulation entrusted many works related to access and distribution of water for irrigation and other purposes including construction of wells and maintenance of water *pandals* (sheds) to the village *panchayats*.

[21] Interview with Mohan.

[22] Vandana Shiva, "Building Water Democracy: People's Victory Against Coca-Cola in Plachimada," https://zcomm.org/zcommentary/building-water-democracy-peoples-victory-against-coca-cola-in-plachimada-by-vandana2-shiva/. A copy of this article is also part of the court records.

the overall development of the Panchayat."[23] Their proposal was to work with the Panchayat for the "betterment" of the area.[24] This included offers to supply water to those neighborhoods within the Panchayat's area that faced a shortage of water and to contribute to the development of schools and hospitals. Mohan recalled that a proposal for supplying water was also mentioned by the company's counsel during proceedings in the High Court.

None of these proposals were acceptable to the Panchayat according to Mohan because:

> If the company alone can do everything for the people in the Panchayat, there is no need of a *panchayat* or an elected body in the area. We also said this in the court. So at any cost this cannot be agreed upon. The Panchayat has its own powers and privileges as a local self-government body. The Panchayat has to protect its people, their wealth, land, and their rights and is bound to do its duties towards the people. And that we are aware of our rights and we are not going to deviate from doing our duties.

Mohan also alleged that the company asked the Panchayat to soften its stand in court so as to ensure a resolution of the dispute in the interests of Coca-Cola, while allowing the Panchayat to keep up the pretense of not having backed down from its responsibilities toward its residents. Toward this end, the company is also alleged to have suggested that the Panchayat change its counsel. The Panchayat rejected these proposals.

It is not surprising that Coca-Cola was willing to go to great lengths to ensure the plant's continuing operation. While in court it has consistently denied allegations of depletion of groundwater and pollution, violation of any existing statute, legal requirement or conditions of its license, and has asserted that as the owner of the land, it has a right to the water that lies underneath,[25] a representative of the company had explained to Mohan that it was not just Plachimada that they were worried about. The stakes were much higher. Closure of this unit for reasons related to the exploitation and pollution of water would set a very harmful precedent, not just in India but worldwide. Access to fresh water is indeed absolutely necessary for the industry, and even the slightest of indications that its operations harm the environment or communities would both affect its image in the eyes of its consumers (most of

[23] Interview with Mohan.

[24] Ibid.

[25] Asserting its property rights is part of its litigation strategy and statements to this effect are also reported to have been made by the company's officials. See Nityanand Jayaraman, "Coca Cola Parches," *Global Policy*, May 28, 2002, accessed September 21, 2010, http://globalpolicy.org/component/content/article/162/28046.html.

whom usually do not live next to the beverage plants) and open it to similar legal proceedings in other places.

All of this would of course be unacceptable to some of its shareholders. In fact in 2006, one of its shareowners had made a specific reference to the agitations in Plachimada, the ongoing litigation, and the cancellation of its license by the village council, while calling for a report on the environmental impact of the company's operations in India. The Board of Directors had at the time recommended a vote against this proposal as it felt that such an exercise would be a "redundant use of Company human and financial resources".[26]

Mohan admits there have been times when he was scared, but emphasized that he could not have acted in any other way. As someone who "come[s] from a family of agricultural labourers," he says, he could not "take a decision [that would amount to] cheating all those who have placed their faith in [him]."[27] While speaking about a meeting with a representative of the company, Mohan stated:

> There was determination in his words and voice, and I could read that from his face. Though I got frightened a bit, I did not show that on my face. I watched him carefully, and also his expressions. I understood why he threatened me like that, but I never showed any emotions. I told him that if any such thing happens, I will think that is my destiny. I took things lightly then. When these kinds of things happen, we, as the representatives of the people, can only stand for the people's cause. We are elected by these poor people. The faith that these poor people put in us – it is very difficult to forget all that and do things that the company wants us to do.[28]

As mentioned earlier, Mohan believes that a *panchayat* must have the "full rights" to protect the land, wealth, and drinking water of its people.[29] According to him, its role as a local body would be meaningless without such rights. Any decision striking down a *panchayat*'s autonomy and right to make decisions of this nature is viewed as fundamentally corrosive of its proper functioning. Thus the stakes are high for the Perumatty Panchayat as well. The larger issue is that of local self-governance – the very essence of the *panchayat* system in the country.

Unlike Coca-Cola, however, pursuing the litigation all the way up to the Supreme Court of India has not been easy for the Perumatty Panchayat. The

[26] "Item 7: Shareowner Proposal Regarding Environmental Impacts of Operations in India" in The Coca-Cola Company Notice of Annual Meeting of Shareowners (March 10, 2006), 61–63.
[27] Interview with Mohan.
[28] Ibid.
[29] Ibid.

number of petitions, appeals, and countless interlocutory applications filed by the company would be daunting for any village council with limited resources. In addition to the requirements for obtaining approvals from the government prior to pursuing any litigation, meeting the cost of litigation has been a big challenge for the Panchayat. Mohan laughed as he talked about the Rs. 500 [$9.00 approx.] that a *panchayat* is allowed to spend on legal fees, when "[e]ven for getting a legal opinion you need to pay thousands."[30] Fortunately for the Panchayat, the lawyer who represented it in the High Court, like a few others involved in this litigation, cared less for his fees than for the principle over which the Panchayat is pursuing litigation.

The Panchayat's decision to not renew Coca-Cola's license was a unanimous one. Each of the elected members of the Perumatty Panchayat voted in favor of the cancellation. Mohan and a few others emphasized the significance of this fact. It is noteworthy that every member of the Panchayat rose to the occasion, and set aside their personal views and party positions (members of the Panchayat support different political parties), in order to take a stand in the interest of the residents. Some people I spoke with feel that Mohan's commitment to his duty, as the president of the Panchayat at the time, was a major factor that made this possible.

Mohan is no longer the president of the Panchayat but he remains concerned about the litigation and its outcome. After my conversation with him, I could not help wondering how this litigation and the repeated encounters with the court processes and conversations with lawyers have affected him. I was most struck by how much his manner of speaking reminded me of former clients who had been involved in litigation for long periods of time. He repeatedly referred to specific documents and made an effort to recall exact dates and details of events, even asked others present to confirm some, almost in the manner of offering evidence, when none was asked for. A lot of what he said and particularly emphasized during our long conversation seemed to be a response, through documented facts, to allegations and arguments made by Coca-Cola.

My thoughts returned to this conversation later when some lawyers I spoke with mentioned how much the Panchayat had learned from its mistakes. These early mistakes, they feel, were due to their ignorance of legal process. Amit, one of the lawyers, noted that the "Panchayat was not experienced in law," explaining further that it did not have the benefit of a lawyer's advice at the time.[31] One example of the Panchayat's mistake offered is the Panchayat's first

[30] Interview with Mohan. See also "Conduct of Cases and Payment of Fees to Legal Advisors" in *The Kerala Panchayat Raj Rules*.

[31] Interview with Amit.

notice to Coca-Cola regarding cancellation of its license. The notice refers to Adivasi protests as one of the reasons it could not renew the company's license. This has allowed Coca-Cola to allege over and over again that the Panchayat's decision was motivated by a desire to appease some people, rather than being based on any scientific evidence. Given the significance of the doctrine of irrelevant consideration in evaluating administrative decision making, this reference to Adivasi protests by the Panchayat is generally considered a mistake. "Not a fatal one," a lawyer pointed out, "but [it is] not something to [be] put in a notice."[32] From a lawyer's point of view, "[d]epletion of groundwater is the *clear* reason."[33] The Panchayat appears to have learnt this lesson well.

Another argument advanced by the company that Mohan was keen to meet is that once allowed to operate in the area, it could not be subsequently denied a license given the financial investments it has already made. Mohan pointed out that it was not the Panchayat that allowed the company to set up the beverage plant within its area. It was the state government, more specifically the Left Democratic Front, which gave the company permission to set up the plant initially. In his words:

> It was the policy of the government to attract companies, willing to invest in the state and thereby contributing to the overall development of the state. The state government gave permission for the company to operate in the state. The company came directly through the green channel system of the state government. Then, the Panchayat was compelled to permit the company to operate in its area.[34]

The "green channel system" that Mohan and several others mentioned is the "single-window clearance" or fast-track licensing process for industries in Kerala under which Coca-Cola obtained an initial approval.[35] It later completed the process of buying land in Moolathara village where Plachimada is located. It was only after this, in June 1999, that the company informed the Panchayat of its plans to set up a nonalcoholic beverage plant and submitted a request for the approval of its building plans.

Like everyone else in the area, all that the Panchayat knew at the time was that a "big international company" was setting up the plant, and that it would provide employment to residents and contribute to the "development of the area," leading to "a better life."[36] At the time no information

32 Ibid.
33 Ibid.
34 Interview with Mohan.
35 See note 88 in Chapter 2.
36 Interview with Mohan.

was available about how much water the company would be using.[37] In fact no impact assessment investigation seems to have been carried out by any public or private agency at the time. No one I spoke with – residents of the area, lawyers, government officials, or activists – is aware of any discussion, consultative proceedings, or investigation conducted before the Coca-Cola plant was set up. No one seems to have a clear idea of why not even the most basic questions regarding water availability or usage were asked before a plant requiring large quantities of water, not only as its primary raw material but also for its other procedures, was allowed to begin operations. Most opined, however, that the single-window clearance system by its very nature does not offer room for any time-consuming procedures. This is not something to which attention has been paid in the litigation, but Sumit, a lawyer who represents one of the parties in the Supreme Court, remarked that, if indeed no prior assessment was done, it "could have been one of the best grounds" for the Panchayat to "challenge the functioning of the company."[38] The impact of the company's operations on the environment, however, appears to not have been on the Panchayat's (or anyone else's) mind at the time.

4.1.2. *Litigation Begins*

On April 9, 2003 the Perumatty Grama Panchayat issued a notice that called upon Hindustan Coca-Cola Beverages Pvt. Ltd. to show cause why its license to operate in the area should not be cancelled.[39] The notice referred to the various complaints received about excessive extraction and depletion of groundwater by the company, "environmental problems," agitations held by "political and mass organizations," and as mentioned above, to the year-long sit-in agitation by Adivasis in front of the company's plant.[40] In the words of Mohan, the president of the Panchayat at the time, the company's response was to "straight away [go] to the High Court." Thus began the long drawn-out formal legal battle that after several rounds of litigation and administrative proceedings now awaits what many involved hope will be the final resolution of the dispute by the Supreme Court of India.

37 Ibid.
38 Interview with Sumit.
39 The translated notice is reproduced in *Perumatty Grama Panchayat* v. *State of Kerala*, 2004 (1) KLT 731 at para 2.
40 Ibid.

4.1.3. *In the High Court of Kerala – Part 1*

In response to the Panchayat's notice, Coca-Cola approached the High Court of Kerala on April 16, 2003. It challenged the show cause notice as being illegal, arbitrary, and in violation of principles of natural justice.[41] On April 22 the High Court directed the company to respond to the Panchayat's notice. It also directed the Panchayat to take an appropriate decision after considering the company's response. The court also ordered that the status quo be maintained until the Panchayat made a decision. After considering the company's written response and meeting with its representative, the Panchayat cancelled its license on May 15, 2003 and directed the company to stop operations from May 17, 2003. Coca-Cola returned to the High Court.

On May 16 the High Court passed the final order in the company's petition before directing the company to approach the statutory authority designated to consider appeals to a Panchayat's decision by the government of Kerala.[42] In rushing to the High Court in the first instance, the Company had in fact by-passed this administrative process. Mohan believes that the company preferred to approach the High Court instead of the government because they wanted to put an end to any further challenge to their operations. In fact his view is that once the representatives of the company realized that the Panchayat was serious about preventing excessive extraction of water, they were not prepared to enter into any dialogue with the Panchayat. The people running the plant felt that the Panchayat was unnecessarily interfering with its operations. In their view the role of the Panchayat was limited to issuing the license, and did not involve looking into the groundwater, health, or pollution issues. Separate government departments were responsible for these other issues and they would, according to the company, handle any issues raised by the people. Although the Panchayat felt it was its duty to look into these issues, the "company's stand" according to Mohan, "was to just ignore the Panchayat."[43] Coca-Cola has consistently denied this and claims even now to be ready and willing to engage with all stakeholders.[44] A major difference in the two positions is, however, that the Panchayat does not consider itself as a

[41] *Hindustan Coca-Cola Beverages Pvt. Ltd.* v. *Perumatty Grama Panchayat & State of Kerala (Secy, Department of Local Administration)*, O.P. No. 13513 of 2003.

[42] See *The Kerala Panchayat Raj Act* (1994).

[43] Interview with Mohan.

[44] "Kerala House Passes Bill to Form Plachimada Tribunal," *The Hindu*, February 24, 2011, http://www.thehindu.com/news/cities/Thiruvananthapuram/article1485861.ece. There is no indication, however, that the Adivasis are regarded as stakeholders.

stakeholder but rather as an elected body that is authorized to make a decision to disallow the company's operations in the interest of residents of the area.

Following the directions of the High Court, Coca-Cola submitted a petition to the Local Self Government Department (LSGD) of the Government of Kerala against the Panchayat's order of May 15. On June 12 the LSGD stayed the operation of that order until the issue could be finally decided. The company continued its operations in Plachimada during this time.

While the secretary of the LSGD was considering the company's appeal, word about the continuing protests outside the company's premises continued to spread. BBC Radio's feature on the pollution being caused by Coca-Cola was aired. Samples were tested in Britain and found to contain cadmium and lead in excess of safe limits. Around this time, the Kerala State Pollution Control Board (KSPCB) also swung into action. In August 2003 it informed the company that a sludge sample taken from its premises was found to have cadmium in excess of limits prescribed by the *Hazardous Waste (Management and Handling) Rules*. Due to this, the sludge was to be treated as hazardous waste. It directed the company to stop using or distributing the sludge as manure in the area. This began a parallel track of litigation that intersects the Coca-Cola/Panchayat litigation story at many points. This litigation too has wound its way to the Supreme Court of India.

On September 18, 2003 the Panchayat issued another show cause notice to the company stating that the "functioning of the company is not only harmful to the residents of the Panchayat but also [...] forbid[s] the Panchayat from discharging its constitutional and other mandatory obligations."[45] Once again Coca-Cola challenged the validity of the Panchayat's notice by invoking the writ jurisdiction of the High Court.[46] During the time this petition was before the court, the Panchayat invited Coca-Cola to explain its position. As per the Panchayat's records, the company's representatives chose not to take up that offer and instead requested the Panchayat to not proceed in the matter and to withdraw its notice.

Coca-Cola may have been hoping for a favorable order in the High Court, or simply looking to stall proceedings, but as it turned out, the court dismissed its petition as being premature. The judge who heard the matter on

45 Special Grade Secretary Perumatty Grama Panchayat, Letter to Hindustan Coca Cola Beverages Pvt. Ltd., Show Cause Notice No. B3-378/02, September 18, 2003, accessed August 7, 2014, http://www.pbs.org/now/transcript/transcript_perumattyletter.html.

46 Writ Petition No. 31286 of 2003 filed by Hindustan Coca-Cola Beverages Pvt. Ltd. on October 6, 2003. See Article 226 of the *Constitution of India* that empowers the High Courts to issue writs in the nature of *habeas corpus*, *certiorari*, *mandamus*, prohibition, and *quo warranto* for the protection of certain rights.

November 14, 2003 felt that if the final decision of the Panchayat was against the company, it could challenge it in appropriate administrative or judicial proceedings. On the very next day, the Panchayat once again invited the representatives of the company to explain their position. The company in turn asked the Panchayat for reports and documents on which its second show cause notice was based, invoking principles of natural justice called for in such proceedings. Simultaneously, on November 26, 2003, Coca-Cola also appealed the judgment of the High Court dated November 14, 2003 to a larger bench of the same court.[47]

Coca-Cola's contention was that the second show cause notice issued by the Panchayat was an abuse of the process of law, given perhaps that the matter was being considered by the LSGD. Another main contention of the company was that its fundamental rights under Articles 14 and 19(1)(g) of the Constitution of India had been violated.[48] It asserted that its right to carry on business had been grossly violated despite the fact that it was running the factory in accordance with conditions of its license and relevant statutes. Relying upon the principles of equality and freedom guaranteed in the Indian Constitution (to "persons" under Article 14 and to "citizens" under Article 19), the company contended that its rights were being violated "not in the interest of general public," as required by the Constitution but "merely to respect the susceptibilities and sentiments of a group of people."[49] This is the kind of argument that seems to have led some lawyers to suggest that the reference to Adivasi and other protestors in the Panchayat's notice was a mistake.

While these appeal proceedings were before the High Court, on October 13, 2003 the LSGD made a final decision on Coca-Cola's appeal against the first cancellation of its license. It concluded that there were indications that both the quality and quantity of the water in the area had been affected and directed the Panchayat to constitute a committee of experts from the departments of Ground Water and Public Health and the State Pollution Control Board that would conduct a detailed investigation into the allegations made against the company before arriving at a final decision. The company was allowed to continue its operations in the meantime.

47 *Hindustan Coca-Cola Beverages Pvt. Ltd.* v. *Perumatty Grama Panchayat* and Another, Writ Appeal No. 1962 of 2003.

48 See *Constitution of India*, Article 14 that guarantees "equality before the law or the equal protection of the laws within the territory of India" to "any person"; and *Constitution of India*, Article 19(1) (g) that guarantees to all citizens the right "to practice any profession, or to carry on any occupation, trade or business."

49 *Hindustan Coca-Cola Beverages Pvt. Ltd.* v. *Perumatty Grama Panchayat* and Another, Writ Appeal No. 1962 of 2003.

The Perumatty Panchayat filed a petition in the High Court against this order of the LSGD because it did not have the financial capacity to conduct the scientific study called for by the LSGD.[50] It also brought this fact to the notice of the government even as it offered to do what it could. The government then asked Coca-Cola to deposit Rs. 5 lakhs ($9,000 approx.) to meet the expenses for the study.

The lack of adequate funds was, however, only one of the reasons for the Panchayat's objection to the directions from LSGD. Mohan explained to me that the Panchayat also felt that as elected representatives, they did not have to follow the LSGD's directions. The Panchayat, according to him, is "committed to the people" and the LSGD did not have "the authority to issue orders to the Panchayat."[51] It appears that the Panchayat felt that it was in the best position to assess the situation and make decisions in the interest of its residents. This is the position the Panchayat seems to have taken in the High Court as well. While deciding the Panchayat's petition on December 16, 2003, the court notes:

> According to the Panchayat it is the ultimate authority to decide on the matters covered by the impugned order. The protection and preservation of water sources are the exclusive domain of the Panchayat. When the Panchayat takes a decision based on relevant materials, the Government cannot interfere with it and dicta[t]e how the Panchayat should act in the matter.[52]

The counsel for the Panchayat argued at length about its rights and responsibilities under the *Kerala Panchayat Raj Act*.[53] He argued that the "preservation of water sources is on[e] of the mandatory duties of the Panchayat."[54] The position of the government, which was also a party in this litigation, was that it was trying to protect the interests of both parties.[55] While it was "sensitive to the concerns of the people in the locality," it also had to consider the "interests of industrialization."[56] The government therefore felt that in order to resolve the disputes between the Panchayat and the company, it was necessary to get "expert opinion."[57] At this stage the Government of Kerala does not appear to have expressed any opinion on the jurisdictional claim of the Panchayat.

50 Writ Petition No. 34292 of 2003.
51 Interview with Mohan.
52 *Perumatty Grama Panchayat* v. *State of Kerala*, para. 3.
53 As noted in para. 5 of the judgment, ss. 218 and 166 read with the Third Schedule of the *Kerala Panchayat Raj Act* were specifically mentioned.
54 *Perumatty Grama Panchayat* v. *State of Kerala*, para. 5.
55 Ibid.
56 Ibid.
57 Ibid.

Coca-Cola, on the other hand, made detailed arguments supporting the order of the government and challenging the Panchayat's petition. Its main contention was that the Panchayat had made the decision of canceling its license in a quasi-judicial capacity and could not now challenge the order of the appellate authority (LSGD).[58] It argued that there was in fact no illegality in the government/appellate authority's decision-making process, and therefore the Panchayat's petition seeking the issuance of a writ of certiorari was not tenable.[59] Coca-Cola also argued that its license could only be canceled if it violates any conditions of the license and not under other circumstances.[60] It also maintained that in fact "no ill effects of the extraction of groundwater ha[d] been proved."[61] In support of this, the company relied on scientific reports that, contrary to their intended purpose, were read by the court as proof that the company was extracting "substantial quantity of ground water."[62]

On the basis of the contentions of the parties before it, the court framed the issue before it as that of the legality of the Panchayat's decision "to cancel the licence of the industrial unit and order its closure."[63] Connected to this was the issue of the government's "interference" with the Panchayat's decision in its capacity as the appellate authority (LSGD). In the court's view, the order of the Panchayat directing the closure of the Coca-Cola plant on the ground of excessive extraction of groundwater was "unauthorized."[64] It opined that the Panchayat could, "at best" deny permission to the company to extract any more water and ask it to seek "alternative sources for its water requirement."[65] Having decided that the Panchayat could not direct the company to stop operations, the court turned to the legality of Panchayat's decision to deny permission to the company to extract groundwater.

Coca-Cola's position on this question was that since there was (at the relevant time) "no law governing the control or use of ground water," it was "free to exact any amount of ground water which is available underground in the land owned by it."[66] Further, the company contended that "[a]s a good neighbor, it may have the moral obligation not to make excessive use of ground water," but "legally" there were "no fetters" to its right to extract water.[67] The court

58 Ibid.
59 Ibid.
60 Ibid., para. 11.
61 Ibid., para. 9.
62 Ibid.
63 Ibid., para. 10.
64 Ibid., para. 12.
65 Ibid.
66 Ibid., para. 13.
67 Ibid

rejected these contentions. Relying on Article 21 of the Constitution of India that guarantees the right to life, Principle 2 of the Stockholm Declaration, the common law doctrine of public trust as extended by the Supreme Court of India in a previous decision to a state's duty to protect natural resources including running water and forests, and the relevant provisions of the *Panchayat Raj Act*, the Kerala High Court upheld the Panchayat's decision to prevent further extraction of groundwater by the company. The court held that the company could not be allowed to continue extraction of groundwater as before but would be allowed to withdraw an amount equivalent to that used by an owner of 34 acres of land for domestic and agricultural purposes. It ultimately directed Coca-Cola to find alternative sources of water required in excess of that amount.[68]

Coca-Cola filed an appeal challenging this decision the very next day.[69] The two-judge bench of the Kerala High Court that heard preliminary arguments noted that "a proper adjudication" of the case called for "more scientific data."[70] Its prima facie view was that the government's decision to constitute a committee of experts for a detailed investigation was correct,[71] but instead of the experts from the government departments suggested by the government, the court appointed the Centre for Water Resources Development and Management (CWRDM), a part of the Kerala State Council for Science, Technology and Environment based in Kozhikode, to conduct an investigation into the allegations of overexploitation of groundwater by Coca-Cola. The company was to bear the expenses for this investigation.

In January 2004, the Panchayat also filed an appeal challenging some portions of the judgment of December 16. This was, at least in part, a response to the company's appeal and the order of the appellate court on December 19. The Panchayat had initially felt that the judgment of December 16 was in its favor. Its purpose was to address the grievances of the residents of its area, which required it to restrict the extraction of groundwater: the judgment of December 16 served the purpose to this extent. However, the company's appeal mentioned in the preceding paragraph, and the legal advice the Panchayat received, led it to believe that the matter could not be fully resolved without clarification of rights of a

68 Ibid., para. 15.

69 *Hindustan Coca-Cola Beverages Pvt. Ltd.* v. *Perumatty Grama Panchayat and Others*, Writ Appeal No. 2125 of 2003.

70 Kerala High Court, Order dated December 19, 2003 in Writ Appeal 2125 of 2003 against judgment in Writ Petition 34292 of 2003.

71 Ibid.

panchayat in such matters. The following extract from the Panchayat's Memorandum of Appeal makes this clearer:

> 7. A learned judge of this Hon'ble [sic] Court accepted the contention of the panchayat that it can regulate and restrict the use of ground water in the event there is over exploitation. However, the learned Single Judge has observed that the panchayat has no right to cancel the licence on that ground. To that extent the learned Judge held against the panchayat. The panchayat has now received advice that in view of the far reaching consequences of the observations made by the learned Judge against the interests of the panchayat it has to necessarily file an appeal as the licensing powers and the power of cancellation enjoyed by local bodies will directly arise in the appeal and the judgement [sic] is concluded, it will impinge on such powers of the local bodies.[72]

The most important "legal point" from the perspective of the Panchayat now was whether or not it was "empowered under the provisions of the Kerala Panchayat Raj Act" to cancel the licence of a unit that posed "health hazards to its residents."[73] The issue had by now moved beyond the specific dispute in Plachimada, with the focus clearly on the determination of the authority of an elected *panchayat* in a broader context. This shift from the specific to the abstract is commonplace since appeal proceedings require a question of law to be involved, as courts of appeal normally do not reopen questions of fact. But it also means that the case before the court was now only partly about the Coca-Cola unit in Plachimada, or about members of the two Adivasi communities that had worked for generations on the land the unit was built on, their wells, the rashes on their skins, or the inedible rice in their pots. The dispute before the court was now over the interpretation of the *Kerala Panchayat Raj Act* and the Constitution of India.

The Panchayat began to focus its energies on defending its power to cancel a unit's license to ensure the safety and well-being of its residents. It argued that it was legally responsible to ensure access to potable water for its residents, and therefore its actions were a bona-fide exercise of the powers set out in the Constitution and the *Kerala Panchayat Raj Act*.[74] The shift from the language of water shortage and Adivasi protests in its initial notice to Coca-Cola to that of statutes is a significant aspect of the legal process through which the Adivasi concerns and stories have remained outside the purview of the courts.

72 *Perumatty Grama Panchayat* v. *State of Kerala*, WA 215 of 2004 filed on January 29, 2004.

73 Ibid., 2.

74 In support of its arguments, the Panchayat has primarily relied on Article 243 G and Eleventh Schedule of the *Constitution of India*, and sections 218 and 234(C) of the *Kerala Panchayat Raj Act*.

As mentioned above, the Government of Kerala had initially tried to balance the interests of residents of the area with its goal to attract more industry to the state. Fortunately, for the Panchayat's case, the state government began to change its position while the litigation was still before the Kerala High Court. On February 21, 2004 the government issued an order directing Coca-Cola to stop withdrawing groundwater until the onset of southwest monsoons.[75] The drought in Chittur *taluk* at the time appears to have prompted the government to take this action. Since the company could not have continued production without water, it challenged the validity of this order by way of yet another writ petition before the Kerala High Court.[76]

In this petition the company alleged that the state government's order violated the principles of natural justice as it had been issued without hearing the company. It also alleged discrimination and denial of equality before law, interference with the administration of justice, and an *ultra vires* exercise of power under the *Kerala Groundwater Act* of 2002. The company could not deny the drought in the region. It argued, however, that the drought conditions had been prevailing in the area for almost a year, during which the government had not taken any action. Moreover, according to the company, there was no evidence that the scarcity of water would be addressed if the bottling plant ceased its operations.

The judges who heard the parties on March 8, 2004 acknowledged that the company had "raised some important legal issues," at that preliminary stage.[77] Nonetheless, they held that the decision of the government appeared to be prima facie correct given the severity of the drought in the region generally, and the extreme hardship being faced by the people in Chittur *taluk* in particular. The court noted that given the "acute scarcity of drinking water in the area," there was no reason to doubt that the government had issued the impugned order to "protect the people's right of drinking water and to tide over the difficult situation caused by the drought and non-availability of water even for the basic human needs."[78] In the circumstances, the court felt that consideration of "difficulties of the people"[79] had to take precedence over

75 Order of the State Government, G.O. (Rt). No. 1179/2004/RD, February 21, 2004.

76 *Hindustan Coca-Cola Beverages Pvt. Ltd.* v. *State of Kerala*, WP(C) No. 7077 of 2004. The District Collector of Palakkad, the president of the Panchayat, the HCCBPL Employees Association, and four of the company's employees were also named as respondents in the petition.

77 Kerala High Court, Order dated March 8, 2004 in WP(C) No. 7077 of 2004, para 3.

78 Ibid.

79 Ibid.

any difficulty that the company might face due to a temporary closure of the factory and refused to grant the injunctive relief sought by the company at the time.

Even with regard to the company's contention that other units functioning in the district had not been asked to stop withdrawing water, the court noted that this would be a reason to direct the government to take similar action against the others, and this could not be justification for allowing Coca-Cola to function. The court's observation in this regard is worth quoting here:

> While removing the illegality of hostile discrimination the Court's anxiety should be to minimise the problem and hardship of the people and not to aggravate them.[80]

Subsequently on March 23, the court noted that had the company approached the government for a review of its decision, "instead of rushing to [the] Court to file a writ petition," the government would likely have considered their request "in accordance with law."[81] At this stage, perhaps sensing that the court was unwilling to interfere in the matter, Coca-Cola expressed a willingness to make a representation to the government without prejudice to its contentions in its petition to the court.[82] At the company's request, the court ordered that its petition be kept in abeyance while the company approached the government for a reconsideration of the matter and directed the government to consider the company's representation expeditiously.[83] It appears that the company's purpose here was mainly to ensure it could rush back to the court again if the government's decision was not in its favor.

Meanwhile, the Coca-Cola unit continued to operate, and the company submitted a fresh application for renewal of its license for five years in February 2004. Once again the Panchayat turned down its application, and once again, the latter appealed the Panchayat's decision to the LSGD in Kerala. The LSGD stayed further proceedings before the Panchayat, on the condition that the company comply with the government's order by which it had asked the company to stop withdrawing groundwater until the arrival of monsoons. The Panchayat challenged the validity of this order in the High Court of Kerala, which passed an interim order in favor of the Panchayat. Availing itself of what Galanter has described as the "lavish provisions for

80 Ibid.

81 Kerala High Court, Order dated March 23, 2004 in WP(C) No. 7077 of 2004. para 2

82 Ibid para 3.

83 Ibid., para. 4.

multiple interlocutory appeals" in India that had been "designed for colonial supervision of unreliable locals," the company appealed this latest order of the High Court.[84]

Around this time, the High Court passed another order directing that several of the separate petitions and appeals related to the multiple legal disputes that had arisen over the Coca-Cola unit in Plachimada be heard together by one bench of the court. Given the sheer volume of petitions, replies, counter-affidavits, and memoranda of appeal involved, this was perhaps the only way to manage the litigation, especially given that by this time the legal issue had crystallized around the question of the authority of a *panchayat* vis-à-vis the interests and rights of a corporation.

In May 2004 the Investigation Team appointed earlier by the High Court submitted its interim report. This report indicated that there was in fact unregulated extraction of groundwater by Coca-Cola, adversely affecting the availability of drinking water and water for agriculture. It proposed regulating the withdrawal of groundwater by the company. However, some questions were raised about its methodology, and in particular the data relied upon. The Panchayat placed before the court a report by the Centre for Science and Environment, New Delhi that raised significant questions about the correctness of the interim report. The Panchayat also informed the court that the Kerala Pollution Control Board had asked the company in April 2004 to show cause why it should not be directed to close down since it did not have on site a satisfactory facility for disposal of the hazardous waste generated by it. This action of the Board was in compliance with a direction in separate legal proceedings by the Supreme Court of India to all state pollution control boards in October 2003.

The investigation team presented its final report to the High Court on February 11, 2005 recommending that Coca-Cola be allowed to withdraw groundwater. The Panchayat claimed that it was not given enough time to prepare a detailed response to the final report, and on March 17, 2005 the court directed the Registry to furnish copies of the report to the parties in the case. In fact this was one of the reasons why the court felt it could not yet issue directions that the company be allowed to withdraw water as recommended in the Report, and set a date later that month for hearing arguments. Subsequently, the Panchayat submitted its preliminary objections to the court along with a report by the Centre for Science and Environment. In the meantime, the

84 Marc Galanter, "When Legal Worlds Collide: Reflections on Bhopal, the Good Lawyer, and the American Law School," *Journal of Legal Education* 36 (1986): 297.

company approached the Supreme Court of India seeking leave to appeal the High Court's order of March 17. It subsequently withdrew this petition after the High Court's decision in its favor in April 2005.

4.1.4. *In the High Court of Kerala – Part 2*

On April 7, 2005 the High Court of Kerala handed down a common judgment in all the various appeals and petitions that had been filed by Coca-Cola and the Panchayat.[85] Taking note of the various proceedings and contentions, the court identified the issue before it as follows:

> [...] the issue very much revolved around balancing of ecological rhythm, the aspirations of the people in the locality, the duties and responsibilities, that were expected to be discharged by a Grama Panchayat, especially in the wake of decentralisation of powers and the predicament of an industrial unit, which had been cordially invited to invest substantial funds, ensuring them freedom of functioning.[86]

As is typically the case, all specificities are missing from this abstract statement of the dispute that refers to "the people," "a Grama Panchayat," and "an industrial unit."[87] Having engaged in such exercises many times during my years in the practice of law, I cannot but acknowledge the usefulness of this practice. Re-articulating complex issues in a language that has "trans-situational applicability"[88] facilitates decision making by allowing lawyers and judges to connect the particular dispute before them to other similar disputes and to their outcomes available as precedents. The "familiar stories of the law," the "approved 'verdict categories'," and the "already legally processed" narratives that guide what follows once the specifics of a particular dispute are set aside to make room for legal reasoning,[89] in fact, go a long way in transforming complex, contradictory sets of facts in messy disputes into narratives that courts can recognize and respond to. Moreover, by not "seeing" the Adivasi protestors, the Perumatty Grama Panchayat, and the Coca-Cola Company, courts also attempt to minimize possibilities of bias. These practices also, inevitably,

85 *Hindustan Coca-Cola Beverages (P) Ltd.*, (2005).

86 Ibid., para. 9 at 556.

87 Ibid.

88 Cain, "The General Practice Lawyer and the Client," 335.

89 For the way in which the familiar and already processed stories constitute the dominant narrative in a trial before a judge and the "powerful hold" of the doctrine of *stare decisis* over fact and law, see M. Meehan, "Law and Literature: Reworking the Master-Plot," in Ruthven, *Beyond the Disciplines*, 117.

eclipse the identities, specific experiences, and relations of power that bring the different entities to a court.[90]

Having framed the issue, the court proceeded to recount the "background of the dispute."[91] Here the court narrates the story about the setting up of the plant by the "industrial unit," the initial grant of license to it by the Panchayat, and its subsequent decision to not renew it.[92] The judgment further mentions the "serious shortage of drinking water," "[e]cological problems," and the fact that the Panchayat had no option but to take note of agitations over the functioning of the bottling plant by "early settlers" and "certain organizations."[93] The court also noted the company's surprise at being in the "bad books" of the Panchayat as according to the company, its "hands were clean."[94] In order to substantiate its claims, the company pointed out that it had "conceived and introduced environmentally friendly policies" worldwide, that it was its practice "to comply with safety standards and [that it was] frugal while dealing with natural resources," that it placed a "special emphasis" on waste management, and that it recycled water in its plant.[95] It also emphasized its commitment to "community development programmes for the people living in the locality in the field of education, health and drinking water supply."[96] One example of this that finds mention in the judgment is the "laboratory facility" provided by the company for the students of a high school run by the Perumatty Panchayat.[97] In sum, the company's position was that the allegations being made against it were "factually not sustainable," and the agitations that had, at that point, been going on for over three years were "stage managed and for extraneous reasons."[98] As part of the background to the dispute, the court of appeal also devotes several paragraphs in the judgment to recounting the litigation initiated by the company and the Panchayat.

Once it had determined the issue that needed to be addressed and the main events as recorded in the various legal notices, petitions, replies, judgments and appeals, the court isolated what it apparently saw as the root of the problem: "the assumption, which almost stands transformed to a conviction harboured by the Panchayat, that consumption of any amount of water for the

[90] See Mertz, *Language of the Law School.*
[91] *Hindustan Coca-Cola Beverages (P) Ltd., (2005)*, para. 54 at 557.
[92] Ibid., 557–558.
[93] Ibid.
[94] Ibid., 557.
[95] Ibid.
[96] Ibid., 558.
[97] Ibid.
[98] Ibid.

industry would be detrimental to the general interests of the Panchayat."[99] According to the court, the most appropriate way to resolve the conflict that seemed to arise from the Panchayat's assumption was to rely on the report prepared by the investigation team that had been appointed for the task by the court in December 2003.[100] On the basis of the findings of the team of experts, the court held that the company was entitled to draw up to 500,000 liters of groundwater per day for its use. It further held that the Panchayat's decision to cancel the company's license without a "scientific assessment" was "not justified."[101] Consequently, it overruled the judgment dated December 16, 2004 by which the company had been directed to stop withdrawing groundwater in excess of what may be generally withdrawn by a landowner for agricultural or domestic purposes.

In reaching its decision, the court placed considerable weight on two things: property rights and the report it had commissioned to decide the issue of adverse impacts of extraction of groundwater.[102] With respect to the rights of the company to extract groundwater, the court disagreed with the reasoning of the first court. The appeal court's concern with protecting private property rights is evident in the following passage (as is its concern over setting the right precedent):

> 35. We have to assume that a person has the right to extract water from his property, unless it is prohibited by a statute. Extraction thereof cannot be illegal. We do not find justification for upholding the finding of the learned Judge that extraction of ground water is illegal. It is definitely not something like digging out a treasure-trove. We cannot endorse the findings that the company has no legal right to extract this 'wealth'. If such restriction is to apply to a legal person, it may have to apply to a natural person as well. Abstract principles cannot be the basis for the Court to deny basic rights, unless they are curbed by valid legislation. Even reference to mandatory function [of panchayats], referred to in the third schedule of the Panchayat Raj Act, namely "Maintenance of traditional drinking water sources" could not have been envisaged as preventing an owner of a well from extracting water therefrom, as he wishes. The Panchayat had no ownership about such private water source, in effect denying the proprietary rights of the occupier and the proposition of law laid down by the learned Judge is too wide, for unqualified acceptance.[103]

[99] Ibid., 562.
[100] Ibid., 556.
[101] Ibid., 571.
[102] See especially *Hindustan Coca-Cola Beverages (P) Ltd., (2005)*, para. 35 at 565, para. 43 at 567, and para. 9 at 556 and 557.
[103] Ibid., 565.

The only "permissible restrictions" on a landowner's right to extract water "as he wishes," according to the court, were that such extraction "not bring about a drought or any imbalance in the water table."[104] This is where the report of the team of experts appointed by the court became significant.[105]

The investigating team's report emerged from a detailed "scientific investigation" carried out over a period of one year. The team of experts met at least six times between January 2004 and January 2005. Members also visited the area and inspected the Coca-Cola premises. During these visits the patterns of groundwater extraction were examined. An expert nominated by Coca-Cola was one of the members of the team. This representative of the company was present at every meeting, along with other experts. Although nobody is specifically mentioned as representing the Panchayat on this team, according to its former president, the Panchayat felt their interests would be well protected by the Centre for Water Resources Development and Management since the Panchayat had proposed its appointment.

There is no record that indicates that the members of the investigating team ever consulted any of the protesting Adivasis outside the factory premises. No one I spoke with in the hamlets remembers being asked to give their opinions to this team or to any of the many others who continue to visit the area in order to collect samples of water from their wells. As Maariamma said to me, the visitors look at the water, collect samples, but they never drink the water. It is with great amusement that she mimics the reactions of such visitors every time she suggests that they stop looking at the water and drink it instead. The reactions seem to lie somewhere between horror and panic. If they drink the water, she says, they would know she and her people are not lying.

The report notes that groundwater is the main source of water in the area and that the reserves are recharged predominantly by rainfall. It then goes on to note that while the deficiency in the rainfall in the past two years could be the "most significant factor" responsible for the scarcity of water in the area, the "unregulated withdrawal of groundwater from the wells within the Coca Cola factory complex and also outside" during this period had definitely "aggravated" the situation.[106] However, based on existing rates of groundwater withdrawal, detailed study of the rainfall patterns, and estimates of expected

[104] Ibid., para. 43 at 567.

[105] The Investigation Team, Constituted vide Order WA/2125/2003 dated 19.12.2003 by the Honourable High Court of Kerala, "Final Report on Investigations on the Extraction of Groundwater by M/s Hindustan Coca-Cola Beverages Private Limited at Plachimada," (February 11, 2005).

[106] *The Investigation Team Report*, 1.

increase in demands for various purposes up to the year 2025, its conclusion was that "under normal rainfall conditions," Coca-Cola could withdraw groundwater at the rate of 500,000 liters per day.[107] Interestingly, one of the facts "safely assumed" by the experts in arriving at this conclusion is that the Coca-Cola plant "will be the only major industrial user in the Plachimada watershed."[108]

The report contains a number of maps and tables with large amount of data. There are also some calculations premised around the "value of X" that is meant to determine the range of water Coca-Cola can withdraw during monsoon and non-monsoon periods. There are also some basic facts. For example, one of the tables shows clearly that six of the total seven bore wells with energized pumps within one square kilometer of the "Coca-Cola factory" are for industrial use. The seventh one is used for irrigation. There are also eleven "dug wells" in this area that draw water with pumps for domestic-cum-irrigation purposes.[109] Seventeen other "dug wells" used for domestic purposes are without pumps. Since Coca-Cola is the only industrial establishment in the specified area, and it is noted elsewhere that there are six bore wells on its premises, it is obvious that six out of the seven bore wells with energized pumps in the area belong to it. The ownership and use of most of the open wells without pumps in the said area are also quite apparent. Several of these are in Adivasi homes right next to the Coca-Cola plant. While noting the unregulated withdrawal of groundwater in the area as a cause of shortage in its summary of findings, the investigating team did not explicitly comment on where the responsibility for such withdrawal must lie despite having noted elsewhere in the report that Coca-Cola was the major industrial user in the area. Instead, it notes that there had been unregulated withdrawal of water from wells inside as well as outside the company's premises.[110]

The report concludes with an observation that its recommendations will not only "protect the interests of domestic and irrigation water supply sectors adequately" but also "ensure that the developmental opportunities, which industrial establishments can create in an area that is otherwise predominantly agrarian, are fully utilized."[111] Unfortunately, given that the task with which the court had entrusted the investigation team was limited to conducting a scientific investigation into the allegations that the operations of Coca-Cola

[107] Ibid., 16.
[108] Ibid.
[109] Ibid., 20.
[110] Ibid., 16 and 21.
[111] Ibid., 23.

had caused scarcity of water, this exercise in balancing interests of "domestic and irrigation water supply sectors" and "development opportunities" afforded by "industrial establishments" did not raise for the expert members the issue of seeking the opinion of those who live in the place.[112] In these circumstances, the complete silence in the report about the residents of the hamlets around the premises, is regrettable, but hardly surprising. Although "development" was considered by many, the fact that the Adivasis who started the protests might have something to say about the agriculture/industry trade-off that was being considered was not, it seems, considered by the committee, the court that appointed it, the government, or the Panchayat.

On April 20, 2005 the Panchayat applied for special leave to appeal the High Court's decision of April 7 to the Supreme Court of India.[113]

4.1.5. *In the High Court of Kerala – Part 3*

After its victory in the High Court, Coca-Cola again applied to the Panchayat for renewal of its license. On April 26, 2005 the Panchayat once again rejected the company's application on the ground that it did not have the required certificate from the Kerala Pollution Control Board or the one necessary for its operations under the *Factories Act*.

In May 2005, Coca-Cola challenged this decision of the Panchayat by way of an interlocutory application in the appeal that had already been decided by the High Court of Kerala on April 7.[114] This application was contested strongly by the Panchayat's lawyer. His main argument was that the company could not be granted the license, as it did not have the necessary clearances. He also vehemently argued that the company had not only once again bypassed the statutory remedy available to it, but it had also inappropriately approached the High Court by way of an application that was not tenable under the rules of procedure, given that a final order in the main appeal itself had already been made. To the Panchayat, the company's action once again pointed to the high-handed attitude of a multinational corporation with enough resources to engage in yet another round of litigation.

Both sides argued the matter at length in the court. Coca-Cola asserted that it had been subjected to prejudice and discrimination. The company believed that it had all the requisite licenses and certificates, and therefore the Panchayat's refusal was uncalled for, especially in light of the judgment

[112] Ibid.
[113] Special Leave Petition No. 9385 of 2005.
[114] IA No. 1347 of 2005 in WA No. 2125 of 2003.

passed by the same court on April 7, 2005 allowing it to extract 500,000 liters of groundwater per day. The Panchayat, on the other hand, insisted the company had violated procedural rules of the court and that its application was not maintainable. Its substantive objection, however, was that a *panchayat* could not be directed to issue a license but only to consider the company's application properly, which it had done.

The court considered the Panchayat's procedural objection but felt that in the circumstances, it had to address the substantive issues. The court saw the Panchayat's action as an attempt to circumvent its earlier order and expressed concerns that its directions "had been trifled with."[115] The judges felt that though "[c]ourts seldom chase their orders, as they are meant to discharge their obligations with a total sense of detachment," in the circumstances "if further directions are not issued, it may tantamount to shirking of responsibility [by the court].[116] They felt compelled to "ensure that lawful orders are obeyed."[117] Even though the Panchayat could continue to "hold an opinion," it had to "gracefully accept the verdict" once the court had "pronounced upon rights and liabilities."[118] "This," the court observed, "is the rule of law."[119]

The court directed the Panchayat to renew the company's license within a week.[120] It further held that if this was not done, the company would be *deemed to possess such a license* and could carry on operations for the next two years, provided they had other clearances. The Panchayat felt that it was being forced to issue the license against its better judgment,[121] which as mentioned before, it perceived as an unwarranted interference with the performance of its statutory duties. The Panchayat met to discuss the latest order of the High Court on June 6, 2005. On that day it decided to issue a conditional license for three months to the company. According to Mohan, the Panchayat took this decision only to comply with the order of the court. They were considering filing an appeal against it, but in the meantime, they did not want to be held in contempt of court.

As per the conditional license, the company could function for the duration of the license provided it fulfilled the thirteen conditions mentioned in the license. The conditions set out by the Panchayat covered a range of issues such as pollution, extent of groundwater extraction, production, and

[115] Order dated June 1, 2005 in I.A. No. 1347 of 2005 in W.A. No. 2125 of 2003, para. 14.
[116] Ibid., para 15
[117] Ibid.
[118] Ibid.
[119] Ibid.
[120] Order dated June 1, 2005 in I.A. No. 1347 of 2005 in W.A. No. 2125 of 2003, para. 16.
[121] Interview with Mohan.

distribution of drinking water to the nearby residents by the company. It is clear that unlike the situation when the company started operations in the place, the Panchayat now wanted to keep a close watch over it. The company rejected this conditional license on the ground that not only was the imposition of such conditions *ultra vires*, but the Panchayat was also not complying with the directions of the High Court, and that its actions were thus "in total disregard of the Rule of Law."[122]

The Panchayat's decision was also not welcomed by the protestors who remained opposed to the reopening of the plant. On June 8 several hundred residents and supporters marched to the Coca-Cola premises, demanding that the facility be shut down permanently.[123] The march was organized by the Plachimada Solidarity Committee and the *Coca-Cola Viruddha Samara Samithi* (Anti–Coca-Cola Struggle Committee).[124] Many in the area talk about the large cordon of the local police that was present in front of the factory gates that day. Between 300 and 500 protestors were reported to have been arrested.[125] They were, however, released by the end of the day. It was also reported that a woman who was beaten up by the police had to be taken to the hospital.[126] One newspaper reported that the "police had to use force when the agitators turned violent and tried to forcibly open the gates of the company."[127] The Adivasi women do not remember the date, but they recall the demonstration. They also recall how some of them were dragged by their clothes, forced into a jeep, and taken to the police station. Amma, an Adivasi elder, recalled how a girl from Plachimada was beaten up by policemen for questioning them and refusing to go with them to the police station.

The Panchayat, on the other hand, felt that it was acting properly within its rights, given the circumstances. In a petition filed by it seeking review of the High Court's directions, it argued that it could not be compelled to issue a license, especially given that it was trying "to ensure that the residents of the area, most of them who are under privileged, illiterate, and poor and large number of them being Adivasis, get drinking water [...]."[128] Under

[122] "Coke Rejects Conditional License," *The Hindu*, June 10, 2005, accessed September 21, 2010, http://www.thehindu.com/2005/06/10/stories/2005061002380700.htm.

[123] "500 Anti–Coca-Cola Demonstrators Arrested in India," *Newswire*, June 2005, accessed November 30, 2005, http://www.ens-newswire.com/ens/jun2005/2005-06-09-02.html.

[124] "Anti-Coke Agitators Held, Released Later," *The Hindu*, June 9, 2005, accessed September 20, 2010, http://www.thehindu.com/2005/06/09/stories/2005060903050700.htm.

[125] See ibid. and "500 Anti–Coca-Cola Demonstrators Arrested in India."

[126] "500 Anti–Coca-Cola Demonstrators Arrested in India."

[127] "Anti-Coke Agitators Held, Released Later."

[128] Review Petition filed by the Perumatty Panchayat seeking review of the order or the High Court of Kerala in IA 1347 of 2005 in Writ Appeal No. 2125/2003, para. 6(h).

these circumstances, the Panchayat felt it had "a right to decline the issuance of license" for the production of "bottled water and drinks."[129] Although its review petition was dismissed on July 5, 2005, the same arguments about its rights were also the basis for two fresh applications it made for leave to appeal to the Supreme Court of India.[130]

Coca-Cola on the other hand maintained that it was not in violation of any laws, and therefore the attitude of the Panchayat, especially in granting a conditional license for three months, was unreasonable, hostile, and high-handed. In order to ensure that the Panchayat followed the directions of the court properly, the company sought further clarifications from the same bench of the High Court that had issued directions for grant of license to the Panchayat on June 1, 2005. The company argued that since the Panchayat had failed to grant a license as directed by the court within the time prescribed, it now had a deemed license under the terms of that same order. The court, however, disagreed, holding inter alia, that in issuing the license for three months the Panchayat had in fact followed its directions. The company could nevertheless apply for another license or a renewal, which would have to be considered afresh by the Panchayat.[131]

This order led to yet another petition seeking leave to appeal to the Supreme Court, this time, interestingly, by the Kerala State Pollution Control Board. In exercise of its powers under the *Water (Prevention and Control of Pollution) Act* of 1974, the Board had withdrawn the consent given to the company to operate on August 19, 2005. This decision was taken by the Board for two reasons – firstly, because of the presence of cadmium beyond permissible limits in the effluents generated by the unit, and secondly, due to the company's non-compliance with the Board's direction to it to provide clean drinking water to the residents of the hamlets near the plant. The High Court's directions to the Panchayat to consider fresh applications for renewal of the company's license despite the Board's actions were seen by the Board as raising doubts over the Board's power to regulate.

To add to the number of appeals, the state of Kerala, through its Local Self Government Department, also applied for a leave to appeal the High Court decision to the Supreme Court in order to seek a clarification of the powers of a local authority in such circumstances. Relying on national and international legal principles of ownership, reasonable use, and rights, it is

129 Ibid.

130 SLP Nos. 15680 of 2005 and 15681 of 2005 against orders passed on June 6, 2005 and July 5, 2005, respectively.

131 Order dated November 16, 2005 in I.A. No. 2981 of 2005 in W.A. No. 2125 of 2003-C.

seeking the Supreme Court's opinion on the question of interference with a decision taken by a local body – a *panchayat* – in the public interest. An application for intervention was also filed by the Research Foundation for Science, Technology and Ecology, a nongovernmental organization (NGO) engaged in research and advocacy and headed by well-known author and activist Dr. Vandana Shiva.

4.1.6. *In the Supreme Court of India*

At the time of writing, all the appeals mentioned above are pending before the Supreme Court of India. It is not clear when the Supreme Court will decide these appeals. Most lawyers involved do not expect the matter to be taken up by the court anytime soon, unless one of the parties moves for an early hearing. Aside from some issues raised over procedural propriety (regarding proceedings before the High Court), the most important questions of law raised by all the appellants in the Supreme Court revolve around determination of the nature of the authority of a *panchayat* and its rights to intervene in and decide matters such as this. Some questions also relate to the ownership rights of "people," "residents," or a "local community" versus the rights of a multinational corporation. The available pleadings and conversations with lawyers indicate that the Supreme Court is being called upon to weigh private property rights against common and collective rights, even as rights and powers of a *panchayat* remain central to the litigation. An acknowledgment of a human right to water also underlies some arguments being made. Environmental rights are significantly highlighted, and some have also raised the issue of right to life guaranteed as a fundamental right in the Constitution of India.

Almost all the lawyers involved in the litigation in the Supreme Court that I had an opportunity to speak with concur on the "questions of law" that need to be resolved at this stage. In fact, it is *only* questions of law that need to be addressed at this stage, as is typically the case in appeal proceedings. As one lawyer, Ravi, pointed out, "[n]ow it's basically a question of law."[132] He emphasized that nothing "remains on facts."[133] The facts are well established at this stage of the litigation. One of those established facts, according to him, is that this has been a "long struggle between Coke and Panchayat."[134]

[132] Interview with Ravi.
[133] Ibid.
[134] Ibid.

4.2. FRAMING LEGAL CLAIMS: LEGAL PROFESSIONALS AS TRANSLATORS

> The tribal question has never been an issue in this litigation. We wouldn't want to make it an issue.

This was the unhesitant response of a lawyer who represents one of the parties in the Supreme Court of India to a question I had posed about the relevance of the Adivasi protests to the litigation over the dispute in Plachimada. He added that "[a]s lawyers, [they will] argue statutes, not tribal rights."[135] The explanation offered for this was that, "[i]t is hard to make the Supreme Court understand," and that tribal rights "don't cut much ice" in the court.[136] These statements about the Indian Supreme Court can be read as reflections on what has been described as the neoliberal turn that over the last two decades has seen the court lean away from rights of the people and toward market-led economic development,[137] but they also offer very valuable insights for understanding why claims are translated into certain languages, framed around specific words, and re-presented in particular ways. They allow us to examine critically the process of translation between normative worlds as disputes are restated in the language of state law, its categories, and legal issues.

None of the legal professionals, including the one quoted above, spoke of the significant role of the Adivasis in this dispute and most did not even mention them, until specifically asked. As indicated by the account of the litigation presented in the first part of this chapter, except for the isolated reference to the "early settlers" in one of the High Court judgments, Adivasis who began the protests are absent from the formal legal narratives of the dispute. The complex questions their histories and their present raise and the answers they seek remain on the margins of relevance in processes and practices that focus on abstract questions of law. The issues that seem to matter most to Adivasi protestors have not been translated into any questions of law that the Supreme Court is so far being asked to respond to in the Plachimada litigation. This is not because those who have framed the legal issues are oblivious to either the existence of Adivasis in Plachimada or to their prominent role in beginning and sustaining the protests against the company. It is also not always because they do not care. Most of the lawyers and judges I spoke with do

[135] Ibid.

[136] Ibid.

[137] See for example, Mayur Suresh and Siddharth Narrain, ed., *The Shifting Scales of Justice: The Supreme Court in Neoliberal India* (New Delhi: Orient Black Swan, 2014).

seem to care, both about the pursuit of justice as a desirable goal for a society and about ensuring justice for those whose lives are currently farthest from its realm. Adivasis are absent, therefore, not because they do not matter here, but because speaking about Adivasis is, as the lawyer indicated, considered neither necessary nor desirable for an effective framing and resolution of the dispute.

Three overlapping logics explain how the Adivasis' accounts have been eclipsed in the legal narrative of Plachimada, and more crucially, why they will continue to be excluded.

4.2.1. *The Legal and the Social*

The legal issues identified by all the lawyers I spoke with relate to the conflicting positions of Coca-Cola and Perumatty Panchayat over the use of groundwater for the company's operations, and involve the question of whether and to what extent the decision of the Kerala High Court undermines a *panchayat's* ability to make decisions at the local level. For most the central legal issue that needs to be decided by the Supreme Court is the role and powers of a *panchayat* in the decentralized system of governance envisaged under Part IX of the Constitution of India, in general, and the *Kerala Panchayat Raj Act*, in particular. Related questions, emphasized to varying degrees by each of them, are those of determination of rights over groundwater and environmental pollution. Resolution of these issues and questions calls for a definitive interpretation of constitutional guarantees, property rights, and the various statutes invoked by all parties to the litigation. The energies of the lawyers are therefore focused on presenting the best arguments based on legal enactments and precedents in support of the respective positions of their clients, that is the Perumatty Grama Panchayat, Local Self-Governance Department, Kerala Pollution Control Board, state of Kerala, NGOs, individually named activists, and a farmers' organization. Each of these, in turn, claims to be representing the best interests of "the people" who are also opposed to the functioning of the company in Plachimada. Application and interpretation of the statutes and precedents will ultimately determine the outcome of the dispute. The lawyers are therefore doing all that they are required to do to win the case, as they are expected to in an adversarial legal system.[138]

The lives of those who reside in Plachimada and other nearby hamlets are what one lawyer referred to as the "social issues" that underlie the legal dispute. These social facts are particular lives of particularly situated peoples that

[138] See Cain, "The General Practice Lawyer and the Client," 343. Cain notes that a "good" lawyer is one "who accepts his client's desired outcome as his own objective."

are not considered an integral part of the legal story. As facts not material to the legal case, they can be, and are, viewed collectively as abstract social issues perhaps because *everyone* opposed to the company would like for it to wind up its operations and leave the place. The different reasons for this opposition, arising from what the company represents to each group, are eclipsed in pursuit of the common goal. This enables the legal professionals to frame questions of law that can be most effectively and successfully argued in court, that is, constitutional guarantees, statutory provisions, procedural irregularities, and national and human imperatives for preserving water.

Raising complex questions of dispossession, displacement, and legal and social processes through which Adivasis have been impoverished, when (as will become clear in the following two chapters) the law does not often recognize these as violations, cannot be sound litigation strategy. Even though related, the "social" and the "legal" thus remain external to each other.[139] The "social" presents the dispute but does not determine the "questions of law," which are determined by and in the language of the law that requires the translation of the specific into abstract.[140] The legal violations are named and framed by the law.[141] Thus framed, the questions are also then determined by applying the law. There is no room here for the complex issues invoked by the expression "tribal rights." Issues and questions that a court cannot recognize are considered best left out.

4.2.2. *The Tribal Question and Tribal Rights*

The expression "tribal question" is generally, and for far too long has been, used as shorthand for the simplistically framed assimilation-versus-isolation debate over the place, role, and future of tribes in India.[142] For many Indians

[139] See for example, Christopher McCrudden, "A Common Law of Human Rights?: Transnational Judicial Conversations on Constitutional Rights," in *Human Rights and Legal History*, eds. Katherine O'Donovan and Gerry R. Rubin (Oxford: Oxford University Press, 2000), 64. McCrudden notes that "lawyers regard vexed questions of what human rights are as best viewed as technical legal questions, in part to distinguish them from the 'political'." McCrudden suggests that this is one of the reasons why the voices of marginalized and disadvantaged sections of the society continue to be absent from the debates over meaning and interpretation of human rights.

[140] See for example, Mertz, *The Language of the Law School*.

[141] See Felstiner, Abel and Sarat, "The Emergence and Transformation of Disputes."

[142] For early debates, see Verrier Elwin, "Do We Really Want to Keep Them in a Zoo," in *The Tribal People of India* (New Delhi: Government of India Press, 1973), 8; and G. S. Ghurye, *The Scheduled Tribes*, 3rd ed. (Bombay: Popular Press, 1963). For an early classification of Aboriginals in India from the "real primitive" and "wild aboriginals" to the "modern" ones, see Verrier Elwin, *The Aboriginals*, 2nd ed. (London: Oxford University Press, 1944). See also S. C. Dube, "Development Designs and Tribal People," in *Antiquity to Modernity in*

the only question to be considered is whether the "tribals" should be assimilated with the "mainstream" or allowed to remain in isolation. This question itself is framed in the narrow language of backwardness/development/uplift of "tribals." This narrow discursive framework underlies the constitutional provisions for Scheduled Tribes and continues to shape judicial opinions and treatment of issues brought to the courts by members of Scheduled Tribes.[143] The idea that the backward/development debate is perhaps better understood as one over alternative visions of democracy remains absent from popular social and political rhetoric in the country.[144]

The expression "tribal rights" is often shorthand for the Constitutional provisions and statutes relating to Scheduled Tribes in postcolonial India. Issues around rights of Scheduled Tribes to lands and forests traditionally occupied and used by them, as well as connected histories of their social marginalization and oppression, underlie these legal enactments. Tribal rights in India, as elsewhere, are therefore inseparable from questions of land. More specifically they are about relationships between tribal peoples and the lands they traditionally live on. The tribal question arises, repeatedly, from their reluctance to end those relationships, from their opposition to attempts by others to disrupt those relationships in ways that are not acceptable to them. It also arises from demands of restoration of these relationships where they have been or are under threat of being disrupted. The tribal question is thus also about the freedom to fundamentally disagree with the vision of the nation's future imagined by others.

In order to explain the comment about the difficulties of successfully arguing "tribal rights" in the Supreme Court of India, the lawyer quoted above referred to the court's decision in *State of Kerala* v. *PUCL*.[145] This case that arose from Adivasi demands for return of alienated lands in Kerala is examined in detail in Chapter 6. I mention it here to point to an important reason

Tribal India: Continuity and Change Among Indian Tribes, ed. S. C. Dube, vol. 1 (New Delhi: Inter-India, 1998); Nandita Haksar, "Law and the Self-Management of Tribal Societies in North-East India," in *Antiquity to Modernity in Tribal India: Tribal Self-Management in North-East India*, ed. Bhupinder Singh, vol 2 (New Delhi: Inter-India, 1998), 161.

143 For a brief history of this discursive framework, of its deployment during the Constitutional Assembly Debates and the resultant limitations of the postcolonial formal legal system in securing justice for those who are sought to be protected, see Parmar, "Undoing Historical Wrongs."

144 See Sundar, *Subalterns and Sovereigns* for the argument that backward/development debate is better understood as a debate over alternative visions of democracy.

145 *State of Kerala & Anr.* v. *People's Union for Civil Liberties, Kerala State Unit & Ors*, (2009) 8 SCC 46.

why Adivasi concerns in Kerala, even when noticed, are not part of the legal narrative. In Kerala, as in other parts of the country, the most important issue that Adivasis continue to face is that of dispossession and displacement.[146] And yet the lawyer, who acknowledged during our conversation that the Adivasis in Plachimada are concerned over the protection of their traditional sources of water, thinks it prudent to not raise such questions of "tribal rights" in the Supreme Court. Precedents like *State of Kerala* v. *PUCL* show that reliance on tribal rights to land or arguments based on Adivasi connections to their traditional lands stand no chance when weighed against statutes. The state law does not recognize any tribal right to maintain connections to traditional lands in perpetuity.[147] In a situation where those lands are required for national progress and development, such tribal rights do not, as the lawyer pointed out, "cut much ice."[148]

The violation experienced by Adivasis in places like Plachimada, when recognized, creates issues that require questions of law and justice to be framed differently than they currently are. The "tribal question" cannot be successfully translated into familiar "questions of law" for courts. The kind of translation that the Adivasi accounts call for – the practice of "hearing-to-respond,"[149] the recognition of the limits of the existing legal language and processes, and the courage to commit to a different vision of the future[150] – is not common. Unfamiliar and messy questions that are inseparable from long and complicated histories of social, economic, and political exclusion offer neither the comfort nor the stability of the familiar categories and narratives of law. For the lawyers, greater possibility of success therefore, lies in translating claims into a language the court can recognize and respond to, that is, in formulating arguments that can be grounded in existing statutes and legal categories of harm, not in the realm of tribal rights. This is especially so when these rights seem to be diverging from the currently imagined future of the nation.

[146] See Government of India, Ministry of Home Affairs, *Report of the Commission on Scheduled Areas and Scheduled Tribes 1960–61*, Volume I [Dhebar Commission]; Government of India, Planning Commission, *Kerala State Development Report* (New Delhi: Academic Foundation, 2008) [Kerala Development Report]; R. M. Sarkar, ed., *Land and Forest Rights of the Tribals Today* (New Delhi, Serials Publications, 2006).

[147] For the manner in which the possibility of articulating such a right was written out of the country's Constitution, see Parmar, "Undoing Historical Wrongs."

[148] Interview with Ravi.

[149] Spivak, "Translation as Culture," 22.

[150] See Cover, "Nomos and Narrative," 7. Cover suggested that it is these "interpretive commitments" that "determine what law means and what law shall be."

4.2.3. *Difference and the Inevitability of Sameness*

Sometimes lawyers and judges do test the boundaries of formal state law. Courts can be persuaded, in the interests of justice, to push boundaries by creatively reformulating existing meanings so as to take the law in unexpected directions. This happens when the existing law appears to not be able to respond to a particular claim in a just manner. It happens when a court's vision of justice requires something more. It happens when lawyers and judges recognize experiences that cannot be translated into existing categories. It happens when justice demands that imaginations be stretched, limitations in existing languages be recognized, and new questions asked and addressed. This only happens, however, when that which is untranslatable is taken seriously. The reason why this has not happened in this case appears to have something to do with how Adivasis are perceived in the country by many.

The Adivasis in Plachimada are viewed as a particularly marginalized, poor, and illiterate subgroup, that is, the "backward tribal" and, at the same time, as an undifferentiated component of "the people" who have been agitating for the closure of the Coca-Cola plant. Although often one view was emphasized more than the other during different conversations, this view of Adivasis as particularly different, but also ultimately the same, emerges from all my conversations with lawyers and judges. Even though expressed separately at different moments during a conversation, these two seemingly contradictory views are in fact held simultaneously.

With the exception of one lawyer, none of the lawyers and judges I interviewed has either been to Plachimada or actually met any Adivasi protestor. One of them, the one who asked if they were "real Adivasis" – "short" and "dark" – seemed not even sure how to imagine them. And yet he shares the confidence of all the others in their knowledge of what the Adivasis must want and what is good for them. This knowledge rests on the confident assumption that the Adivasis' interests are well represented by the activists, the Panchayat, the state government, and its various departments and sundry functionaries. This faith in their own knowledge does not allow any room either for recognizing the radically different meaning of the protests for the Adivasis or for reflecting on the possibility of framing different questions of law.

Adivasis are viewed as nothing more than poor, illiterate, unskilled, and "backward" peoples. The word "tribal" itself connotes for many a state of social, cultural, and economic "primitiveness" to such an extent that the two words – tribal and primitive – are unreflectively used as a synonym.[151] For example, a lawyer used the expression "totally indigenous people" while speaking about their lack of expertise in successfully connecting the functioning of the Coca-Cola plant to the pollution and depletion of water.[152] This odd expression – totally indigenous – was meant to convey a particular deficiency, with the word indigenous standing in for words he used at other times in relation to them: illiterate and ignorant. This lawyer does not actually know any of them, but he can say they are ignorant with complete confidence because that is what "indigenous" or "tribal" signifies for many Indians. It appears that to be illiterate is also to be ignorant about everything, even your own life and surroundings.

If backwardness is assumed, it follows that Adivasis need to be represented and spoken for by the literate, advanced, and modern sections of the society. Some lawyers and judges I met believe that it is in fact the literate outsiders who mobilized and led the agitations against the company. It is unimaginable for many that this action could have been conceived or carried out by the poor and illiterate Adivasis on their own. Any agency on their part is inconceivable.

One reason why radical difference in visions of the future is not recognized for what it is lies in the confident belief in the ability of what is conceived as modern to represent fully what is viewed as not-yet-modern. Within this view, everyone is (or must be) traveling on the singular path toward the same future. By attributing any difference of worldviews to "backwardness" that can and must "catch-up" with that which is "modern," "progressive," and "developed," it is possible to discount it. The Adivasis can therefore be treated as the same, albeit a little behind everyone else. As an undifferentiated constituent of "the people," Adivasis in Plachimada are ultimately viewed as the same, with their perspectives, desires, and hopes indistinguishable from all the other groups protesting against the company. They are poor as some other groups in Plachimada, and they need water to live like everyone else in the area. They are also entitled to all rights as any other citizen of the country. They must therefore mean what everyone does, and even if there are some differences, those can be reconciled without any prejudice to them as long as the common goal of removing Coca-Cola is achieved. The difference that shapes Adivasi

[151] Even though this seems to consign certain peoples to a state of perpetual "not yet," postponing their being regarded as equals forever, the Constitutional enablement and level of access to public funds that are tied to the extent of a group's "primitiveness" have also interestingly led to a situation where ever more communities in India demand that they be declared as "backward."

[152] Interview with Surendra.

protests and sense of injustice, and gives meaning to their claims here therefore remains eclipsed because of the disregard of the untranslatable by those who re-present their claims.

Regardless of the degree to which each of the above lines of reasoning – the separation of the legal and the social, the problematic "tribal question," and the untranslatability of the claims of the tribal viewed as particularly different but ultimately (bound to become) the same – is followed by the legal professionals, eventually they lead to the same conclusion. To the extent that the Adivasis' story diverges from the narratives recognizable in state law and policy, it is best left out. For the same reason, they are also best represented by others.

4.3. CONCLUSION

As many concerned about or connected with the events in Plachimada wait for the final determination of the various questions of law by the highest court in the country, the Coca-Cola facility in Plachimada remains closed. Although the company suspended operations in 2004, it refuses to leave. The main entrance to the facility is locked and the premises guarded by a security agency. The company won the last round of litigation in the High Court when it was allowed to withdraw a certain amount of groundwater for its use, and it continues to deny any wrongdoing. The former president of the Perumatty Panchayat, on the other hand, is confident the company "cannot survive in the area".[153] He strongly feels "[t]he company has lost the opportunity to operate in the area."[154] Since the issue first arose, evidence has accumulated indicating that the area is not suitable for the operations of companies like Coca-Cola that rely primarily on water.[155] The significance of this fact is not lost on the members of the Panchayat.

The dispute is clearly far from resolved. Given the nature of the litigation so far, the number of parties to the litigation at present, and the stakes involved, the battle in the Supreme Court is likely to be long and bitterly fought. What impact the various developments subsequent to the High Court decision in 2005 will have on the appeals already before the Supreme Court is something only time will tell. Whether the latest move by the Kerala Government to set up a tribunal for adjudicating claims for compensation will lead to a fresh round of litigation is also an open question.

[153] Interview with Mohan.

[154] Ibid.

[155] See "*Report of the High Power Committee*", 18, 19, http://www.scribd.com/doc/80063693/Plachimada-High-Power-Committee-Report-PDF.

In this chapter I have presented the stories of the dispute in Plachimada as they emerge from the records of the litigation and as understood and described by the litigants, lawyers, and judges involved. Those who began the protests in Plachimada are not present in these stories. On the rare occasion that they are mentioned, it is only as examples of the people who need to be protected from a powerful multinational corporation. As their protests are translated for the courts and given legal expression, their stories, presented in the following chapters, are eclipsed. This means that even when the Supreme Court decides the case before it, it inevitably will address only the issues and questions presented to it in the language and categories it is familiar with. It is no doubt true that even if the Adivasi stories and concerns had been placed before it, the court could have ruled, as it has in the past, that economic development of the nation must trump concerns over displacement of those already marginalized. It could have ruled that the Adivasis had no right to say whether they wished to stay or leave their homes. It could have ruled, as in another case, that they would be better off living elsewhere.[156] But it could also have ruled, as it has recently, that it is time now to undo the wrongs of centuries.[157] It could have, while "hearing-to-respond"[158] to unfamiliar stories, recognized the limits of its own language.

As the lawyers on all sides prepare to argue the law and the statutes, and I read regular news updates to keep up with the ongoing saga and note the latest quotes from both the opponents and supporters of Coca-Cola's operations in Plachimada, my thoughts always return to the *samara pandal* and to the old woman who sits there all day everyday. I am reminded over and over again of the faraway look in her eyes when she said: "I don't know if I will also die like Mylamma did – without seeing an end to this *samaram*. Who knows for how long it will go on!"[159]

[156] See *State of Kerala & Anr.* v. *People's Union for Civil Liberties, Kerala State Unit & Ors*, (2009) 8 SCC 46; *Narmada Bachao Andolan* v. *Union of India*, 2000 INSC 518; AIR 2000 SC 3751.

[157] See *Kailas & Ors* v. *State of Maharashtra*, 1 *SCI* 94, (2011), para. 4.

[158] Spivak, "Translation as Culture."

[159] Interview with Maariamma.

5

Claims and Meanings

> The Adivasi community has not achieved anything. An example of this is the old woman sitting in the *pandal*.[1]

When asked what he meant by that, Kannan, a thirty-nine-year-old Adivasi man, described by another activist as the "key leader" of the Adivasi youth in the area, said he could not tell me. He said I would know when I spoke with those who sit in the *samara pandal*. By that time I had been speaking with Maariamma, the old woman Kannan referred to, for several weeks. I had also been speaking with other women and men in the area. Everyone of them had said that they did not want the Coca-Cola unit in the area. The fact that the Coca-Cola plant is not currently operational is a success – one they had fought hard and long for. While talking about the time when the protests began, an activist recalls that the Adivasis were "very clear" about driving Coca-Cola out.[2] They are still determined to not let it reopen. Had they not achieved, to a considerable extent, what they had set out to accomplish? Why then does Kannan feel that the Adivasis had not achieved anything? In this chapter I present stories that offer some answers.

My conversations in the village revealed that the Adivasis' reasons for opposing the company's operations are inadequately understood when the inquiry begins with presumptions about aspirations of those who began the protests. The dreams and desires expressed in unfamiliar languages, sometimes through stories, at times in silences, have a way of challenging and displacing such presumptions. In learning to be attentive to these stories, we are confronted by other more important questions, foremost among which is: What *had* they set out to accomplish?

[1] Interview with Kannan.

[2] Interview with Madhavan.

The answers to this question, unfortunately, are neither contained in the activist, media, and lawyers' accounts presented in Chapters 3 and 4 nor in the hundreds of pages of documents related to the litigation between the Perumatty Panchayat and Coca-Cola. These stories are also missing in the numerous reports, scientific studies, and other material about the Plachimada Struggle. The answers are instead in the absences, in the voices that are lost as the dispute and the Adivasi protests over the last decade are translated, and in the silences that the various processes of translations have produced. The answers are in the stories that Kannan says no one is interested in. The answers are in the lives of the Adivasis in the various "ST colonies" around the Coca-Cola plant, and in the accounts of the Plachimada Struggle they share with those who are prepared to listen. Some are in the rifts in the community over the dispute with Coca-Cola. Others are in the pain that wells up in the eyes of the elders in the community when they talk about certain events and people; they are in the deep hurt that some deny and most do not share easily. Some answers are in the layered histories of the area, connected with other histories in other places; they are in the complex interplay of the global and the local, and in relationships to land and water that are shaped by all these connections and disconnections.

This chapter presents some of these excluded accounts and meanings.

5.1. THE SEPARATION

By the time Kannan responded to my request for an interview, I had heard from many Adivasis about the ones who had "separated" when Mylamma "left." It took me a while to realize that the frequent references to Mylamma's "leaving" were not always to her death, as I had initially assumed, but to her estrangement from the *samara pandal* she had helped build. Soon after I met Maariamma, she mentioned that while the Adivasis had been sitting in the *samara pandal* for eight years, Mylamma had "left." Speaking for herself as well as others in the *pandal*, she added that they did not know the reason for her leaving. She repeated this a few times during our subsequent conversations as well. Over time, a few other women also made references to Mylamma leaving the *pandal*. Several weeks after Maariamma first mentioned Mylamma's departure from the *pandal*, she told me that on the day she left, Mylamma had said: "I told you not to call anybody else. Now I will not sit here till I die."[3] Repeating, once again, that they did not know what happened, Maariamma

[3] Interview with Maariamma.

added that there could have been a misunderstanding between Mylamma and Subramaniam, the activist whose significant role in the Plachimada Struggle is described in Chapter 3. Although Maariamma suggests that she does not know that for a fact, what she does confirm is that Mylamma had been angry when she left the *pandal*, and that she never returned.

In the evening on the day Mylamma left, she had announced her decision to stop the agitation, and asked all the women to do the same. Maariamma remembers thinking at the time that they could all "start going to work" the next day.[4] That of all the possible reactions to such a development, Maariamma's first thoughts were about going back to work is very significant. It speaks to how difficult it must have been for people living on daily wages to give up work to sit in the *pandal*, not for a few days or weeks, but for years. Several Adivasis, including Maariamma, mentioned this fact of not being able to go to work because of the protests during conversations, but nothing seems to convey this more clearly than Maariamma's first response to the possibility of ending the agitation in the *samara pandal*.

Later that night, Subramaniam spoke to Maariamma, her son, and a few other people. He had insisted that "the struggle was not over."[5] What happened immediately before and on that day is not entirely clear owing largely to the hesitation among most to talk about that time. What is clear, however, is that on August 12, 2006 Mylamma and a few other Adivasis made a public statement calling off the agitation outside the gates of Coca-Coca. They were ending their *pandal samaram* or the sit-in agitation in the *pandal*. It is also clear that Maariamma and others who continued to sit in the *pandal* after Mylamma left did so because they did not wish to let Subramaniam, and others who had supported them, down. Speaking of Subramaniam specifically, both Maariamma and Amma (another respected elder from a nearby hamlet) said that since he had joined them in their hour of need – when their water was affected – they could not end the protests unless the decision was acceptable to him too.

At the time, several elders in the community were of the opinion that any differences should be resolved by "talking it out directly."[6] These unspecified differences were mainly between Subramaniam and Mylamma along with all those who decided to leave the *pandal* with her. Most Adivasis were reluctant to say anything more. Even what little was shared was accompanied by statements indicating that talking about Mylamma's separation was not meant as

4 Ibid.
5 Interview with Maariamma.
6 Interview with Amma.

a criticism. Mylamma was related to several of them, and in Amma's words, "was a good woman."[7] What stopped me from pursuing answers beyond what was volunteered was the extreme discomfort, hurt, or what seemed to be some inner conflict that appeared on faces every time names of those who had "separated" came up during conversations.

The non-Adivasi supporters of the anti–Coca-Cola struggle are also reluctant to speak about this. Many of them feel betrayed by what Mylamma and others did, even though most do not know (or as I suspect in some cases, do not wish to share) the exact reasons for the separation. Some of them acknowledged the personal sacrifices she made as a leader of the Adivasi protests. Each one of the activists confirmed that she was committed to driving Coca-Cola out. Some suggested that she remained committed to this cause until the very end, and according to them, the decision to "withdraw" could not have been Mylamma's. They suggested that Mylamma was induced, pressurized, threatened, or misled by someone.

Subramaniam, who said that Mylamma did not have the "confidence to continue the struggle" anymore, also indicated that her decision was influenced by the promises made by the Left Democratic Front, a major political coalition commonly referred to as the LDF.[8] Several others also mentioned the possible role of the LDF. The degree of this influence on Mylamma and other Adivasis, however, varied from one account to another. Kannan, the Adivasi leader who also "left" the *pandal*, confirmed that they had relied on the assurance of the LDF at the time when they decided to end the agitations in the *pandal*.

The LDF is one of the two major political coalitions in the state of Kerala and is led by the Communist Party of India (Marxist).[9] It had won the assembly elections in May 2006 defeating the other major political coalition in the state, the United Democratic Front (UDF), led by the Congress party, by a considerable margin.[10] The newly appointed chief minister of the state, V. S.

7 Ibid.

8 Interview with Subramaniam.

9 The Communist Party of India (Marxist) [CPI(M)] emerged after a split in the Communist Party of India in 1964. The party has a strong presence in Kerala, where it has been in and out of office since its formation. According to the party's web site, "[t]he CPI(M) was born in the struggle against revisionism and sectarianism in the communist movement at the international and national level, in order to defend the scientific and revolutionary tenets of Marxism-Leninism and its appropriate application in the concrete Indian conditions. The CPI(M) combines the fine heritage of the anti-imperialist struggle and the revolutionary legacy of the undivided Communist Party that was founded in 1920. Over the years, the Party has emerged as the foremost Left force in the country." See: http://cpim.org/.

10 In keeping with what according to many residents of Kerala is a tradition in the state, in the elections held in 2011, the UDF won by a slender margin.

Achuthanandan, had been a vocal supporter of the protests against Coca-Cola in Plachimada before the elections. As the leader of the opposition in the Kerala Legislative Assembly, he had repeatedly raised the issue of groundwater exploitation by both Coca-Cola and Pepsi in Palakkad district, calling upon the government to take action.[11] In fact, according to a report published soon after the election in 2006, as the leader of opposition in the state legislative assembly, "Achuthanandan had fashioned his hugely popular image of a 'lonely warrior' by single-handedly taking up cudgels for environmentalists and tribals" in Plachimada.[12]

On August 9, 2006 the Achuthanandan government issued an order banning the production and sale of colas in the state. This could have been an attempt by the LDF to fulfill its pre-election promises made in Plachimada, but some reports in the Malayalam media indicate that at least some people involved in the protests viewed the decision as a sign of the government's reluctance to find a "permanent solution to the problem."[13] Some even saw this as a "weak action" and an attempt to "influence the activists".[14] Although closer to Plachimada the government was criticized for not doing enough, this ban reportedly prompted Franklin Lavin, the U.S. Undersecretary for International Trade, to write to the Indian Commerce Secretary "seeking a level playing field for its cola companies."[15]

To many others, including Achuthanandan's colleagues, the decision to ban seemed "hasty," and unlikely to "stand judicial scrutiny."[16] These people were proved right subsequently when the government's order was successfully challenged both by Coca-Cola and Pepsi in the High Court of Kerala.[17] In

[11] See for example, "Check Exploitation of Groundwater: Achuthanandan," *The Times of India*, February 6, 2006, accessed May 15, 2006, http://timesofindia.indiatimes.com/articleshow/1402847.cms.

[12] M. G. Radhakrishnan, "Capital Convert," *India Today*, August 28, 2006, accessed September 14, 2010, http://www.indiatoday.com/itoday/20060828/kerala.html

[13] "Interview: N. P Johnson Chairman, Co-ordination Committee, Plachimada," trans. Jiss Verkey, *Keraleeyam* 129 (April 2008): 19–20. See also Nizar Ahmed, "Justice through Decentralized Democratic Struggle," *Keraleeyam* 129 (April 2008): 41–43.

[14] Sunny Paikada/ Janaadhikaara Rashtriya Samithi, "The Politics and Future of Plachimada," trans. Jiss Verkey, 129 *Keraleeyam* (April 2008): 33.

[15] "Kerala Court Lifts Cola Ban: Coke, Pepsi Relieved," September 22, 2006, accessed September 21, 2010, http://www.siliconindia.com/shownews/Kerala_court_lifts_cola_ban_Coke_Pepsi_relieved-nid-33226.html

[16] Radhakrishnan, "Capital Convert."

[17] See "Kerala Court Lifts Cola Ban: Coke, Pepsi Relieved," September 22, 2006), accessed September 21, 2010, http://www.siliconindia.com/shownews/Kerala_court_lifts_cola_ban_Coke_Pepsi_relieved-nid-33226.html, and Statement from Coca-Cola India, "High Court of Kerala Quashes the Ban on Coca-Cola in Kerala," *New Delhi*, September 22, 2006, accessed April 7, 2007, http://www.coca-colaindia.com/quality/fact_sheet.asp.

August 2009, however, it seemed to many in the Plachimada area that the newly elected government was committed to fulfilling the pre-election promises made to the protestors.

To those who had been foregoing daily wages to take turns to sit in the *samara pandal*, the government's action seems to have brought some hope. As one well-respected activist remarked, many of these people were "tired" and under "financial burdens."[18] By then it had been four years since the protests began – four years during which those who have separated feel the Adivasis in the hamlets had become worse off than ever before. To begin with, the setting up of the Coca-Cola plant on farmlands had resulted in loss of daily work close to where they lived. This disproportionately affected women, especially those with young children since they could not go far from home for work. Depletion and pollution of water in the wells had made life extremely difficult in many ways, as described earlier. In this too, women's ability to work outside their homes has been affected more than that of men. Since they are paid lower wages than men, women are the ones who often forego work to stay at home to fill pots of water brought in lorries. The sit-in agitation also led to more lost wages as large numbers of women and men took turns to sit in the *samara pandal*. Many of them faced police action, were beaten or arrested, and some still face criminal charges. They had been humiliated and ridiculed by their neighbors, disbelieved by many, and had faced disappointment and failures, including the blow dealt by the decision of the Kerala High Court in April 2005.

Moreover, ever since the dispute became the symbolic "people's movement" it has attracted reporters and others with cameras, politicians, activists, representatives of all kinds of organizations, and last but not the least, researchers like me. While all this attention has ensured that many across the world now know about the residents, this relentless attention is also intrusive in ways not evident right away.[19]

It is quite possible that in these circumstances, Mylamma and others with her decided to hold on to whatever hope was offered by the government. Their

[18] Interview with Sreejith.

[19] For example, a local non-Adivasi teacher remarked that many Adivasis here had begun to "dress properly" only after the protests began. Several women now wear blouses with their *sarees*. The men wear shirts even when they're not going out, not surprising since the "outsiders" are now a constant presence in the hamlets unlike ever before. While none of the Adivasis I spoke with complained about this change, I had an opportunity to reflect upon this after Maariamma asked me how I could be all covered up in the hot and humid weather. She declared she could never wear a blouse. My conversation with her indicates that perhaps she has been asked to, but refuses to wear one.

decision made sense to some outsiders as well. According to Vaasu, activist and prominent member of the Plachimada Solidarity Committee, Mylamma's decision had been to stop the particular "form of struggle" they had been engaged in up until that time.[20] Explaining this further, he says that initially the protests were against the functioning of the plant, as well as the inaction of the government. After the government issued the order banning the production and sale of the colas in the state, it seemed that the government was on their side. Some of them felt that it was time to change the form of protests.

Mylamma left the *pandal*, but had no intentions of abandoning the Adivasi demand for removal of the plant. As Ottukan a senior member of the *Adivasi Samrakshana Sangham* emphasized, they will start the agitation again if the Coca-Cola plant is reopened. Given all that the community had gone through, it is not hard to see why Mylamma and others may have thought it was time to end the sit-in protests outside the gates of the company. It was their everyday lives that had been affected after all. To her, the decision may have seemed to be in their best interests. Those who understand this consider the subsequent criticism of Mylamma's decision as "very unfair."[21]

Ultimately, it was this decision that led to a split between Adivasis who were with Mylamma and many "outsiders" who supported continuing the sit-in agitation, including Subramaniam. It also resulted in a rift in the close-knit Adivasi community. Before I explain the nature of this split and the significant insights it offers into what the protests against Coca-Cola really mean for the Adivasis and their "outsider" supporters, a fuller account of those who had left the *pandal* with Mylamma and their reasons for doing so is called for. As I have mentioned before, their names came up regularly during conversations about the *samaram*. However, for a long time none of them seemed to be interested in speaking with me, until the day Kannan called to say he wanted to meet.

5.2. THE ONES WHO LEFT

It was almost six weeks after I had first met Kannan that he responded to my request for an interview. On the day we first met, he had heard me out patiently, albeit perhaps disinterestedly. After I finished describing my research, he had smiled and remarked, pleasantly, that many researchers had been there and much had been written about the place. And then he had tacked my interview

20 Interview with Vaasu.

21 Ibid.

consent form to a wall, on top of what looked like an electricity bill. I didn't hear from him again until the day he called to ask if I still wanted to speak with him.

Arriving at the designated spot, I was taken aback to see Kannan with a tall man who introduced himself as an officer of the "State Intelligence Bureau." He informed me that he was visiting Kannan who was a "friend." The officer had heard about two women who had been talking to people in the area for some time and was merely curious – a claim belied by the manner in which he interviewed me for the next several minutes. He wanted to see any documents I might have from my university confirming what I claimed to be doing in the village. I showed him the consent form printed on the university letterhead with addresses and other contact information and a brief description of my research. He read it and later placed it in his bag. He asked about my research, my nationality, which part of India I "originally" belonged to, and where I was staying in Palakkad. He also asked who I was doing this research for and whether any "foreign agency" was involved. He was also curious about the interest of my doctoral supervisor in the project since his name and address were also printed on the consent forms. He seemed to be satisfied with my explanation about that being a requirement under the university's research ethics regulations.

When I wondered aloud about his department's interest in the small hamlet, the officer repeated he was merely passing by and had stopped to catch up with his friend. To my further amazement, he then asked me if I had read about the alleged links of some members of the Dalit Human Rights Movement to a recent murder of an elderly man out on a morning walk in another part of Kerala. On learning that I had missed that piece of news and had never heard of the organization, he summarized the events and the ongoing investigations. He then spoke for a few minutes about what he described as the centuries of oppression of Adivasis and *dalits*, and how sometimes there is no option but to rebel. He also brought up the "oppression" of "Dravidians" by "north-Indians," referring to the "Aryan invasion" of the Indian subcontinent and persecution of Dravidians that is believed to have followed.[22]

I can only speculate on his reasons for raising these issues or declaring his sympathy for those who are oppressed to me or to his "friend." Perhaps this

[22] For the emergence of this theory in Europe in the nineteenth century, its role in the reconstruction of Indian history, and its subsequent entanglement with Indian politics, see Romila Thapar, "The Theory of Aryan Race and India: History and Politics," *Social Scientist* 24:1 (1996): 3–29.

was a reminder to a "north-Indian" researcher of the ways in which she too was implicated in histories of oppression. It could have been a reference to my outsiderness vis-à-vis those he referred to as "all Dravidians," a category that for him obviously included both Kannan and himself (despite the differences of caste, tribe, or class that separated them) but excluded me. Perhaps it was a reminder of the layered history of the subcontinent, and the many injustices across time and space, or of the many ways in which we are all implicated through our collective and individual actions and inactions. The interview could also have been a test that I either passed (since the officer never sought me out again) or failed (if he had anything to do with the group of unidentified men who came looking for the "woman who speaks Hindi" two days before I left the place).

There could also be other explanations for the officer's visit. I have wondered if it is a mere coincidence that this interview took place soon after local land disputes began to come up more frequently in my conversations with Adivasis in the hamlets. It also did not strike me until later that this happened just two days after the first time I spoke with some Adivasis who had separated. Were his declarations of support for the oppressed a ruse and an attempt to lure me into revealing views and sympathies that everyone interested in listening to Adivasis in the country is suspected to hold?[23] Was he merely interested in what I was doing there or in what Kannan had to say to me? This "chance" encounter could even simply have been an opportunity for the officer to strengthen his networks in the area. Perhaps this conversation with an outsider gave him an opportunity to declare his support for the "oppressed" to the group of men that slowly gathered around us. His concern could be genuine or simply something that his job required him to say in an effort to reach out to the community, or to build rapport, or such other exercises that the "intelligence" departments engage in. I have no reason to believe one explanation more than the other. Similarly, I can only speculate on the reasons for Kannan's insistence on being interviewed that day – something I had considered inappropriate and out of the question as soon as the officer introduced himself. Kannan too must have his reasons for saying what he did during that conversation in the presence of the officer.

[23] In the last few years a number of activists and researchers working in and with Adivasi communities have been accused of sympathizing with and supporting "Maoist/ Naxalites". See for example, "Named for Naxal 'Nexus,' Delhi Prof, NGO Call Chhattisgarh Police Fascist," *The Indian Express*, July 13, 2010, http://www.indianexpress.com/news/named-for-naxal-nexus-delhi-prof-ngo-call-chhattisgarh-police-fascist/645692/.

Whatever lay behind the officer's visit, in retrospect, I can only thank him for bringing out into the open issues that until then had only lingered in uncomfortable silences, unfinished sentences, and unclear references I had been struggling to decipher. As it turned out, I learned much from my subsequent conversations with Kannan and other Adivasis who until then had seemed disinterested in talking with yet another "outsider." I have wondered if being questioned by a "police officer," as the man is referred to in the area, and being asked to produce documents had made me a little bit of an insider.

I did not hear anything about the officer again. The next time I met Kannan, he simply smiled when I asked if his "friend" had paid another visit. He did not seem to be willing to say any more. I decided not to bring it up again, even though, of the many questions this encounter raises, the one that I would have most liked answered is why had an officer of the intelligence department sought the "friendship" of an Adivasi leader in this place?

As an active member of the *Adivasi Samrakshana Sangham* (Adivasi Protection Council) and a founding member of the *Adivasi Samara Samithi* (Adivasi Protest/Struggle Committee) in Plachimada (renamed as the Anti–Coca-Cola People's Struggle Committee), Kannan has been at the forefront of the agitation against the company. He was among the first few to call for action against the depletion and pollution of water. Maariamma, who sits in the *pandal* everyday, says he was one of the "boys" who brought everyone together on the issue and convinced those who thought they could not do anything against the "big company" to join in.

An activist recalls Kannan's determination in the early days of the protests. One of the things that most impressed him on his first visit to the place was that despite concerns among others in the hamlets, the youth along with their "key person" Kannan, had been determined to "[s]hut down the plant, and drive [Coca-Cola] out."[24] Something else he remembers is that most people seemed to be unsure about the possibility of achieving anything through the government or "by law."[25] The events of the next decade do not seem to have offered them a chance to alter this opinion. Ottukan, another Adivasi leader, says they have no hope of redress from any political party or any court. "Everything is a formality," he says, before going on to describe the injustices in the everyday encounters of Adivasis with the local courts, the local police, administration, and elected representatives.[26]

[24] Interview with Madhavan.
[25] Ibid.
[26] Interview with Ottukan.

And yet, in August 2006, Mylamma had decided to rely on the LDF. Kannan still believes the LDF is in a position to do something about Coca-Cola. After all, he recounts, it was the LDF government that had initially "brought the company" to the place.[27] Surely they could now ensure that it leaves. The chief minister of the state at the time, as stated before, had openly supported them during his visit to the place. Along with Mylamma, Kannan and others believed in the promises made to them. They expected the newly formed government to do "whatever they have promised."[28] Their faith also came from their belief in the stated ideologies of the LDF, especially those of its lead party, the Communist Party of India (Marxist). Kannan explained the reason for this in these words: "LDF is considered as the party for [the] poor. There is no caste there."[29] After a pause, he added: "earlier."[30] Despite indications that they have begun to doubt the government's commitment to address the issue, it is clear that at the time, in 2006, they had faith in the LDF. It was in these circumstances that they had decided to end the *pandal samaram* – the agitation in the *pandal*. However misplaced her faith in the government of the day may have been, it was a decision Mylamma made as a leader of her community. Subramaniam disagreed, although it appears from my various conversations, not for the first time.

There is no doubt that the members of the *Adivasi Samrakshana Sangham* spearheaded the protests, and that Mylamma was in the forefront. Even those who insist this be understood essentially as a "people's movement," acknowledge that it was the Adivasis in the area who started it. It was the *Adivasi Samrakshana Sangham* that had led the community and brought together Adivasis from "five different *panchayats*" in the area.[31] Mylamma, Kannan, and Ottukan were prominent leaders of the protests. Subramaniam's role at the time was described as that of a patron of the *Sangham*.

About a year after the protests were formally launched outside the gates of the company, Subramaniam was expelled from the *Adivasi Samrakshana Sangham*. According to its president, this decision was prompted by the fact that Subramaniam had started making "his own decisions" without regard to the opinions or views of others involved.[32] In addition, a few other organizations that had lent their support to the protests also parted ways over differences

[27] Interview with Kannan.
[28] Ibid.
[29] Ibid.
[30] Ibid.
[31] Interview with Ottukan.
[32] He, however, clarifies that Subramaniam was expelled from *Adivasi Samrakshana Sangham*, the Adivasi organization, not from the "protest committee."

with Subramaniam, even as they continue to support the protests, albeit from a distance.

Subramaniam's growing affiliation with the "main political party" in the area, a reference to the Janata Dal (Secular), was also a cause for concern for the *Sangham.*[33] The exact reasons for the *Sangham's* concern over Subramaniam's association with the party remain unclear. There is also no information available on the exact nature or extent of Subramaniam's affiliation with the party, but it is a fact that the local leaders of the party had begun to support the protestors after initial disinterest and, in some cases, even opposition. Given that at the time the Janata Dal was an ally of the Congress-led UDF, it is possible that it was not too pleased with the influence of the leader of the Communist Party (M) and LDF among the Adivasi protestors in Plachimada.[34]

5.3. MYLAMMA

Mylamma, a grandmother from Vijaynagar, described often as someone "people listened to," emerged as a prominent leader of the agitation against Coca-Cola. Kannan says she "came to the struggle" with "no education" and "more sincerity."[35] "She was a stubborn woman," he adds, "who stood for the place and the people."[36] Her leadership was recognized by many, not just in Kerala, but also beyond. In October 2005 Mylamma traveled to New Delhi to receive an award from a "big person," something proudly mentioned to me by several Adivasis. Few Adivasis recall the name of Sonia Gandhi, the president of the Congress party who handed the award to Mylamma,[37] and most do not know about *Outlook*, the national weekly magazine behind the *Speak Out Award* that Mylamma received. Each one of them is, however, proud of the fact that Mylamma was honored. Her trip to New Delhi and the trophy that is now in her daughter's home means a lot to all of them, despite all that has since happened.

It was some time after this trip that rumors about Mylamma having received a large amount of money, much more than what accompanied the *Speak Out*

33 Interview with Ottukan.

34 Interestingly, the local Janata Dal leader and long-standing supporter of the Plachimada Struggle has since parted ways with Janata Dal (Secular) and formed a breakaway party known as the Janata Dal (Left) [JD(L)]. The JD(L) is now part of the LDF.

35 Interview with Kannan.

36 Ibid.

37 "Speak Out Winner: Mylamma," *Outlook*, October 11, 2005, accessed November 4, 2010, http://www.outlookindia.com/article.aspx?228877.

Award, began to surface in Plachimada. These unverified rumors hurt and angered many Adivasis. Several Adivasi women who sat with her in the *pandal* "turned against Mylamma."[38] It was also around this time that serious differences arose between the *Adivasi Samrakshana Sangham* and Subramaniam. The *Sangham*, which had earlier expelled him, wanted him to stay out of their action against Coca-Cola as well. Although some Adivasis were with the *Sangham* on this, others did not agree for reasons set out below. It is not clear what happened on the day Mylamma left the *pandal* in anger. However, the fact that "Mylamma was [being] portrayed very badly to the outside world" had also played an important role in the *Adivasi Samrakshana Sangham's* decision to withdraw from the *pandal samaram* or the sit-in agitation in the *pandal*.[39] According to a senior leader of the *Sangham*, the "outsiders" could not accept Mylamma's leadership. My conversations with some "outsiders" suggest he has good reason to believe so.

Adivasis in Plachimada and nearby hamlets regarded Mylamma as their leader because she raised the question of their right to live on this land and because she remained committed to that issue.[40] Others, in Kerala as well as outside the state, know Mylamma as the face of the Plachimada Struggle. As Easwaran, a senior politician, stated, she was "the symbol of the battle."[41] Posters with her picture can still be seen on some walls in the area. One is prominently displayed in the *anganwadi* preschool in Vijaynagar. Her role in spearheading the protests is highlighted and celebrated in campaigns. Despite this, there are those who refuse to acknowledge her leadership. In the words of Gopal, a local activist, Mylamma "was projected as a leader in all the newspapers just because she was a woman, and that too an Adivasi."[42] This attention to her seems unfair to him, since it was the "Struggle Committee" that "made all this possible."[43] He did not wish to talk further about why she separated, but he emphasized that she had been "thankless."[44] It was obvious that her decision had hurt and upset this committed Gandhian peace activist, as it had several others. He admits not having a "clear picture of what actually happened," but he did not explain why he or others had not bothered to find out.[45]

[38] Interview with Ottukan.
[39] Ibid.
[40] Interview with Kannan.
[41] Interview with Easwaran.
[42] Interview with Gopal.
[43] Ibid.
[44] Ibid.
[45] Ibid.

Mylamma's "ungratefulness" was also specifically mentioned by Easwaran, the senior politician, even as he described her variously as "an Adivasi Dalit woman," "a very poor woman," and "a very simple woman."[46] According to him, "she only knew one thing," something she had said at the World Water Conference: "I want water, my children want [water]."[47] He also recalls her wish to meet the prime minister of the country. On being asked by him why she wanted to meet the prime minister, "[s]he said she wants rights for her water wells."[48] Like many supporters of the Plachimada Struggle, Easwaran has not felt the need to look beyond what he refers to as her "simple truth."[49] What matters to him is that she was totally committed to this truth. This is what makes her "a great fighter" in his eyes.[50] She was "a great woman" who inspired others, he said, and she deserves to be remembered for this.[51]

There are other "outsiders" who would rather remember Mylamma as a "great woman" who led the protests against Coca-Cola, and not for later events after she left the *pandal*. On the other hand, Adivasis in Plachimada, those who continue to sit in the *pandal*, and those who refuse to sit there remember her for all that she was, which was more than a symbol of a resistance movement against a multinational corporation. The Mylamma that emerges from any of the "outsider" accounts is not the mother, grandmother, cousin, sister-in-law, a respected elder, or a woman who is remembered by her community as someone who stood for the place and its people. For Easwaran and others like him who wrote about her, Mylamma had ceased to be, if she ever was, a living person of many strengths and, perhaps like the rest of us, some weaknesses. To them she was instead "a Mylamma" that, in Easwaran's words, *they* had "created."

Mylamma's position is not very different from Plachimada, which for many is no longer a real place where people live, but the name of a "symbolic struggle," a "battle," and a "resistance movement" – words that recur in so many outsider accounts. Similarly, the *samara pandal* too has acquired a powerful symbolic significance. It is no longer a small shed to protect the protestors from the sun and rain (the reasons why the protestors built it) but a symbol of the small and poor taking on the big and powerful, an integral element of a larger global story. This reduction of real people and real places to nothing

[46] Interview with Easwaran.
[47] Ibid.
[48] Ibid.
[49] Ibid.
[50] Ibid.
[51] Ibid.

more than symbols, however powerful, is evident not only in a lot of what has been written about Plachimada, but often also represented in pictures accompanying such texts.

In the symbolic battle of some of the most marginalized peoples against a powerful multinational company, Mylamma too was no longer seen as a real person who had a voice, perspective or opinions. She had become a symbol with a designated role in the story of the Plachimada Struggle, a role that for those who feel betrayed by her decisions, did not perhaps involve being herself anymore. Symbols, after all, do not have a voice of their own. They can only be interpreted or reinterpreted by others. The significance of a symbol lies less in what it is and much more in what it stands for. Moreover, what was there for Mylamma to say anymore? Those who had assumed the role of translators already knew her "simple truth," and they remain, as I have emphasized before, committed to conveying that truth to the world. This is why the Adivasi leaders' decision led to much of what Gopal called "confusion" not just at the local level but also elsewhere. As the activist pointed out, questions were raised by people from within as well as outside the country about some Adivasis' decision to end the sit-in agitation in Plachimada.

Mylamma is not around to respond to the charge of having betrayed those who helped her people. There is also no way of knowing what it meant to her to be alienated from some of her closest allies, friends, and relatives who continued to sit in the *samara pandal* after she left. The change from being the one chosen by the Adivasis to lead the protests, and the one who got to have the "final word,"[52] to being accused of betraying the struggle, must have been a significant one in her life. Although there is no way of asking her how she dealt with it, there is enough to indicate all the ways in which she too may have felt betrayed.

Maariamma recalls that for some time after leaving the *pandal*, Mylamma stayed inside her house and refused to return to the *pandal*. After a month, she "joined some political party," the name of which Maariamma does not know.[53] One day, she says, Mylamma was "given a black flag, and a hundred people joined her."[54] Maariamma does not know who these people were or "what they were shouting."[55] All that she knows is that they were not from the area and were not Adivasis. None of these people entered the *pandal*, she says. They

52 Interview with Kecharan.
53 Interview with Maariamma.
54 Ibid.
55 Ibid.

walked past it and stood under a tree she pointed out to me. Mylamma had, she says, decided to "start her own *samaram*."[56]

The Plachimada Struggle on the other hand, continued as before, even though, as Maariamma notes, Mylamma did not share the stage with visiting dignitaries anymore. That responsibility was Maariamma's now. She continues to sit in the *pandal*, watches stages being erected and taken down, is invited to go up on them from time to time, lights lamps at events in Plachimada and, at times, in Palakkad town, poses for pictures, and speaks about the struggle. Ironically, but unsurprisingly, she talks about the same things that Mylamma and others who left the *pandal* speak about – separation from land and livelihood, water, home, education, and jobs. Unfortunately, much of what she says is also lost in news and analysis of the struggle.

About five months after leaving the *pandal*, Mylamma passed away. She had been suffering from an illness that, according to several accounts, appeared as some kind of "rash," first on her face and then all over her body. No one seemed to know what exactly it was. Some say it was the polluted water that caused it. Her children, who continue to live in the shadow of her "betrayal," must know more but do not wish to share. Their discomfort was visible even during my very brief conversations with her son and daughter. On more than one occasion, Maariamma expressed concerns about their predicament as she sees it. She feels that even if Mylamma left the *pandal* in anger, she should have allowed her children to continue to sit there. This is important to Maariamma, and to the other women who sit in the *pandal*. They view this as a significant omission on Mylamma's part. Although all their reasons for regret are not entirely clear, this indicates, at the very least, how much the exclusion of some members of the community from something they started together continues to bother many, especially the elders.

Maariamma had an anxious, almost haunted look on her face when she talked about the day Mylamma died. Her body was not brought into the *samara pandal*. It was placed, instead, in a separate *pandal* set up outside the Coca-Cola plant. It was then taken away in a car decorated with flowers by "people who came from other places."[57] There were many other cars too. She was buried in a burial ground nearby. Maariamma and others went to the burial, but they could not perform the customary last rites or "rituals [they] perform" for the deceased.

Although Maariamma does not know the people who came in many cars from other places that day, an editorial published at the time suggests that the

[56] Ibid.

[57] Interview with Maariamma.

CPI(M) and the DYFI[58] appropriated Mylamma's death for political ends by proclaiming her as "a martyr for their parties."[59] The piece is particularly critical of the CPI(M), and LDF, the political coalition it heads, which, according to the author, does "not have any actual wish to solve the Plachimada issue." It goes on to note that it was not the people in the *samara pandal* who showed disrespect to Mylamma's body on that day. It was the LDF, which offered no support to the agitation and yet "raised claims on the dead body," that had in fact disrespected her.[60]

Maariamma gave me three reasons why Mylamma's body was not brought inside the *pandal*: Subramaniam was against this; Mylamma had herself said she would not enter the *pandal* "even if she dies"; Mylamma should have "directed her children to participate" in their struggle.[61] All of these reasons point to the sense of betrayal as well as the anger and hurt on all sides at the time. But the last one in particular indicates the ways in which the split has affected the community where most people live in huts within a few feet of each other. Mylamma did not live long after she left, Maariamma says, but she should have asked her children to return to the *pandal*.

The tears in Maariamma's eyes every time she mentions the fact that Mylamma's sons and daughter refuse to talk to those in the *pandal* are proof that despite all differences, anger, and hurt, the rift in the community is not what it might seem to outsiders. Her concern for their well-being is obvious when she worries about them being left out of any compensation that might materialize as a result of the protests, since they had not until then filled out the claims being submitted to the High Power Committee set up to ascertain Coca-Cola's liability.[62]

It seems that when Mylamma left in anger, those in the *pandal* had hoped that she would eventually return. The memory of Mylamma

58 The DYFI or the Democratic Youth Federation of India is an organization committed to mobilizing young men and women "to fight against the forces of authoritarianism and dictatorship, and in defence of the uncurtailed democratic rights and freedom[s]." According to the preamble available on the web site of the organization's Kerala State Committee, it is "a forward looking and progressive youth organisation inspired by anti-imperialist, democratic and socialist ideas." The web site, which carries a picture of Che Guevara, also states that the organization is "not a wing of any political party." See http://www.dyfi.in/ and http://www.dyfikerala.net/.

59 "Editorial," trans. Praveen Hariharan, *Keraleeyam* 4–6 (January 2007).

60 Ibid.

61 Interview with Maariamma.

62 The committee has since determined the compensation that the residents of the area are entitled to for the losses incurred due to Coca-Cola's operations. I could not determine if any of Mylamma's sons or her daughter had subsequently submitted the forms required for the process.

standing outside the *samara pandal*, shouting that she would never ever enter it again haunts many women who sit there. Her death and events of the day when she was buried had made her "leaving" final and irreversible in ways that they had perhaps not expected. But it is clear that they have not given up on the possibility of reconciliation with others who had also left. This was visible in the joy and hope on several faces the day after a public meeting called by the High Power Committee where Kannan (one of those who had separated) spoke on the same stage as other Adivasi leaders and their many supporters. To those in the *pandal* it was a sign that they were together again.

Kannan too pointed out to me that the community is like a family. "Eravalans are all related," he said, echoing what I had heard from many other Adivasis.[63] "Even before the struggle started, we were all together," he told me before adding: "There are small problems in families, like there are everywhere."[64] These were, however, "not much," he assured me. "The pain [of separation] was for them," he said with a nod in the direction of the *samara pandal*.[65] But he seemed to betray his own hurt when he said, "[n]obody can compensate for the split [pause] therefore the pain."[66] Recognizing the damage done to the relations in the community, Kannan sees little hope of reconciliation in the near future. He hopes that the "future generations might come together because they will not know what happened."[67]

5.4. DIFFERENCES

In the outsider accounts that refer to it, the separation of some Adivasis from the *pandal samaram* or the sit-in protest in the *pandal* was caused by the assurances given by the government of the day to take action against the company. References to unspecified early "problems," "tensions," and "differences" between Adivasis and non-Adivasis, however, find mention in some editorials and articles written in Malayalam, and surface occasionally in some activists' accounts of the split as well. In the accounts given by the Adivasis, the process of separation had certainly begun long before the events of August 2006, which were really a culmination of deep differences that had begun to divide protestors much earlier.

63 Interview with Kannan.
64 Ibid.
65 Ibid.
66 Ibid.
67 Ibid.

As described before, initially the group of Adivasis who began to question Coca-Cola's operations and its impact on their well-water had formed themselves into the *Adivasi Samara Samithi* or the Adivasi Struggle Committee. This name was subsequently changed to *Coca-Cola Viruddha Samara Samithi* or Anti–Coca-Cola Struggle Committee. According to Kannan, the name was changed "because if [the word] 'Adivasi' is used, only Adivasis will support."[68] He says they decided to change the name because a number of non-Adivasis also supported the agitation.

Ramesh, owner of a small business near the Coca-Cola plant, also mentioned this change in name. While recounting the events around the time when the protests began, he said it was primarily the Adivasis who started agitating about the contaminated water. However, subsequently, it turned into a *janakeeya* [of the people] struggle. He explained that "[i]f the struggle was done in the name of Adivasis we cannot join them."[69] But after it became a people's movement, "every one gathered together."[70] As everyone in Kerala is aware, the long-standing "Adivasi struggle" in the state is over alienated tribal lands. The words invoke images and recall pasts that most would rather forget.[71] The change in name – from an Adivasi protest to a people's protest or struggle – could in these circumstances have also been aimed at overcoming some of the barriers that the Adivasi demands for return of their lands have created in the state.

The change in name did not, however, alter the fact that the protests held different meanings and significance for all those involved. Madhavan, an activist who does not live in the area but has been supporting the agitation from the beginning, recalls the debates and dialogues that took place in the early days of the agitation. One of the questions raised at the time was: "what exactly is the issue?" As far back as August 2004, just over two years after the protests against Coca-Cola were formally launched, a researcher reported that of the "seventy people from the *samara pandal* in Plachimada" who responded to her questionnaire, 64.29 percent thought "there had been many failures in the agitation."[72] Two other students who later conducted research in Plachimada also reportedly noted in their findings the differences between "natives here in Plachimada and their supporters."[73] At least two other articles published

68 Ibid.

69 Interview with Ramesh.

70 Ibid.

71 Some of this history is presented in the following chapter.

72 Divya K., "The Peoples Establishment at Plachimada: A Special Study about Perumatty Panchayat," *Keraleeyam* 1:7 (January 2005): 66.

73 Vijith Mathew and Eed Muhammed Haneefa, "The Plachimada Issue in Views of Social Work Students," trans. Jiss Verkey, *Keraleeyam* (April 2008): 64.

in Malayalam refer to the differences between residents of the hamlets, and activists and other supporters over the objectives of the agitation.[74]

In an interview published in 2008, another prominent local activist too had indicated the need to resolve the differences over the "social objective of the struggle," without offering any specifics.[75] There is enough to indicate, however, that even though the immediate cause of the split may have been the resolution offered by the Government of Kerala for calling off the agitation in August 2006, the differences that led to the decision to separate had existed for some time. As Sreejith, another local activist recalls, these differences, left unaddressed for so long, had by then "grown to such an extent that people like Kannan [decided] to withdraw."[76]

The Adivasi leaders had initially believed that the outsiders' support extended to all the issues that they wanted to address. According to Ottukan, this was the "big thing", or of most significance in this coalition for the Adivasi leaders.[77] He specifically pointed out that "the people who were supporting the struggle from outside, gave their word that they will intervene in matters related to Adivasis."[78] He believes as do some others that the outsiders have failed to honor their word. This is how he says they "have been cheated."[79]

While Ottukan only says that the struggle they had envisioned when they started was a different one, Kannan explained what they had in mind:

> We are struggling for the lost land. The government is doing everything for the settlers. Not for the original inhabitants.[80]

This "struggle for the lost land," which I shall return to in the next chapter, cannot be separated from the Adivasi opposition to Coca-Cola, because for them these are not two separate issues. The company represents a further alienation from lands they have lived and worked on for generations over centuries. Its presence in this place is another chapter in the continuing story of their dispossession. This is why they are committed to ensuring that Coca-Cola leaves. The significance of the protests against Coca-Cola for the Adivasis therefore lies in the fact that it is an inextricable part of their struggle for land. Their agitation against Coca-Cola does not make sense in their lives

[74] See S. Anand, "Industry Is a Human Vocation," trans. Praveen Hariharan, *Keraleeyam* 1:5 (January 2005): (page numbers missing in translated text); "Interview with N. P. Johnson," 19–20.
[75] "Interview," trans. Jiss Verkey, *Keraleeyam* (April 2008): 17–18.
[76] Interview with Sreejith.
[77] Interview with Ottukan.
[78] Ibid.
[79] Ibid.
[80] Interview with Kannan.

when separated from their struggle for land. It is this that they had expected the 'outsiders' to support when the latter gave their word to get involved in all "matters related to Adivasis."[81]

The events of last several years have led many Adivasis to believe otherwise. In fact, according to Ottukan, "[n]ow the agitations are going on in the interest of some other people."[82] Unlike Kannan, however, he does not blame Subramaniam alone. There are many others who have taken over the direction of the agitations and possible solutions. Without naming anyone in particular, Ottukan refers to those who have provided funds over time, others who "come here, take out the camera, take photographs, and give them to the press."[83] In this context he also mentioned the World Water Conference held in Plachimada in 2004.

That was the time when "a lot of people" congregated in Plachimada.[84] In talking about the time, Ottukan mentions several well-known activists. There were also "people from ruling and opposition parties," and many "people from America," the last being a general reference to activists from Canada and the United States.[85] His account of the Conference was very different from others I had heard or read until then. Unlike the accounts published in print and electronic media, or narrated by activists and politicians, Ottukan does not speak of it in a triumphant voice. Nor does he speak of antiglobalization or the resistance to multinational companies (MNCs) – words and phrases that frame other accounts. The following is the version that was left out of all that has been said about the Conference, and is the only one that appears to matter from his perspective:

> It was two–three days program. They put up big *pandals* and there were lights all around. And in the Adivasi *samara pandal*, they lighted a kerosene lamp even on that day. At that time, there were almost fifteen women who would regularly sit in the *samara pandal*. They used to make *kanji* [rice gruel] together in Mylamma's house. That day they did not have anything to eat with the *kanji*. There were people who had just *kanji*. In the Conference *pandal* all kinds of facilities were there. The *pandal* was made air-conditioned. The *pandal* was completely air-conditioned, and [food according to] each person's liking [was made available] ... from the dam they brought fish, then different kinds of meat. [Pause] They use the name of Adivasis, and they come here in the name of Adivasis, but those people

81 Interview with Ottukan.
82 Ibid.
83 Ibid.
84 Ibid.
85 Ibid.

> don't know the difficulties faced by the Adivasis. They were all doing that for somebody . . .[86]

It is experiences like this that have perhaps led Ottukan to conclude that in Kerala, "all the Adivasis' *prashnams* [translated as problems, questions, or issues] can be addressed only by the Adivasis."[87] Having said that he returns to talking about the Adivasi "struggle for land," indicating once more the centrality of the fact of their continuing dispossession and displacement to their perspective on Coca-Cola's presence in Plachimada. And it is in addressing this issue that they have been let down by everyone – the various social activists, religious organizations, the administrators who represent the secular state, and the political representatives of "the people," who in Kerala, belong to political parties representing every possible political ideology ranging from the right to the left.

It appears that in this vast range of social, political, and religious ideologies and discourses aimed at addressing social inequality and issues of social justice, there is no space to include what Adivasis in this area are saying on its own terms. Their aspirations and claims for justice must be transformed and translated into more recognizable languages, or left out. The complete silence over the land issue in every other account of Plachimada indicates that most consider the latter to be the best course.

It is a fact that Mylamma belonged to one of the most marginalized communities. It is also true that Adivasi protests against Coca-Cola pitches those among the world's most dispossessed peoples against a company that at the end of the year 2010 reported total assets of over $729 billion.[88] Increasing corporate control and acquisition of rivers, forests and mountains are worrying trends, just as protection of the environment is a serious issue that calls attention to much that needs to done.

All these facts, however, hold particular meanings for Adivasi protestors because of who and where they are. Coca-Cola has enclosed with walls the land the Adivasis lived and worked on. It has changed the water in the wells in ways that they had never imagined possible. Their water is like "dead water" now; it is there but they cannot drink it. Separated from their land, they are now forced to look for work far from their homes. Coca-Cola has altered their place and their lives. The state has allowed all of this to happen. Those who

86 Ottukan did not complete that sentence or specify who the "somebody" he was referring to was.

87 Interview with Ottukan.

88 The Coca-Cola Company, "2010 Annual Review," accessed August 2, 2011, www.annualreview.thecoca-colacompany.com.

have lived in the place for centuries were never given a choice in any of this. All of these facts hold significant meanings for Adivasis because of the specific history of alienation of tribal lands in Palakkad and other parts of Kerala. These are the specific facts that all Adivasis here speak about, regardless of whether they are inside or outside the *pandal*.

It is the loss of these particular situated meanings that Mylamma and others protested against when they decided not to sit in the *pandal* anymore. It appears that just as the *pandal* they had built was no longer theirs, their protest was also no longer theirs. Just as they could not stand by silently as Coca-Cola destroyed their wells and their place, they could not simply look on as the Plachimada Struggle drifted further away from the most significant aspects and objectives of their protests as outsiders continued to speak for them.[89]

The concepts of globalization, environmental and other rights, corporate invasions, American hegemony, and so on, all capable of multiple interpretations, are wide enough to represent many events in Plachimada. The dispute in Plachimada is certainly about water rights, corporate control, and many other issues being raised. As discussed in Chapter 3, those who speak on behalf of the protestors use this language because of its global recognition and resonance. But when the dispute in Plachimada is narrated only as being about these issues, what is lost is the ways in which these issues connect to the lived realities in Plachimada. Just as in legal translations, languages of "trans-situational applicability"[90] are useful, but not always to the one whose specific experience is lost in translation.

Contrary to the unacknowledged assumption of many outsiders I spoke with, Mylamma and other Adivasis are not voiceless symbols. They are not living out a chapter in a story written by other people in other places. They have their own stories to tell – ones that cannot be reduced to footnotes. Mylamma and others with her seem to have refused to be bound by any given script of resistance. Most of all, they wanted to make their own decisions and speak about the things that mattered the most to them. They did not want Subramaniam or any other outsider to speak for them. They had their own goals to pursue, ones that, contrary to initial assurances, the outsiders appear to have considered best put aside for the time being.

Seen in this context, Mylamma's act of leaving the *samara pandal*, does not seem to be a betrayal as understood by some outsiders, but rather represents

89 The fact that at least some Adivasis were unhappy about outsiders like Subramaniam speaking with visiting officers on their behalf was clear during my conversation with Ottukan.

90 Cain, "The General Practice Lawyer and the Client," 335.

her refusal to be silenced. It seems that the woman described as stubborn wanted to continue speaking about her community's right to live and work on that land, even if it meant losing the support of some of their most committed allies like Subramaniam. She could not stop talking about this because, as Kannan said, it is because she spoke of their right to live there that she was their leader. Repeated references to not leaving their land indicate that for Adivasis in the area, this remains a central concern.

Even as some Adivasi leaders refused to be sidelined, what they had perhaps not anticipated is the manner in which the separation with outsiders would also create rifts in their close-knit community. As it turned out, their decision to separate from the outsiders also ended up dividing the community into those who supported Mylamma and others who felt they could not "betray" the people who had stood by them in their hour of need – between those who thought she was right to leave and those who felt differences ought to be resolved by sitting together and talking about them.

The resolution of differences was important to Maariamma and others who chose to stay. She mentioned that the first time Kannan spoke to her about protesting against the company, she had told him once the agitation begins, they will all have to see it through to a conclusion. "Even if it is for another ten years," she had said, "we should all be together."[91] Everyone had agreed at the time. Amma, another elder, also emphasized this. She said they had given their word to stay together. Her sentiment, that they cannot "separate" after "saying that [they] are one," is shared by others who feel that Mylamma and others should not have left, whatever the reason.[92] They cannot desert Subramaniam who had come to help them when they "did not have water."[93] He stepped in "just because [their] land was slowly turning into a desert."[94] They could not ask him to leave.

Moreover, as Maariamma further points out, Subramaniam "is doing so much" for the residents of this place.[95] She mentioned ration cards and loans for building houses that he had helped apply for, and his campaigns for demanding closure of liquor stores in the area. They cannot abandon someone who she believes is even risking his life by taking on the powerful for their sake. That Subramaniam's efforts be acknowledged is something that matters a lot to her. It matters more to her than perhaps her own doubts about "what

[91] Interview with Maariamma.
[92] Interview with Amma.
[93] Interview with Maariamma.
[94] Ibid.
[95] Ibid.

is on his mind," and other similar thoughts that surfaced at times during our conversations.[96]

Maariamma's response to my question about why some Adivasis were against Subramaniam despite all he had done was: "They don't like him because this is our place. He is not from here."[97] She and several others do not agree with that view. As Amma pointed out, he came to help them, "not to do something bad to them."[98] According to Maariamma, if there were concerns about him being an outsider, it should have been pointed out to him at the very outset "that this is our land," and that he was not wanted here.[99] Saying that to him now amounts to "cheating" – a position several Adivasi elders agree with.[100] Unlike what has been said about some members of their community, they do not cheat or betray outsiders. It was important for them to make sure I understood that, just as it is important for them to resolve differences with those who left the *samara pandal*.

5.5. INSIDERS AND OUTSIDERS

Kannan, who is among those who "left," speaks about those who sit in the *pandal* with a sense of disappointment, frustration, and compassion, never with anger. He directs the anger at the "outsiders" who he says have used the struggle against Coca-Cola "for their own ends."[101] It is the outsiders who, according to him, believe that some "people are born to obey" them.[102] They are the ones who continue to deny others "freedom."[103] These are the people he holds responsible for the rift in the community. When asked why the outsiders would want to separate them, Kannan recited a saying in Malayalam, which can be translated as follows:

> We should recognize who you are; you should recognize who we are;
> Until that recognition dawns, gaps cannot be filled [or bridged].[104]

96 Ibid.
97 Ibid.
98 Interview with Amma.
99 Interview with Maariamma.
100 Ibid.
101 Interview with Kannan.
102 Ibid.
103 Ibid.
104 Ibid. The "we" here can also be translated as "I" depending on the context. This is the translation several Malayalam speakers I consulted agreed with most. All of them required an explanation of the context before translating the words into English, confirming the difficulty of translating such locally situated expressions.

These gaps or differences between "outsiders" and "insiders" are what according to Kannan cannot be bridged until the two sides recognize each other. The "gaps" or the meaning of "recognition" is not something Kannan elaborated upon directly, but much of what he, and later Ottukan, spoke about offers insights into understanding the differences as well as the kind of recognition they feel is missing.

To begin with, recognition of the other requires knowledge of oneself. "Unless you know who you are," Kannan had explained to me, "you cannot escape."[105] He followed that observation with an example, perhaps because my struggle to understand what he meant reflected on my face. He mentioned Nelson Mandela, and the struggle he led. As a consequence of that struggle, he explained, "[n]ow there is an American president from there."[106] According to him, "Obama from Africa is now president because they knew what they are."[107]

I could not help noting here that of all the global stories that have found their way into the village via the Plachimada anti–Coca-Cola struggle, the ones that speak to Kannan are about the movement led by Mandela in South Africa and the election of Barak Obama as the president of the United States. Also worth noting here is how he connects a spiritual quest to know oneself with the two men's political struggles that he also sees as connected. In a similar linking of the spiritual and political quests, Kannan also mentioned Gandhi, the influence of whose ideas both Mandela and Obama have acknowledged, albeit to express his disappointment with Gandhi's followers in India, who according to him have deviated from the path followed by Gandhi.

Kannan believes in the power of knowing who you are, and he desperately wants his community to understand the significance of this. This is what, according to him, will facilitate their "escape," and will enable them to recover "all that [they] have lost."[108] Kannan's words and the deep sense of betrayal that he almost seems to deny most clearly show the connections between assertions of identity and a community's quest for recovering what they have lost. As the stories in the next chapter indicate, what they have been losing is not just the lands they lived on but also a voice in history, ways of living, and worldviews.

It was after this conversation with Kannan that I began to think more about the insiders and outsiders in the area. These categories are inevitably complex

[105] Ibid.
[106] Ibid.
[107] Ibid.
[108] Ibid.

in these hamlets located in a layered place only a few kilometers from the border that separates the states of Kerala and Tamil Nadu. Kannan's understanding of "us" and "them" of "insiders" and "outsiders" is not what it may seem at first. He pointed out that all residents of the area are not "from the same group."[109] There are "OBCs, Muslims, Eravalars, and Malasars."[110] But he also added that he does not "believe in caste or religion, as human beings are just human beings."[111] These distinctions, he feels, were "made up by some people for their own comfort."[112] The same people, he notes have "divided not only human beings but also the power that controls the earth."[113] The distinctions that matter most to him, are those between insiders and outsiders. This distinction is different than those of religion, caste, race, and ethnicity. To begin with, a sense of place and time has something to do with being an insider.

As mentioned earlier, most Adivasis I spoke with self-identified as members of the Eravalar tribe. A few simply said they were "ST" or Scheduled Tribe. Many also said they were Adivasis. It was also pointed out repeatedly to me that they are all related. Their lives have been connected to the place since the time of their ancestors. The non-Adivasi residents of the area are not generally referred to as outsiders, owing perhaps to the recognition of a sense of belonging or being part of a place as a marker of insiderness. As mentioned in Chapter 2, the most common words of reference for those who have settled in the hamlets in the last few decades are "settler" or "Malayali," a word that generally denotes the linguistic identity of people who speak the Malayalam language. Occasionally, the word "mappila" is used to refer to Muslim settlers. "Malayalis" or "settlers" are therefore in the most part Hindus belonging to the scheduled castes, communities classified as Other Backward Classes (OBCs), or Muslims who have settled on small pieces of land allotted by the government. A large number of these settlers are employed as agricultural and construction labor on daily wages.

Unlike the settlers, the other group of non-Adivasis who live in the area are the landowners who have been around for generations. They are referred to either by their individual names or as *jenmi*, Rauther, Pattani, or Gounder. Just as none of these settler and other groups of non-Adivasi residents in the area are not simply outsiders, other Adivasis might not simply be insiders. Here again, a sense of place and belonging seems to play a role. According to

[109] Ibid.
[110] Ibid.
[111] Ibid.
[112] Ibid.
[113] Ibid.

Kannan, Adivasis live "[e]verywhere in the world," but they are not the same in all respects. "Customs and traditions differ," and these differences, according to him, are "based on the place they live in."[114] He mentioned Naga tribes, who live in the northeastern parts of India, as an example of this. And then he added something else to the mix that determines belonging: relations "based on love."[115] He mentioned this while talking about the caste system in Kerala. It "was severe here," he noted explaining further that relations between people belonging to different castes "were not based on love."[116] But things have changed. "Now," he says, "everyone can take any job."[117] Caste according to him is "not so much of a problem now."[118]

This change, however slight, is reflected to an extent in the social relations in the hamlets. Significantly, the protests have brought the residents together on a common platform. I could not help wonder if this is also something that the Adivasi elders who chose to stay in the *pandal* do not wish to lose. Recognition from those who have traditionally occupied positions of power in the social hierarchy must hold significance for some elders, who unlike Kannan and others of his generation, remember the time when they or their parents worked as *adima* or slaves. The *samara pandal* is where all the others came to sit with them, transcending traditional social divisions. Leaving it would therefore perhaps not only be a betrayal of that support but a loss of respect.

As mentioned before, the various non-Adivasi residents of the area are rarely referred to simply as outsiders. The nonspecific general outsiders are mostly the non-Adivasi nonresidents; most of whom the Adivasis have come in contact with after the protests against Coca-Cola began. Subramaniam, who is considered by many as a leader of the protests and who has been working to help the residents of the area in many aspects of their lives for years, remains an outsider. The innumerable men and women who have supported the Adivasis are outsiders. The political representatives, government officials, and the reporters with cameras are outsiders. All the people who take samples of water from the wells, but never drink it, are outsiders. The numerous researchers like me, who have visited the area in the decade, are outsiders.

[114] The centrality of place to Indigenous identity has been noted by scholars as well. See, for example, Patrick Wolfe, "Settler Colonialism and the Elimination of the Native," *Journal of Genocide Research* 8(4) (December 2006): 388, where Wolfe notes that *where* Indigenous people are "*is* who they are."

[115] Interview with Kannan.

[116] Ibid.

[117] Ibid.

[118] Ibid.

Many of these outsiders have much in common. Kannan explained that several of these "outside people came in and got involved" in their struggle, "but they did not stay long with [them]."[119] Referring to the time when they were on their own, Kannan said Adivasis here had "a particular set up" and "a way of functioning."[120] But then they "brought in" Subramaniam, and with him came many more.[121] And soon these outsiders began to speak for them. They began to translate their lives for all visitors, officials, activists, ministers, lawyers, and researchers, often in languages the visitors could understand. These visitors, in turn, began translating the already translated lives and claims for their respective audiences. It is these outsiders that Mylamma appears to have rejected when she left the *samara pandal*. It is many of these outsiders that Maariamma and others in the *pandal* do not wish to betray. It is also these outsiders that according to Kannan "can destroy the relations [the Adivasis] share."[122] Each group appears to have made different choices about the paths to be followed in encounters with outsiders.

5.6. STORIES AND MEANINGS

The accounts of the dispute in Plachimada as narrated by the Adivasis who began the protests against Coca-Cola offer important insights into the significance of the dispute for the Adivasis. These narratives also reveal what has been eclipsed in the popular and legal accounts presented in the previous chapters. The stories that the Adivasi protestors tell about their protest against Coca-Cola, as well as stories they tell about the place, its insiders and outsiders, are crucial for understanding the ways in which the re-presentation of their protests has alienated the Adivasis from their own *samaram*. It is only in the context of their stories that the meanings lost in translation become visible. Finally, the accounts presented here indicate that while it is important to recognize the role of insiders and outsiders in such situations, it is difficult, perhaps impossible, to recognize the outsiders and insiders independent of the stories that give meaning to the difference between them, or make the difference meaningful.

[119] Ibid.
[120] Ibid.
[121] Ibid.
[122] Ibid.

6

Law, History, Justice

I have so far presented multiple accounts of the dispute in Plachimada. Each of these narratives, re-presentations in different languages and organized around particular words fundamental to those languages, is important.[1] In a world of unequal languages, however, they are not considered equally valid. As a result, Adivasi accounts of the dispute have been eclipsed in the narrow claims that have been put forward on their behalf. I have earlier suggested that much of the particular and situated meanings that appear to have been lost in translation are connected to the place, its complex social relations, its layered histories, and the stories that the Adivasis in the area tell.[2] In this chapter I present a few such eclipsed narratives that are critical for a fuller and more meaningful understanding of the dispute in Plachimada.

I begin with accounts shared with me by two elder Adivasi women that provide glimpses of the community's remembered pasts and offer important insights for a better understanding of local social relations and Adivasi dispossession in Kerala. Next is a brief account of the more recent Adivasi struggle for restoration of alienated lands traditionally occupied by them in Kerala. This is followed by a critical examination of the law's account of this Adivasi struggle through a close look at litigation over the legality of a legislation aimed at restoring alienated Adivasi lands. While the outcome of this litigation can be seen as yet another local iteration of the global story of the role of formal state law in the dispossession of indigenous peoples, this is also a story of an imperfect encounter between the different normative worlds of common law notions of property and indigenous relationships

[1] See Cover, "Obligation," 65–74 for the argument that "every legal culture has its fundamental words" and that evoking a particular concept locates us in a particular normative universe.

[2] For the importance of recognizing "historical continuities" of protests in the "local," see Ramachandra Guha, "The Unquiet Woods: Ecological Change and Peasant Resistance in the Himalaya," in *The Ramachandra Guha Omnibus*, 2nd ed. (New Delhi: Oxford University Press, 1999).

of belonging to places. In the concluding section I offer some thoughts on the ways in which all these different, often contradictory histories are inseparably connected to the dispute in Plachimada. Nonrecognition of these connections can only lead to more injustice.

6.1. ORAL HISTORY

Multifaceted histories of the place emerged from my conversations in Plachimada and other hamlets in the area. Maariamma and Amma, well-respected Adivasi women mentioned earlier, shared two accounts that are significant for the challenges and opportunities they present. The first is a story Maariamma had heard from her elders. The second, an account of the Eravalans' arrival in the place, has been passed on from one generation to the next. These accounts from a community's archives are not recorded in any of the written sources of the past of the place or its people recounted in the previous chapters. As evidenced by the footnotes accompanying the histories presented before, I found those earlier written narratives of the past, readily recognized *as* history, in libraries, bookstores, and state archives that house old documents, gazettes, manuals, reports of colonial officials, and published accounts of travelers. They comprise what historians refer to as historical facts and establish "historical truths" in accordance with the established disciplinary rules of historical research.[3] Within this particular understanding of history, all other narrations of the past are not historical facts.

Oral traditions, despite their recognition as archives that are used to produce previously unrecognized histories,[4] generally have a harder time meeting the

3 See Dipesh Chakrabarty, "History and the Politics of Recognition," in *Manifestoes for History*, eds. Keith Jenkins et al. (London: Routledge, 2007), 77–87. While critiquing the discipline of history, Chakrabarty explains the distinction between "historical truths" and what he names "historical wounds." The former, according to him, are "broad, synthetic generalizations based on researched collections of individual historical facts. They could be wrong but they are always amenable to verification by methods of historical research." Historical wounds, "on the other hand," are a "mix of history and memory" and therefore their "truth is not verifiable by historians." They are a result of a "social consensus" in a community/polity that a certain marginalized group has been wronged or oppressed in the past. And given the fact that these historical wounds are "cultural formations," they "live precarious lives." The specific example of a "historical wound" he gives here is that of the act of calling the generations of aboriginal children forcibly removed from their homes in Australia as the "stolen generation." The historical verifiable truth is that children were in fact removed. But the use of the word "stolen" in this expression, according to Chakrabarty, packs "into the expression an emotional intensity that could not be measured by the historian's scale."

4 See Jan Vansina, *Oral Tradition as History* (Madison, WI: University of Wisconsin Press, 1985). For the significance as well as limitations of this approach see Ajay Skaria, "Some Aporias of History: Time, Truth and Play in Dangs, Gujarat," *Economic and Political Weekly* 34:15 (1999): 897–904.

requirements of historical truths.[5] Not really treated on par with written histories, they are, at best, used to produce authoritative written histories that "adhere to the norms of western professional history writing,"[6] or simply disregarded as all that does not meet the requirements of disciplinary history: myth, story, memory, or "historical wounds" that use "present experience as a guide to the past" and are therefore unacceptable to historians who privilege "historical objectivity" and separation of the past and the present.[7] It is perhaps this perceived difficulty of proving the reality or truth of oral traditions that lies behind the continued privileging of written histories even as subaltern pasts are sought to be recovered and retold.[8]

This difference between two dissimilar forms of recording, remembering, and narrating the past, informed by "distinctive sense of pasts,"[9] exists despite the fact that even the available written accounts of peoples, their lives, practices, agriculture, and commerce, and of events, are records of the authors' observation and analysis, as well as their interpretations and reinterpretations of older records in particular places and times.[10] Like oral traditions, written texts are also "created" for the "accomplish[ment] of certain tasks," but they are assumed to be truer representations of the past perhaps because they outlive "the context of [their] production."[11]

5 The said distinction between "truths" and "wounds," while perhaps necessary to maintain for the discipline of history, becomes quite problematic when it has real consequences for real people engaged in legal struggles when memories of a group's past come up against written records created by those whose worlds were constituted by other narratives and truths. See Bruce G. Miller, *Oral History on Trial: Recognizing Aboriginal Narratives in the Courts* (Vancouver: UBC Press, 2011). Miller, an anthropologist who in this book draws on his own experiences as an expert witness in courts in Canada and the United States, shows that if we take oral traditions seriously, and treat oral history with the same respect, we might actually be able to find ways in which they can be seen as meeting the evidentiary thresholds in common law courts (Miller, *Oral History on Trial*, 12).

6 Skaria, "Some Aporias of History," 897.

7 See Chakrabarty, "History and the Politics of Recognition," 77–87.

8 This could, at least in part, explain the very few attempts to engage with oral histories even by scholars connected with the Subaltern Studies project. For notable exceptions see 'True Stories' in Gyan Prakash, *Bonded Histories: Genealogies of Labour and Servitude in Colonial India* (Cambridge: Cambridge University Press, 1990) and Skaria, *Hybrid Histories*, xii. I am grateful to Gyan Prakash for all that I learned from his response to a paper I presented on this theme in 2012.

9 Skaria, *Hybrid Histories*, 1.

10 See Prakash, Bonded Histories, 35 for an argument that all history involves "imagining the past," and requires interpretation.

11 Ibid., 40. For the manner in which oral histories are "intrinsically connected to the present through the [processes of their] production," see Nandini Sundar, "Village Histories: Coalescing the Past and the Present," in *History and the Present*, eds. Partha Chatterjee and Anjan Ghosh (New Delhi: Permanent Black, 2002), 180.

Regardless of how the Adivasi narratives presented in this section are evaluated by anyone who might be interested in verifying the truth within them, I have included them here because I have learned much from them about the people I met and the places they inhabit. These narratives offer invaluable insights that are critical for understanding some of what is happening in Plachimada today.

6.1.1. *Maariamma's Story*

Over a month after I first met Maariamma, she suddenly declared she would tell me a story she had heard as a child from her elders. She narrated this story intermittently over two days. The first time I asked Maariamma if she would speak with me, she had said she would not tell me anything until Subramaniam said it was all right to speak with me. There had been many visitors with questions, and in the past some had written things that she was later blamed for speaking about. She did not elaborate on what those things were or who had blamed her for saying them, but she explained that due to that reason she could not trust every "outsider." In fact, it was only after Subramaniam said that she could tell me everything had Maariamma begun to speak about the protests against Coca-Cola with me. I was surprised therefore by her decision to share a story with me that she did not wish to narrate in the presence of any non-Adivasi residents and "outsiders" (a journalist, some local activists, and a group of concerned men who wished to determine the "facts" about the villagers' lives and the extent of water pollution in the area) who stopped by during the two days over which she narrated the story. She did not even want them to know that she was narrating a story. But she wanted me to share this story. Later she said that she would tell me more stories if people where I had come from said it was a good story, but not if they said, angrily or impatiently: "What is this story you are telling us?" She specifically reminded me to tell her story on the last day I visited her in the *samara pandal.*

Maariamma did not wish for the story to be recorded and signaled that I put away the recorder as soon as I took it out. She laughed when I expressed my concern about not remembering it correctly later; she pointed to my notebook indicating that I could write it down. I did not realize until later when I attempted to write about the story, that my re-telling, as well as all future renditions of the story, would inevitably be re-presentations of her story.

This is the story that Maariamma would only tell her way, without any interruptions from me for questions or clarifications. "Just write it as I'm telling it.

You will understand," she had said. I could not therefore ask her the many questions that arose in my mind at the time of narration or later on. Twice in the following weeks I asked her if I could ask something about the story, but she had refused to say anything. On the second occasion, she even said she would stop talking to me if I asked any questions about that story again.

Every time I read Maariamma's story, I see new things and make new connections. The meanings I continue to discover with each reading make it a new story every time. At first I struggled with the multitude of interpretations that the story offered. I was troubled by the renewal, the fecundity, often because I was not sure which of these meanings she had wanted me to convey to others. How could I be certain about her intent and meaning? The responsibility of telling the story that she had placed on me made me anxious to the extent that I avoided writing about it for a long time.

As I read and re-read this story and thought about many of my other conversations with her, I began to acknowledge that my anxiety arises not from what she said to me but rather from my own desire for certainty. I was looking for a fixed set of meanings that a story, whether written or oral, cannot provide beyond any given moment. Narratives generate meanings through processes of telling and listening, and these meanings change with each narration and each act of listening or reading.[12] Meanings often emerge in what each narrator or listener sees in the narrative, and in each other. None of this can be news to anyone who has read and re-read favorite books, even pieces of fiction. And yet I struggled with the new meanings that Maariamma's story offered. I suspect this is because I did not see Maariamma's story either as a novel or as a theoretical treatise, in which I would expect to find new meanings every time I return to them with new experiences and knowledges. As in the other narratives of past that I recorded in the place, I was searching for facts in her story – *historical facts* – that I could connect, either by way of corroboration or challenge, with other facts about the place and its people I had found in other archives. I felt it was these connections or discontinuities that would make her story significant. Maariamma would have none of that. She refused to connect it to any person, place, or time. Here lies an epistemic rupture that I do not know how to bridge.

Maariamma's instruction to me was that I write her story and that I will understand (at some point). Her refusal to indulge my desire to find a

[12] See Sundar, "Village Histories," 180, where in the context of the process of recording oral histories, Sundar suggests that different accounts may be produced by "different fieldworkers" and in "different fieldwork periods."

definitive meaning in her story was deeply unsettling for me as a lawyer. Such uncertainty is also troubling to courts that are increasingly called upon to adjudicate indigenous claims that challenge the limits of the language of state law, because meanings have to be determined and cases have to be decided in the here-and-now. However, if the epistemic ruptures between indigenous/oral and nonindigenous worlds are taken seriously, seen for what they are, and respected rather than overlooked or dismissed, this uncertainty can be a productive one.

For all these reasons, I present here the text of the story narrated by Maariamma, translated by Shiny, and written down by me; re-presented twice before you read it.

> There is a Gounder.[13] His wife was pregnant. As he was out grazing cattle, he thought about how he would manage everything. "There will be a lot of work in the house", he thought. As he walked further, he saw a seven-year-old boy. He asked the boy where he was going. The boy said: "I'll see where I'll go. I'm just walking." The Gounder said: "I'll take you home and take care of you like a son." So the boy went with the Gounder. While the Gounder took care of work at home the boy went out to graze cattle. The Gounder's wife had a child. A cow also gave birth to a calf. The Gounder said: "Now my family is becoming better. If it gets even better, I will give cows to the temple."
>
> The calf got bigger. The boy also grew up. The Gounder's wife said: "Since we have promised to give a cow to the temple, we will give the calf that is now grown up." The Gounder said: "Why are you saying this?" Then he wondered which caste the boy belonged to. The boy wears a thread. He is a Brahmin. Why should we go to the temple? We'll just give the calf to the boy. So the calf was given to the boy. Now, the boy has to be married. He was married, and he brought a wife.
>
> I don't know where the Gounder and his wife went. Now the boy, his wife and the calf, which is now a cow, were living together. A calf was born to the cow. The wife used to milk the cow. She didn't leave any milk for the calf. There was no milk for the calf. The cow would tell its calf to drink milk. The cow's child said: "I don't know how mother's milk tastes. Is it sweet, or what?" The cow said: "we cannot do anything." Then the cow's child said: "After milking you the woman will let me out to play. At that time I will hide." The cow asked: "What will we do if we hide? What will happen?" The calf said: "After I hide they will tie you somewhere, like they normally do. I will

[13] As mentioned before, Gounder is a Tamil caste name used by certain landowning communities in western Tamil Nadu. Many have bought land in this border area over the last few decades. In Plachimada, the man referred to as "Gounder" lives in the only large concrete house with a clearly demarcated boundary and seems to enjoy a status of power and authority. References to him are usually in lowered voices or by a nod or gesture toward his house.

come back at midnight and untie you and we'll go somewhere." The cow agreed, and that's what they did. Everyone looked for the calf after it hid, but they couldn't find him. At night he came back and untied the cow. The mother and child ran away. After a while they came to a big garden, where they drank water. They grazed and lived there.

One day, after grazing and after the calf had milk from its mother, they were sleeping. A tiger came there and cut the mother cow's throat and drank all the blood. Then the tiger's child came. The calf, on seeing the cub, thought that just like how the tiger had killed his mother, the cub will kill him. The calf ran from there. Seeing that, the cub also started running after the calf. The cub said to the calf: "Please stop! I won't do to you what my mother did to your mother. We will live together. You eat grass. I'll eat something, and we'll drink water." Like that they lived and became friends. The cub would catch a cat or dog and drink water, and the calf would eat grass and drink water. After this both of them would sleep together under a tree.

Shiva and Parvati[14] passed by the tree and saw the cub and the calf sleeping together. Parvati said: "When they wake up, the cub will eat the calf." She asked Shiva to do something. They placed four *shankh* (conch shells) next to the two and left.[15] When the cub woke up he turned into a human being. The calf also turned into a human being. Both were as elder and younger brothers.

Now that they had turned into human beings, what were they to eat? So they went in search of food. After a while they reached a place of many flowers. They saw a big tree and rested under it. An old woman like me was going for her bath. She told the boys not to go there. She said: "We cannot pluck flowers because there is a big snake with five heads there." The boys wondered what they would do if the snake came out. In that area there was a king with a daughter. Nobody came to the palace to ask for her hand because of the snake. The king had declared that his daughter would be married to whoever kills the snake.

The boys saw the snake approaching them. Remember they had the *shankh*? They showed one to the snake who then died. The old woman saw this and ran to the king's palace. The king asked her why she was running. She said: "My son has killed the snake. The princess should be married to my son." The king discussed this with the family. Why should they give their child to ordinary people? They thought: "We have raised her like a princess!"

[14] Shiva and his wife Parvati are widely regarded as Hindu deities. Some sources suggest that the worship of Shiva predates the advent of Vedic Hinduism in the subcontinent and that Shiva and Parvati were in fact tribal gods that were absorbed into Hinduism.

[15] Conch shells have a significant place in Indian mythology and rituals of worship in Hindu temples. One of the powers that conch shells are believed to possess is that when blown they get rid of negative energy in a space.

So he decided to see for himself what had happened. He went to the spot and found these two boys. He asked them who had killed the snake. The cub-boy said: "my elder brother calf-boy has killed the snake". The king took the two boys to the palace. The princess was married to calf-boy.

Now the cub-boy was left alone. It was not good for the elder brother – cub-boy – to live with his younger brother and his wife.[16] So, he decided to go out. Calf-boy asked cub-boy: "where are you going? If something happens to you, how will I know and how will I see you again?" The cub-boy took a pot filled with water and lit a lamp, and kept these there and said to the calf-boy: "If I die, or something happens to me, the water will disappear and the lamp will be blown off." He gave these as a symbol, and started walking.

The cub-boy reached a town called Buboothinagaram. There was an old woman there with a lot of wealth and a big house. He went in and asked for drinking water. The old woman asked: "Where are you going? I don't have anyone to take care of my wealth." Then she gave a pot of buttermilk to him to drink. She said: "Wherever you go, don't settle down. Come back to me." The cub-boy said: "I cannot stay back. I have to go." The old woman said: "Don't go to the west. You can go to the east, north and south." He didn't ask her why.

He went towards west. There was a small pond full of water there, and a big tamarind tree. There was a beautiful lotus flower in the middle of the pond. He wanted to take the lotus. He went into the pond and saw some steps going down. Earlier, there had been a pregnant woman sleeping under the tamarind tree. A tiger came and took the child from her womb and took it inside the pond, and raised the girl in there. Now, this boy plucked the flower, put it in his pocket and walked down the steps. He saw a big palace there. There was no one around. On the steps of the palace he saw the head of the girl and her body lying at different spots. The cub-boy thought: "What is happening here? What is this?" He took the head and placed it near the body. He placed a *shankh* next to it. The girl came alive. He asked her: "What is your name?" She said: "My name is Rajammal." "And where are your parents?" he asked. She said: "My mother is not there. My father has gone to the forest." "Why are you kept like this?" he asked. She said: "My father goes out. And if someone does something bad to me, my father will be sorry. So, every time he goes out, he does this to me. It is time for my father to return. You go and hide yourself. My father is a tiger. He will kill you."

The boy separated the girl's head again. He said to the girl: "When your father comes back, give him food, and when he is resting, ask him what will happen to you and all your wealth if something happens to him while he

[16] It is not clear which of the two brothers was the older one, and whether this reference to both as the "elder brother" in turn is a mistake or deliberate.

is out. Say to him: 'There will be none to give me back my life if you don't return.' Then tell me your father's reply tomorrow after he goes out."

Rajammal did all this and asked the question: "If something happens to you, you will die there. I will die here. What will happen to all our wealth?" Her father said: "I will not die like that. There is a big banyan tree behind our house. If you cut the top and bottom of the tree and cut it open, there you will find a big insect – that is my soul. I will not die even if I go to far off places. I will die only if this insect is killed and burnt."

The next day he left her in the same manner. The cub-boy brought her back to life, and asked her what her father had said. She told him the story of the banyan tree. She said: "Kill the insect and burn it. Then my father will die." The cub-boy killed the insect and burnt it. Rajammal's father died. They got married and started living together. They had no kids, so they decided to go to the temple and pray for kids. One Friday, they went to the temple. The priest asked them to come back next week. When they went there next week (the temple was in a Gounder's place), they saw a Gounder who was working. His name was Kozhikatt Gounder. He was sitting in front of the temple. He saw Rajammal and thought he had never seen a girl like her. He thought: "She is very beautiful. Where has she come from?" An old woman used to go to this temple to take *pongal*.[17] The Gounder called the old woman and asked her about this girl. He said: "If you bring me and the girl together I will give you all my wealth." She said she would have to see what she could do.

The old woman went to the girl. This girl was pregnant. Seven months. The old woman said to the cub-boy: "I have no one to look after me. Your wife is also carrying. You don't have anyone to look after her. Since I'm alone I'll come and live with you." The cub-boy said: "We have a lot of experience. We don't need anybody. But whatever you need, I'll do for you." The old woman said: "Just give me some water and I'll come with you." They took her home.

The next day the cub-boy said to Rajammal: "We'll have to go to the temple today." The girl said: "It is close by. I'll go alone." So the cub-boy stayed back. The old woman was in the house. She mixed poison in the boy's tea. He died. The girl came back. She thought the boy was sleeping. As she was going to wake him up, the old woman stopped her and said: "Don't wake him up. Let him sleep." The girl also slept by his side. When she woke up late in the evening she wondered why he was still sleeping. Then she found out he was dead. She started crying. The old woman said: "Don't sit here alone and cry. There is nobody around. Some evil spirit may come here. We'll go to my house."

[17] Pongal is sweet food considered to be blessed by the deity.

She had a small house. So she took the girl to the Gounder's house. The Gounder said: "You keep her until she delivers. I'll meet the expenses." After the girl delivered the child, the old woman took the girl to the Gounder. The Gounder asked her to clean her up and then bring her back. After cleaning up, when Rajammal was walking to the Gounder's house, she met a seven-year-old boy. She asked him where he was going. He said "I'm going to see where I can get food." Rajammal took him with her and gave him her newborn baby. She said: "I'm not going to live long. You take care of my child."

Then the girl went to the Gounder. The boy took the child and went somewhere. When the girl went to the Gounder, she was wearing new clothes. The Gounder had taken alcohol and was not in his senses. The old woman left the girl there and went away. The Gounder who was in a drunken state pulled her sari and asked her to come near. She gave him an end of her sari, which he started to pull. She took off the sari slowly and tied the other end to a pillar-like thing near the window and ran away.

As she was running for her life she came across seven thieves who were dividing the day's loot. She fell right in the middle of where they were sitting, and asked for help. She only had her skirt on. The seven of them gave her their clothes and took her home. They were thieves. They had small houses in a big space. They said since the seven had taken her home, she would have to be the wife of all seven.

Rajammal set up a competition. She asked them to bring seven vessels and fill them with thorns and flowers. She said she would marry the one who fills his vessel first. They couldn't fill the vessels in one day as the flowers and thorns were very small. Every night they went out to rob, and during the days they tried to fill their vessels. One day when they were out robbing, the girl escaped on a horse with all their gold.

Rajammal started a new town called Pudupattanam[18] as she now had a lot of money and a horse. She built a big palace. She had enough water. She had people to cook food, and was enjoying life with all luxuries. If poor people like me go there, she will give food and water. You can live there and have a good life.

That area was mainly used for grazing cattle. After six or seven years her baby who had been given to the boy, also grew up into a boy. The small boy was crying and the big boy was pulling him along. Some boys who were grazing cattle saw this and asked why the small boy was crying. The big boy said: "Because he is hungry." The boys grazing cattle said there is a place called Pudupattanam over there. Go there and you'll get free food. The two boys went there. They got food, clothes and everything they needed, and they started living there.

18 The word translates as "new town."

The Gounder Rajammal had left behind came looking for her. Rajammal asked her people to capture the Gounder, shave his head and apply sandalwood paste on his head. She asked them to make him sit on a donkey and let him go like that.

Then the seven robbers came to Pudupattanam. They saw her picture in the town and started crying out: "Rajammal, where are you?" She saw them, and asked her people to shave their heads too, and to put them in a horse stable. The seven of them were locked inside that, and they died.

When the cub had left the calf-boy he had left some symbols – the water and the lamp. When the cub-boy died, calf-boy had got the message as the water was gone and the lamp had been blown out. He set out in search of the cub-boy. Calf-boy wondered where his elder brother went.

Like cub-boy, the calf-boy also went to Bibhootipatnam and met the old woman. The woman asked: "Where are you going?" He said: "A few years ago a young man like me came this way. I'm looking for him." The old woman said: "Long ago a boy like you came here. I asked him not to go towards the west." Then without listening to the old woman, the calf-boy also went towards west. There he saw the flower and pond. He went in. Just like the cub-boy had, he also saw the stairs. He climbed down. There he saw cub-boy's body. He put the *shankh* on the chest of cub-boy, who then got his life back. He got up as if he had woken up from a deep sleep. He started crying. "Where is Rajammal?" he asked. The calf-boy said: "Don't cry. Wherever she is, we'll find her."

Both the boys started looking for her. They reached Pudupattanam and saw a number of people grazing cattle. They asked the two boys where they were going. They said: "If you are hungry, over there is a place called Pudupattanam. Go there and have food and water, and rest." Both the boys went there, bathed, and ate food. The cub-boy saw Rajammal's picture there. He cried out: "Rajammal, where are you? Why did you leave me?" Rajammal heard this. She came down and saw her husband and his brother.

Now they are all united and are living happily. Rajammal got her son and husband back. After that calf-boy went back to his house.

In the next few paragraphs I offer some reflections based on what I have learned from Maariamma's telling, from my listening, and later reading and re-reading her story. Although I can offer only these, other readers with other experiences, knowledges, and sensibilities will no doubt see other meanings, directions, and purposes.[19] What follows is therefore not an attempt to give

[19] Individual stories in community archives are often connected to other stories and fuller meanings emerge from other stories and from the connections between them. I am thankful to Roma Chatterjee for our conversations on how stories function in oral cultures, their elusive and polysemous nature, and the importance of knowing other stories in order to understand any one of them more fully.

any definitive meaning to Maariamma's story, but rather it is an invitation to engage further with her story and its significance.

I have not heard the story Maariamma narrated to me before, and yet some parts of it are not completely unfamiliar. At several junctures in the story I was reminded of other events in other stories I have read or heard before. Some of these were about souls of beings residing outside their bodies, of gods interfering in lives of beings on earth, and of humans living in palaces under water. Some of Rajammal's experiences will also remind those who are familiar with the epic tale of *Mahabharata* of events in the life of Draupadi. Interestingly, unlike in the most widely recognized interpretation of the epic in which Draupadi is saved from being completely disrobed by divine intervention, Rajammal manages to escape in a more earthly manner. She also avoids accepting several "husbands" unlike Draupadi in the widely accepted version of the epic. I have also wondered if this was Maariamma's subversive interpretation of the popular queen she may have encountered in other narratives. Whether or not Maariamma's account of Rajammal's experiences are closer to that of Draupadi's in the many other versions of the epic in the country requires further investigation; however, Rajammal clearly possesses agency that is denied to Draupadi in the popular rendition of the epic.

Maariamma's story points to the significance of interconnectedness of all life forms and, more significantly, offers insights into social relations.[20] There are beings connected by a past violence that agree to live together, and there are relationships of trust that are violated. There are relations of power – of exploitation, oppression, and also subversion. Woven into these many relationships are stories of journeys – some with no apparent destination, some in search of a better place with enough food and water, some in search of lost loved ones, and others in search of freedom. The relationship of all life forms to water as something that sustains and holds life within it is a recurring theme woven into the narrative.

While in Plachimada, Maariamma's story enabled me to think about and understand earlier conversations with her and others in the place in ways that I might have otherwise missed. For example, I began to think about the relationship of the residents with the "Gounder" who lives in a large house to the north of Plachimada. I was particularly intrigued by Maariamma's account of the Gounder who is publicly humiliated by

[20] For the significance of myths in understanding social relations in the past and present, see Sundar, "Village Histories," 146. See also Prakash, Bonded Histories, 35 for useful ways of interpreting the "fantasy, mystery, and magic in [oral] traditions."

Rajammal's "people." Typically, when a man is forced to sit on a donkey in such an act of public shaming, his face is blackened. In Maariamma's narration of this event, however, the Gounder's head is shaved and smeared with sandalwood paste. The immense significance of this emerges in light of the fact that sandalwood paste is an integral part of many Hindu rituals and religious ceremonies as a mark of purity. Everything from the preparation of the paste to its application on images of deities and other temple spaces requires purity, and therefore such tasks are typically carried out by priests or other "upper caste" people considered appropriate for them. Many Hindus in this area wear sandalwood paste on the forehead as a mark of religious piety and purity.

By substituting the popular blackening of the face in this act of shaming with the smearing of sandalwood paste on the shaved head of a powerful "upper caste" man who attempted to rape Rajammal and had her husband killed, this story seems to question the widely accepted understanding of purity. In a society where the practice of wearing sandalwood on the forehead is popular among certain Hindu castes, this story offers a counter-narrative that rejects such markers of piety by drawing attention instead to the deeds of those who wear their claims of spiritual and religious superiority on their bodies.

The fact that the Gounder's humiliation was ordered by a woman like Rajammal, also adds another layer of meaning to this story. Rajammal is her only name. Like most, especially older Adivasis in the area, there is no other name before or after this one name that could have connected her to any house, caste, or village. The name itself is similar to some Adivasi names, but Maariamma did not say if she was an Adivasi. She was taken from the womb of her mother by a tiger whose soul resided in an insect that lived inside a large banyan tree. The tiger raised Rajammal inside a pond. Rajammal goes on to marry and have a child with a man who was earlier a tiger's cub. The ways in which this woman, who does not bear any markers of human society such as caste or religion, is connected to and sustained by various forms of life continues to intrigue.

Another aspect of the story that I was struck by is the recurring theme of children separated from their mothers – of children raised by those who had either taken the child from the mother forcibly, had found a wandering child, or had been entrusted with the care of another's child. Maariamma had earlier told me that her mother had left her even before "cutting the cord." She had been lying there "crying under the hot sun," until her father returned from grazing the cattle. He "found" her covered in a bundle and said: "this is my daughter." He had then washed her, cut the umbilical cord, and raised her along with her older siblings. When she was a baby, he used to carry her in a cloth slung over his back all day as he walked with the grazing cattle. When she cried he would give her *kanji* (rice gruel). I thought about this when Maariamma talked about the calf in her story who did not know the taste of his mother's milk.

Later I met or learnt of a few other older men and women in this place whose mothers had "left." Kecharan, a man with whom I spoke at length, broke down while talking about being abandoned as a young child or infant. He told me that he did not know anything about his biological parents. The parents who raised him had found him abandoned at the end of what I understood to be a gathering where a song was sung through the night in what he called the "ancient days." Another resident of the area later mentioned that Kecharan's mother had abandoned him as an infant, after which his maternal grandfather had raised him.

There are others like Maariamma and Kecharan in the place. I did not learn why these mothers had to leave, or where they went. I do not know therefore if these women left on their own, or whether they, like the calf's mother in Maariamma's story, are "tied up" somewhere, forced to forsake their own children to provide for others. Were some of them forced to part with their children like Rajammal as she made her way to an uncertain future? Did Maariamma, as a child listening to this story, dream of "untying" her mother and fleeing with her to a "big garden" where they could live together? The questions I could have asked are not easy to ask. The couple of Adivasi women that I did ask did not respond in words. My hesitant questions were met with the kind of silence that is best left undisturbed.

Maariamma told me she had heard this story from her elders when she was a child. Perhaps they too had heard it from their elders. I often wonder whether and how far the story has traveled. Is it a tale that wandering children and people like those in the story have carried with them as oral records of the past of a people? Have the narrators over generations woven into the story their own lived experiences to be conveyed to generations to come? This could be one reason why the story is not located in any particular time with Maariamma's narration switching constantly between the past and present tense.

In the National Archives in New Delhi, there is an account of the life and practices of the Kotars, described as one of several "aboriginal tribes" that lived in and around the Nilgiri hills that lie to the north of the Palghat Gap. While reading this account compiled by one Dr. Shortt, who "quietly elicited all the information" during his visits to many tribal hamlets in the Nilgiri hills while "conferring on the unprotected the boon of vaccination,"[21] I came across this entry:

> They never, as a rule, milk their cattle, but leave it all to the calves.[22]

That is all that Dr. Shortt, Superintendant General of Vaccination of the Madras Presidency, was either able to "quietly elicit" or cared to record in his carefully put together account of the "hill-tribes" in 1868. But it is a practice that appears to have clearly stood out as unusual to him at the time.

I am in no position to offer an expert opinion on the possible connections between the Kotars and the Eravalans (the community Maariamma belongs to), except to note the obvious geographical proximity. But this entry raised, once again, questions that I knew Maariamma would not answer, even if I could have returned to Plachimada from the National Archives in Delhi. I did what I could instead – read Maariamma's story again. Could it be that the Kotars left all the milk for the calves because they looked at the situation from the perspective of the cows and their calves? Unlike the Brahmin household in Maariamma's story, where no one seemed to care if a calf knew the taste of its mother's milk, did the Kotars tell each other similar stories about the conversations between cows and their children? Did the account of the calf that wanted to free its mother enter the stories of Eravalans as they came in contact with people who did not leave the cow's milk for the calves? I wonder if the children who grow up listening to accounts of cows and milk from the calves' perspective see an injustice in the cow–human relationship that children who grow up with stories of cows providing for humans do not.

Before concluding this section I want to point to the significance of water in Maariamma's story that indicates the significance of paying attention to possible ways in which certain elements enter accounts or take on a particular significance at certain times. The importance of water to life is emphasized throughout the story as people ask or search for water and even live in water. The fleeing cow and calf drink water once they reach the garden where they decided to spend their free lives. Later, when the cub of the tiger that kills the cow suggests to the calf that they live together in peace, he mentions that while each would eat its separate food, they would both drink water. Further

[21] J. Shortt, An *Account of the Hill Tribes of Neilgherries* (April 11, 1868), Home Department Proceedings, Hon'ble R. S. Ellis, C. B., Chief Secretary to the Government of St. Fort George, to E. C. Bayley, Esquire, Secretary to the Government of India, No. 305, New Delhi, National Archives, 1.

[22] Ibid., 30.

in the story, as he is about to set off on a journey, a pot of water is one of the things he gives to the calf-boy as a signifier for his continuing life. The water would disappear, he told his brother, if he died. Finally, the new city that Rajammal founded had plenty of food and water.

Water is part of everyday conversations in Plachimada and other hamlets today. Expressions such as "there is no life without water," "you need water to live," and "you can live without food but not water" are commonplace. Given that they have lived through a time when their water depleted and changed for the worse, this is hardly surprising. They have had to carry water over longer distances in the last ten years. Waiting for the lorry that brings water to the hamlets is the new reality of their everyday life since they cannot simply pull out a pot of water from their wells anymore. Structures to harvest and store rainwater have been installed in some places.

I could not help wondering if the moments that emphasize the significance of water for sustaining life have entered Maariamma's story over the last decade. She may have told the same story with a different emphasis earlier. It is also possible that the search for water by the various journeying beings has always been a theme in the story. But it must have different meanings and significance for the narrators of this tale and their audiences in Plachimada today.

6.1.2. *Journeys, Places, Belonging*

Amma, a respected elder in her community, says they have been "here" since time immemorial, since the time of their ancestors. "Here" is not, as I had first assumed, the piece of land on which her home stands today. As she continued to narrate the history of her ancestors, "here" became a complicated place. There is a "here" where they have lived since time immemorial, and there is a "here" where her ancestors three (or five) generations before her parents made their home, and there is a "here" – the exact piece of land on which her home stands.[23] Specific times, even when measured in numbers of generations, or identifying specific pieces of land where they have lived before settling in the present "here" do not seem to matter in Amma's relationship with the various "here" she refers to. The questions I posed in an attempt to arrive at these specifics surprised, amused, and even confused her.

[23] For the significance of recognizing the "multiple histories and meanings of and for place," see Renisa Mawani, "Imperial Legacies (Post) Colonial Identities: Law, Space and the Making of Stanley Park, 1859–2001," in *Making Law Visible: Past and Present Histories and Postcolonial Theory*, eds. Nan Seuffert and Catharine Coleborne, *Law Text Culture* 7 (2003): 98–141.

As Amma narrated the history of her people, I realized how meaningless several of my early questions must have seemed to her. While I was trying to locate a tenable claim to land in the language of the law, she was telling me about belonging. Amma's account is a history that has lived for centuries in the community's archive, told and retold without dates, about places that existed before they were numbered, measured or owned. It is an account of homes found and lost, and of people who have journeyed for a long time. The history that Amma recounts offers insights into the many ways in which relationships of belonging in a place are central to her normative universe. It took me a while to understand this. If Amma thought anything of my ignorance at the time, she did not express it.

Amma lives in a hamlet not far from the Coca-Cola plant with her family. She was born here, as were her parents before her. Three (or five) generations before her parents, her ancestors lived in a place called "Kottekkad near Manamplavu."[24] This was the place where they had found "a god of [their] own." But the journeys of her ancestors did not begin in that place. They began much earlier with two orphaned brothers who were beaten and chased away by all whom they approached. Since nobody would take these children "who [had] no parents" in, the two boys went to live "deep in the forest." They sought shelter from rain under the bamboo trees, and "ate whatever they found inside the forest, [like] fruits and some tubers." They drank water "wherever they found [it]."

Since these boys were by themselves in the forest and scared to approach anyone lest they be beaten and killed, "[t]heir hair and beards grew long." At this time, some Koravars who had gone into the forest to get bamboo "saw two boys sitting there like ghosts."[25] And then, with the help of god, these Koravars, who "were all good people," brought the two boys out. This is when the two boys had their hair cut and beards shaved. According to Amma, these events took place somewhere in Palakkad. The boys subsequently began to cultivate land, got married and had many children.

[24] While I have been unable to locate Manamplavu, there is a small town called Kottekkad near the Malampuzha dam in Palakkad. It lies to the north of Plachimada and is close to the edge of a forest.

[25] Upon being asked who the Koravars were, and whether they too were Adivasis, Amma had said that they were not. She had also added: "We are Adivasis." Koravars are in fact one of the itinerant communities who were notified as a criminal tribe by the British in India. They are now listed as a "de-notified tribe." See Meena Radhakrishna, *Dishonoured by History: 'Criminal Tribes' and the British Colonial Policy* (New Delhi: Orient Longman, 2001) for a history of the *Criminal Tribes Act* enacted by the British government in 1871 and its impact on certain communities including the Koravars.

This place somewhere in Palakkad was where Amma's ancestors had found their "own god." The gods were two *kanna* fish – in fact a couple – that lived, romanced, and kissed in a well in the forest. Two girls who had gone up to the well to fetch water had first spotted the two fishes. They ran back home to report this finding to their parents-in-law. The discovery of those magical fishes in the well had surprised Amma's ancestors because "[t]hey did not know that god was in the well." At this point, Amma reminded me that the two brothers had also been discovered by Koravars in the forest after they had been given a flute and a pot by god.

Being worried that someone might take the fishes away, Amma's ancestors decided to protect them. The fish had to be guarded all night, and the many sons of the two brothers took turns to stand guard by the well. This arrangement, however, did not work well for the men who were married, and they decided to kill the fish. As they tried to kill the fish, "the male fish was struck in the ear," and its blood gushed out of the well like a fountain. The fishes died. When the elders found out, they were scared. Surprisingly, what worried them was not divine wrath, but the police. "The police knew about the fish," Amma said, and it was the police that had "asked [them] to take care of the fish." Thus in order to avoid trouble with the police for killing the fish, they decided to leave the place.

They took "thirty cattle," tied up grains like *chama* and *tena*, in bundles and set out in search of a new home.[26] "Like that from Kottekkad, they all came here," Amma said. At the time when they "left all that and came here," the railway track that runs close to Amma's present home had not been laid. Even the road that runs parallel to the tracks here had not been built. This is how Amma described the journey of her ancestors:

> They made a way and they came here. How they made their way was, the boys had long blades. With that they made [a way]. When they came from there, there was nobody here. Our great grandfathers[27] went inside and cut down trees. They cleared [land] for agriculture, and they cultivated *chama* and *ragi*. They cultivated those. That land is nearby. It is here.

Amma's account does not end here, but I want to pause to reflect on several aspects of this oral history that call attention. To begin with, I was struck by

[26] According to Amma, *Chama* and *tena* are names of grains that only her community knows about.

[27] This expression, along with "our fathers," is commonly used by Adivasis to refer to ancestors generally, and not specifically to one's father or grandfather.

the recurring theme of children with no parents and their journeys in both Maariamma's and Amma's accounts. All I have, unfortunately, are questions. The answers will have to wait for another day, if and when Maariamma or Amma decide to share more, or perhaps, when someone else decides to share other stories – such as the elderly woman in Vijaynagar who has on both her legs tattoos of two long fishes facing each other with their mouths touching as in a kiss. She did not acknowledge any connection of the tattoo to the story about the fishes that were gods. Reactions of other younger men and women during subsequent conversations also suggest that they are familiar with the story, but did not wish to say any more. Generally, except for Amma, Adivasis in these hamlets seemed reluctant to speak with me about gods and deities.

Amma's account also tells of another prior dispossession before their ancestors were forced to leave the forests. That is the story of how their ancestors came to live deep in the forests. They were forced to do so because they had no parents or anyone else to protect them from being beaten or killed. Amma's ancestors could have been among people who are believed to be the original inhabitants of the subcontinent thousands of years ago. These peoples were pushed deeper into the forests as successive waves of migrations and invasions from elsewhere within the subcontinent, as well as from the lands to the west of it, continued to increase demands for space and agricultural land. The accounts of violence passed down over generations in Amma's community could bear witness to that often-overlooked displacement.

In more recent times, Amma and other Adivasis in the area have continued to be alienated from lands they had cultivated for generations. Most of it was sold, she told me, by a man who was referred to by some others as a *jenmi*, who as explained below, was one of the stakeholders in the cultivated land under the traditional system of land tenure in the region. Amma told me that subsequently he also "gave" some of the land to her father. She showed me a deed executed on a stamp paper on August 27, 1962 by the man, who she referred to as "Kuttan," which is an affectionate shortened version of his name. The document states that he gave land measuring 1.4 acres as "*daan*" – a charitable donation – to all the "dependants." Amma's father is one of the persons named in the document.

According to Amma, this land was given to them because they lived on it and cultivated it. It was the land "for [them] to stay." They had been offered an alternative spot to live as well, but her grandparents had advised against moving to that place where it would be difficult to get "firewood and anything." Her account does not explain how the lands her ancestors had cultivated for a long time became someone else's to sell or give away.

In an effort to understand the nature of the transaction witnessed in the deed Amma showed me, I asked a few lawyers in the state about it. Some were as intrigued as I was. One suggested that this could either be a transfer mandated by land reforms legislation in the state that required "homestead lands" to be transferred to those who had lived on agricultural land for a long time or it could be one of the ways in which owners of large tracts of land in Kerala had avoided physically parting with lands in excess of what they could legally retain after the state enacted land reform legislation.[28] Another informed me that his grandfather routinely donated land to people who worked on his lands.

Amma never used the word "landlord" for the executor of the deed. Her references to him were always by his two names – his full name or simply "Kuttan." More than once, she repeated that the piece of land where her home stands today, was "given" to them because they "were doing agriculture" on this land, as they have done for a long time. That is how she had described her childhood: "We were doing agriculture. We had cattle, agricultural land and agriculture." When asked who they worked *for*, Amma frowned, in what seemed like an attempt to understand the question. She did not understand it the first time. When the question was repeated, she said: "We worked for ourselves." The conversation that followed revealed an understanding of relationships to land and to others connected to it that cannot simply be translated into any legal categories I am familiar with. From Amma's perspective, they did not work for anyone but themselves. "We did not work for any landlord," she said before adding: "We were doing agriculture." Amma's statement here clearly contradicts the "fact" of slavery and servitude of Eravalans and Malasars recorded in the written accounts of their history I have mentioned earlier in Chapter 2.

Amma mentioned that life became difficult after Kuttan sold the agricultural land to a Gounder from Tamil Nadu. He did that, she says, in order "[t]o get more money." My questions about how he could have sold land that (as I had understood from our conversation so far) belonged to her ancestors did not make much sense to Amma, even as I struggled to understand her responses. What I did understand clearly, however, is that Amma and I understand differently these relationships of belonging – of people to lands and of lands to people.

[28] See *Kerala Agrarian Relations Bill, 1957* (repealed); and the *The Kerala Land Reforms Act, 1963* that includes provisions for fixation of ceiling on land holdings, the vesting of lands in excess of the ceiling in the government, assignment of surplus lands to the landless, abolition of tenancy system, and assignment of proprietary right on land to the cultivating tenants.

For Amma, it is their ability to cultivate land that matters most. It is her family's inability to cultivate land now that has made their life difficult. The idea of land as a commodity that could be owned does not seem to play any role in this relationship. In fact neither the word nor the idea of ownership, as I understand it, appears in her recollection of the past or her understanding of the present. They lived and worked on lands "here," as did the man she calls Kuttan. Even though now her family possesses a document that indicates that they own the piece of land they live on, that is, the land transferred to them by Kuttan, what matters to her is that they cannot cultivate the land her ancestors had cleared when no one else was "here" anymore.

Other elders in the community I spoke with also did not generally speak of ownership in the context of land – either theirs or anyone else's, even as there were several references to "our land," and "our place." The people who are generally regarded as "owners" of farmlands in the area (for example, those after whom some hamlets have been named) were, with a few exceptions, almost always referred to by their names by the Adivasis. Some other words commonly used by the elders are "*swami*" (a reference to Brahmins), "*jenmi*," and "*kudiyan*."" These words denoted particular interests in and relationships to people on lands within the traditional system prevalent in this part of the subcontinent that have been fundamentally altered over the last two hundred years.

According to *The Cochin State Manual*, traditionally in Cochin as well as in neighboring Travancore and Malabar, the "property in soil" did not vest in either the sovereign or the cultivator but rather in an "intermediate class" known as the "*janmis*" (also written as *jenmi*).[29] The *jenmis* in turn leased lands to cultivators on a produce sharing system on a variety of tenures. According to the *Manual*, while several theories have been proposed, the origin of the *jenmi's* "proprietory right" and the system of tenures is considered to be "lost in the mists of antiquity.'[30]

The well-regarded *Logan's Malabar Manual* first published in 1887, however, suggests that the *jenmi's* "property in soil" is in fact a mistranslation. According to Logan, certain "castes and classes" in the state, who were "told off to the work of cultivation," held land "in trust."[31] This, according to Logan,

[29] Menon, *Cochin State Manual*, 385. I am also grateful to Professor N. S. Soman at the School of Legal Studies in Cochin for explaining some of the complexities of the traditional land tenure system of the region to me.

[30] Ibid., 385.

[31] P. J. Cherian, ed., *William Logan's Malabar Manual*, Volume 1 (Thiruvananthapuram: Kerala Gazetteers Department, 2000), 599.

was fundamental to understanding the Malayali land tenures.[32] Another fact he regarded as central to this system was that the "ruling authority" in the region customarily granted lands to Hindu "Brahmans" (as well as to Christians and Jews).[33] The grantees of the land acquired hereditary rights over the lands referred to as "*janmam*" (from "*janm*" meaning "birth"), and were therefore known as *jenmis*. The lands were cultivated under the supervision of another class referred to as the "*kanakkars*." In Logan's view, neither the *jenmis* nor the *kanakkars* were therefore the owners of land in the European sense, but they were merely hereditary holders of lands.

According to Logan, it was these "hereditary holdings" "freely bought and sold for a long time" that were erroneously understood as being equivalent to the "*dominium* of the Romans" by early British administrators, who perhaps imported the changing meanings of land as a commodity in Britain at the time.[34] Logan suggested that in contrast to the "Western or European idea" of property in soil or "ownership *in the soil alone*," the principle feature of the transactions in the region was transfer of "authority" with everything else being "mere appurtenances" to that authority.[35] He noted: "The European looks to *the soil*, and nothing but *the soil*. The Malayali on the contrary looks chiefly to *the people* located on the soil."[36] What the "Malayali" was buying or selling at the time was therefore not "the soil" but "positions with emoluments" and certain authority over different classes of people who lived on such lands.[37] Over time, mistranslation of custom by administrators and civil courts, a process in which the litigants who were mostly *jenmis* and *kanakkars*, and the changing political landscape of the region certainly played an important role as well, appears to have resulted in a replacement of "authority" by "property in soil" in the region.[38] It was through this process that the rights of cultivators of land who, according to Logan, were in fact the "co-proprietors" of lands with the *jenmis* in the region, were "virtually expropriated,"[39] and they began to be increasingly evicted from the lands.[40]

[32] Ibid.
[33] Ibid., 600.
[34] Ibid., 602.
[35] Ibid., 603.
[36] Ibid., emphasis in the original.
[37] Ibid.
[38] Ibid., 606. This is a very brief description of a complex process of mistranslation of local custom that occurred over a long period of time and in specific ways in various parts of the region. For a detailed understanding of the social, political, and legal changes that contributed to this change see Cherian, *William Logan's Malabar Manual*.
[39] Cherian, *William Logan's Malabar Manual*, 608.
[40] Ibid., 619.

The changes in the law relating to land over the last couple of centuries, however, do not appear to have altered many Adivasis' understanding of their relationship to land or to others who are related to the same land. As both Amma and Maariamma told me, they worked *for* themselves. They cultivated the land "here." Their relationship was with the land, and through that with others. In fact, it seems that in their perspective, each holder of an interest in land is still connected to others through these relationships to all the land "here." References to specific pieces of land were usually made when describing specific instances of separation from or denial of access to land.

Contrary to the accounts of administrators and researchers referred to in Chapter 2, most Eravalan and Malasar elders speak of their attachment to land they cultivated generally, not to an individual "*swami*" or "*jenmi*." Some older men described relationships that indicate to me a form of bonded labor, but to them it was an attachment *to the land* not to another person.[41] Maariamma and a few other elders insisted that they were free to work on any part of the land or even to leave, but no one did that because the work in any particular place was never finished; there was always something to be done on the land. The elderly women in particular denied that they or their ancestors had ever been anyone's "slaves" – a word used by some young men who seem to either view these traditional relations differently or understand the idea of property differently than their elders. Maariamma had visibly bristled at the suggestion of slavery. I was reminded of her reaction when I later read an account of "Eravallen" women who in 1909 were reported to have worked for the same wage as men of the tribe, "but [unlike the men] never agree[d] to serve in a state of bondage."[42]

As with the relationships with land, the relationships between humans who lived on the land and between non-Adivasi *jenmis* and Adivasi cultivators were often complex. For example, while speaking of the time when they received grains as payment in kind for their work in the fields, it was mentioned that the grains were never enough to last a week, and many increasingly received smaller volumes of grains from the *jenmis*. One elder also spoke about the encouragement he received for going to school from the man after whom the hamlet he lives in is named, and who appears to have been a *jenmi*. Some also spoke favorably of former *jenmis* than of "Gounders" who have been buying land in the area over the last few decades.

[41] See Murickan and George, *Development-Induced Displacement*, 71, where the fact of existence of bonded labor in Palakkad and two other districts in Kerala has been noted.

[42] Thurston, *Castes and Tribes of Southern India*, 211.

During one of our conversations, Maariamma mentioned that earlier when times were bad, they could go to the *muthalali* and borrow "ten rupees."[43] They could not, however, she said, go "to the *sarkar* [government] or to the police, or *vakkil* [lawyer] to ask for ten rupees." This is what Maariamma had said to a man she referred to as the "minister" when he asked her why they had started the protests against Coca-Cola. This statement clearly indicates how all the changes in the social and political landscape have affected their lives. It also points to the "unfolding agrarian crisis" in the state.[44] More than anything else, it indicates how important it is to understand all that the presence of Coca-Cola means in the place. It also points to the importance of engaging with all the ways in which Coca-Cola has changed the place and lives of those who live here. The minister, like so many others, may have only heard in Maariamma's words what he thought she was saying.

6.2. ADIVASI DISPOSSESSION IN KERALA

There are several moments in Eravalan oral history narrated by Amma that connect with available data and written historical records. According to one source, 1.9 million cases of alienation of "tribals" from lands occupied by them have been "officially reported" in India, of which 400,000 cases were "resolved" by the year 2001.[45] As in other parts of the country, alienation of land has been identified as a "crucial problem faced by Tribals" in Kerala as well.[46] The relationship of Adivasi displacement to processes of state formation in the subcontinent that accelerated during the colonial period, enclosures of forests, revenue measures that disadvantaged itinerant communities, enactment of legislation that restricted cultivation, hunting and fishing practices of communities who lived in forests, and changing concepts of private property as well as to the postcolonial development agenda has been

[43] Depending on the context, the word *muthalali* can generally be translated as landlord, head of a household, or a trade or business owner. It was, however, pointed out to me that earlier *muthalali* was a reference to a man of power, or someone who was favored by the king or upon whom an estate was bestowed by the king. Here Maariamma appeared to be referring to the man who sold the land she had cultivated to Coca-Cola.

[44] Ananthakrishnan Aiyer, "The Allure of the Transnational: Notes on Some Aspects of the Political Economy of Water in India," *Cultural Anthropology* 22:4 (2007): 640–658. Aiyer points out that the "Plachimada struggle" must also be "analyzed as part of the unfolding agrarian crisis" in India (Aiyer, "The Allure of the Transnational," 640).

[45] Govinda Chandra Rath, "Introduction," in *Tribal Development in India: The Contemporary Debate*, ed. Govinda Chandra Rath (New Delhi: Sage, 2006), 44. Further investigation is necessary in order to determine how these cases have in fact been resolved.

[46] Murickan and George, *Development-Induced Displacement*, 71.

documented.[47] Similar processes also took place in what is now Kerala, leading to widespread Adivasi displacement.[48] The journey of Amma's ancestors from Kottekkad could therefore be the history of many such forest communities that were forced out of their traditional homes because they were unable to hunt or fish. They could be the ones who fled their homes to escape the "police" who might hold them responsible for killing the fish as in Amma's account.[49]

Ottukan, an Adivasi man who like Amma spoke about ancestors who cleared the forest and "made land" for cultivation, also mentioned that it was during his father's time that the land was given to the man who had essentially been a supervisor. This is a reference to a dispossession that took place 50–60 years ago, around the time when a series of extensive land reforms were initiated in the state. The purpose of these reforms was to abolish the feudal system of tenancy in the state.[50] The reforms also imposed limits to land ownership, with surplus land to be transferred to the landless in the state.[51] Despite being hailed as "the first comprehensive measure of its kind attempted in India," and perhaps because the transformation they were meant to bring about was so radical and broad, the land reform measures in Kerala have met with both successes and failures.[52] As it turned out, the period since the land reforms have been introduced is also the period when cultivators, such as Ottukan's family, have lost most of their land.[53]

Although the abolition of the tenancy or *jenmi* system in the state is considered as a "remarkable success," that "freed" large numbers of cultivators from

47 For what are identified as the three phases of tribal land alienation in India, see Rath, "Introduction," 44. See also Radhakrishna, *Dishonoured by History*.

48 See Bindu Ramachandran, "Displacement of Land and Identity Crisis: Tribal Situation Today in Wayanad, Kerala," in *Land and Forest Rights of the Tribals Today*, ed. R. M. Sarkar (New Delhi, Serials Publications, 2006), 152–158; J. Devika, "The Capabilities Approach in Vernacular: The History in Kerala," *Economic and Political Weekly* 26–27 (June 26, 2010); Menon, *Cochin State Manual*, 55 and 472.

49 See for example, Kjosavik and Shanmugam, "Property Rights Dynamics," 1183–1260, which provides a detailed narrative of Adivasi dispossession and displacement in Wayanad in Kerala beginning in the fifteenth century. For how these processes worked in Europe, see Thompson, *Customs in Common*.

50 For a history and overview of the land reforms in Kerala, see Leiten, "The Human Development Puzzle," 47–68.

51 Ibid.

52 Ibid. See also Govindan Parayil and T. T. Sreekumar, "Kerala's Experience of Development and Change," *Journal of Contemporary Asia* 33:4 (2003): 465–492.

53 See *Kerala State Development Report 2008*, 359. The report notes that the "most blatant encroachment" on Adivasi lands in Kerala took place in the 1970s, that is, after the land reform laws were passed.

"Feudal subservience," the former *jenmis* were able to use "loopholes" in the legislation, often in connivance with officials who belonged to the same social class and caste, to avoid parting with the lands.[54] In many cases, the ones who replaced the *jenmis* as "owners" of land were not the actual tillers like Ottukan's grandfather, but the "supervisors" who proved their status as tenants on lands "owned" by the *jenmis*.[55] In cases in other parts of Kerala, "settler farmers who had acquired" lands traditionally occupied by tribes succeeded in becoming "owners" by claiming the status of a "tenant" on the lands held by members of tribes.[56] This often-overlooked aspect of the land reforms in Kerala in the last sixty years wherein cultivators were, contrary to the objective of the reform legislation, dispossessed and impoverished requires serious consideration. Whereas more research is called for to understand fully the complex social, political, and historical reasons behind this failure, there is enough to suggest both in available accounts and in the Adivasi narratives presented in this chapter to indicate that land reforms in the state have not prevented, and in some cases have even increased, alienation of Adivasi lands.

According to Ottukan, after their land was "given" to the man who replaced the previous *jenmi*, his father, and subsequently his brother and he himself worked as "slaves" for the new "landlord." They were not paid any wages other than a small quantity of *kambu* grains once a week. That amount did not last more than four days. For the rest of the week they depended on tubers and greens that grew in the area, and sometimes on fish they caught locally. Because they "did not have [their] own land" they had to "obey" the landowners. They were beaten up for taking anything from the land without permission. This is the life Ottukan remembers of his childhood. Things have improved now, according to him, because they can make their own decisions. But the land that was taken away has not been restored.

In the last six decades, Adivasis have been forced or tricked into parting with their lands through various means. As I discovered during my time in the hamlets, the process is continuing. There are several Adivasis who hold documents of ownership to some land. As Amma had explained they

54 Leiten, "The Human Development Puzzle," 59–60.

55 Parayil and Sreekumar, "Kerala's Experience of Development," 473 have argued that actual tillers and agricultural laborers did not benefit from land reforms.

56 *Kerala State Development Report 2008*, 359.

have used and occupied this land for generations, but they received documents with regard to specific pieces of land during the last sixty years. This land was either transferred by the *jenmis* or is the "excess land" acquired by the government from large landowners and transferred to them.[57] Despite being the owners of this land, many of them are unable to cultivate the land because they are denied access to the land by their powerful neighbors, who are the same people who either "donated" the land to them or owned the land before it was taken over and redistributed by the government. Several of these *jenmis* have also been replaced by "Gounders" who have acquired lands in the area in more recent times.

Attukaran, a young Adivasi man, owns an acre of agricultural land in the area, but he cannot cultivate his land because he has no way to access it. It is surrounded on all sides by land that belongs to a Gounder, who does not allow Attukaran to go through his lands to reach his own. But the Gounder can cultivate it, Attukaran explained to me. Since Attukaran's family needed money, they decided to "give" the land to the Gounder for four years in return for less than a hundred dollars. He does not know what will happen now that the period is up. The nature of this transaction remains a mystery as the Gounder has retained the document that was executed, for safekeeping, Attukaran explained.

Those who can muster the courage to approach the police to complain against such unlawful denial of access to their own lands, are turned away with advice to not cause trouble. According to Ottukan, there are over 130 such cases of alienation through fraud or by force in this area alone. He narrated the story of an Adivasi farmer who parted with fifteen acres of land in exchange for a bag of tobacco. It is these lands that Ottukan refers to when he says: "We are struggling for the lost land. The government is doing everything for the settlers. Not for the original inhabitants." According to him, the Revenue Divisional Officer, whom they have repeatedly approached, has acknowledged both the problem and the difficulty of doing anything to address the situation. A "minister" they met regarding these cases also expressed his inability to do anything, even as he agreed with the reality of alienation. According to Ottukan, "[t]he law is like that. Nothing can be done."

57 This was the land held by farmers in excess of the ceiling prescribed under the land reform laws enacted in the state. All such land, referred to locally as *michcha bhoomi*, had become vested in the state as per *The Kerala Land Reforms Act*, 1963.

6.3. LAW'S STORY OF ADIVASI LANDS

6.3.1. A *Law to Restore Alienated Adivasi Lands*

In April 1960 a Commission was appointed for "investigating and reporting on the problems of the Scheduled Tribes" in India.[58] The Scheduled Areas and Scheduled Tribes Commission, also referred to as the Dhebar Commission after its Chairman U. N. Dhebar, presented an extensive report in two volumes with several recommendations covering a range of fields including administration, agriculture, industry, education, and creation of land records in order to protect the interests of Scheduled Tribes in the country. At the outset, the chapter on Kerala in the Commission's report states that nothing had been done in order to "safeguard the rights of the tribals in land or to protect them from exploitation by moneylenders."[59] The Commission specifically noted the fact that tribes were being "pushed out" and "deprived" of "their lands."[60] It also noted the high levels of indebtedness of "tribals" and the existence of bonded labor in parts of the state.[61]

In recognition of the fact that Adivasis were increasingly being cheated or forced out of "their traditional lands," and perhaps realizing that this was a significant cause for their impoverishment, the Government of Kerala enacted *The Kerala Scheduled Tribes (Regulation of Transfer of Land and Restoration of Alienated Land) Act* in 1975.[62] This Act, similar to others enacted in other parts of the country, was based on the recommendations of the Dhebar Commission as well as the recommendations of an Evaluation Committee appointed by the state government in 1961.[63] It has also been suggested, however, that the immediate reason for enacting these laws was an increase in deaths of Adivasis due to starvation in the early 1970s.[64]

[58] The mandate of the Commission is stated in the letter that accompanied its report submitted to the president of India in October 1961. The text of the letter No. 35/36/60-TC is reproduced in the Report. See *Dhebar Commission Report*.

[59] *Dhebar Commission's Report*, 386.

[60] Ibid.

[61] Ibid., 387.

[62] *The Kerala Scheduled Tribes (Regulation of Transfer of Land and Restoration of Alienated Land) Act*, Act 31 of 1975. The reasons are acknowledged in the "Statement of Objects and Reasons" for the Act published in the *Kerala Gazette Extraordinary*, February 20, 1975.

[63] See ibid., "Statement of Objects and Reasons."

[64] Mukundan C. Menon, "A Fact File on Tribal Land," NCHRO, accessed August 10, 2014, http://www.nchro.org/index.php?option=com_content&view=article&id=43:a-fact-file-on-tribal-land&catid=17:campaigns&Itemid=27.

At the time when the Bill was introduced in the Kerala Legislative Assembly, a minister had stated that "the Government treats all the alienated tribal lands as 'stolen property'."[65] Although the "Statement of Objects and Reasons" for the enactment published at the time does not contain the same words, it recognizes two facts of immense significance: the traditional occupation of certain lands by tribals and the taking of such lands by nontribal people. The passage below indicates this unequivocal acknowledgment:

> It has been noticed that the extent of land which has been under the *traditional occupation* of the Scheduled Tribes in the State is steadily on the decrease due to alienation, lease, mortgage and above all, due to *unauthorized occupation of tribal lands by non-tribal people*. In tribal areas the unsophisticated tribals are being dupe[d] into transactions which make them part with their *traditional lands* for very small sums of money. The Evaluation Committee constituted by the Government in 1961 has suggested that special legislation should be introduced to protect the interests of the tribals in lands under their *traditional occupations*; and that this legislation should result in a general prohibition of transfers whether by sale, [m]ortgage, gift or lease of tribal lands to non-tribal people. [emphasis added][66]

The law that was enacted, the Act of 1975, not only restricted the transfer of land from Adivasis to non-Adivasis without prior approvals, it also declared as invalid all transactions under which land had been transferred by "a member of the Scheduled Tribe to a person other than a member of a Scheduled Tribe."[67] It further provided for the restoration of possession of all such land transferred after January 1, 1960.[68] Any consideration that a member of the Scheduled Tribe had received at the time of transfer was to be returned, for which loans were to be made available by the government.[69] Most significantly, under this law the burden of proving the validity of any transfer of land from a member of a Scheduled Tribe to a nonmember was placed upon the person who claimed that the transfer was valid.[70] Given that the lands in question were in possession of nonmembers, this burden in fact lay on the nontribal settlers.

65 Ibid.

66 See *The Kerala Scheduled Tribes (Regulation of Transfer of Land and Restoration of Alienated Land) Act*.

67 Ibid., sections 4, 5.

68 Ibid., section 6.

69 Ibid., sections 11, 12.

70 Ibid., section 8.

Even though this law did not address the issue of land alienated before 1960 at all, it had some ameliorative potential. Unfortunately, but perhaps unsurprisingly, given the entrenched interests likely to be disrupted,[71] this law remained dormant for another ten years. It was brought into effect only in 1986, albeit with retrospective effect.[72] But even then, despite many petitions filed by members of various Scheduled Tribes in the state seeking restoration under the Act, nothing much changed. Of the 166 acres of land under dispute in the Palakkad district where the Coca-Cola plant is located, not a single piece of land has been restored.[73]

The situation in Palakkad is not different from other parts of the state.[74] A report published in 2008 records that the "settler farmers" have resorted to all kinds of action including "physical violence" in order to stall the proceedings for restoration.[75] As I have mentioned before, many Adivasis spoke in whispers about the land that has been taken away from them. One of the elders even warned me to be careful, as talking about these disputes could result in me being "thrown out" by the Gounder. The fear in his eyes said a lot more.

Successive governments in Kerala have failed to act despite repeated demands by Adivasi groups and their supporters. In this inaction there appears to be complete consensus between the two political coalitions in Kerala. Both the Communist Party-led Left Democratic Front and the Congress Party-led United Democratic Front have failed to keep promises made to Adivasi leaders from time to time. Even specific directions from the Kerala High Court in this regard appear to have been disregarded equally by both groups. This is one of those stories about the "model state" of Kerala that is hardly ever told. It is, however, a very instructive story about the realities of addressing historical injustices in a modern liberal democracy – a story that is a familiar one in other similar democracies.

In 1988 a petition was filed in the High Court of Kerala for issuance of a writ of mandamus directing the state of Kerala to implement the Act of 1975. The petitioner was P. Nalla Thampy Thera, a doctor who had been working among the Adivasis in Kerala. Relying on the assurance of the Additional Advocate General who represented the state of Kerala in the proceedings,

[71] A member of the Kerala Legislative Assembly I met in the area comes from a family that owns considerable land. He was most emphatic in his denial of land alienation being an issue in the area.

[72] *State of Kerala* v. *Peoples Union for Civil Liberties*, para. 4.

[73] *Kerala State Development Report 2008*, 172.

[74] Ibid.

[75] Ibid.

that the "Act would be enforced in all its rigour," in October 1993 the High Court directed that all applications for restoration of land be decided within six months.[76]

Thereafter the state sought repeated extensions of time until the High Court issued detailed specific directions regarding the time and manner in which the applications should be processed. At this stage the court also seems to have taken over the role of monitoring the progress made by the state officials.[77] The court also noted the fact that Palakkad was one of the districts where the pendency of applications for restoration of land was "unusually large."[78] After this order, the relevant authorities issued directions for restoration of land in many cases.[79]

However, no actual restoration of land took place.[80] Therefore another application was filed before the High Court against this inaction in 1996. While responding to this application, the Additional Advocate General explicitly assured the court that orders for restoration passed by the authorities "under the 1975 Act would be implemented."[81] In August of that year, the court once again directed that the lands in respect to which no appeal was pending, be restored "within six weeks."[82] In order to enable this, the court also issued the following directions to the state:

> 2. In view of the submission that the officers are meeting with resistance in restoring possession the State and the District Superintendents of Police of all Districts are directed to afford the needed protection to the Revenue Divisional Officers to carry out the duty of restoring possession to the Tribals.
>
> 3. The State and the Collectors of the various districts are directed to make available to the Revenue Divisional Officers the necessary man power and support to carry out the implementation of the orders for restoration passed under the Act.[83]

In a move that demonstrates clearly the entrenched interests and the clout of "settlers" in the government, the state that thus far had been promising to do its utmost to implement an enacted law, filed another appeal. The matter was referred to the Full Bench of the Kerala High Court, which stayed all

76 *State of Kerala* v. *Peoples Union for Civil Liberties*, para. 7.
77 Ibid., paras 7–8.
78 Ibid., para. 11.
79 Ibid., para. 12.
80 Ibid., para. 13.
81 Ibid., para. 14.
82 Ibid., para. 16.
83 Ibid.

proceedings based on the state's claim that it was amending the law. A Bill proposing the amendment of the Act of 1975 was passed by the state legislature with the support of all members across party lines, except for one woman MLA.[84] The Bill was, however, ultimately unsuccessful as the president of India declined to give his assent.[85]

The government managed to delay the matter of restoring Adivasi lands for another two years by seeking further extensions in court. Finally, faced with contempt of court proceedings, the state once again sought to amend the law. In a statement made before the Kerala High Court, it said that the new law would be a "permanent solution to the problem of alienation of tribal lands" that took place between 1960 and 1986.[86] Thus, it was "in the interest of justice" that the state sought yet another extension from the court while it amended the law to bring about a "permanent solution." It was given three months to do so "in the interest of justice."[87]

In 1999 the State Legislature enacted the *Kerala Restriction on Transfer by and Restoration of Lands to the Scheduled Tribes Act*.[88] This new law repealed the 1975 Act.[89] That the new law was meant to undo most of what the earlier law was meant to achieve is evident even from a quick reading of the new Act. Unlike the 1975 Act, the new law applies only to agricultural lands, leaving unaddressed the issue of "stolen" nonagricultural lands. But this is a significant move on more than one count. First, it eliminated the need for a final assent from the president.[90] Second, and more crucially, it ensures the interests of the "settler farmers" in several ways. Under the new law all transfers of lands from tribals to nontribals that are less than two hectares are to be considered valid. Even in cases of transfers of land that is more than two hectares, the nontribal can retain possession of up to two hectares of agricultural lands. A tribal from whom this land had been originally taken could instead get some

84 Menon, "A Fact File on Tribal Land."

85 Ibid. See also *State of Kerala* v. *Peoples Union for Civil Liberties*, para. 18. One of the reasons for this refusal was that the 1975 Act had been included in the Ninth Schedule of the Constitution of India and as such, could not be amended by a state legislature.

86 *State of Kerala* v. *Peoples Union for Civil Liberties*, para. 21.

87 Ibid.

88 *The Kerala Restriction on Transfer by and Restoration of Lands to the Scheduled Tribes Act*, 1999 published in *Kerala Gazette Extraordinary*, April 20, 1999.

89 Ibid., section 22.

90 As per the division of powers between the Union (Federal) government and the states (provinces) set out in the Constitution of India, the "transfer and alienation of agricultural lands" is included in the state list not the Union list. Therefore, states have the power to legislate on this matter. See *Constitution of India*, Seventh Schedule.

other land from the government.[91] This also applies to those lands for which orders of restoration had been made under the 1975 Act, but possession was not effected. All the "settler farmers" who had thus far refused to give up possession did not now have to resort to extra-legal means. The new law validates their former illegal occupation.

Another significant change in the new Act is the absence of the word "alienated" from the title of the Act, eclipsing thereby an entire history and the possibility of any meaningful justice for the Adivasis in the state. The "permanent solution" to the problem of alienated tribal lands arrived at by the state was therefore that both the fact of alienation, and the alienated lands themselves, be forgotten by the Adivasis.

In what is perhaps the biggest setback in addressing historical wrongs, and in keeping with the goal of forgetting, the meaning of 'transfer' has also been altered in the new Act. From being defined in the 1975 law as "an act by which immovable property is conveyed by any documentary or oral transaction" that included "*voluntary surrender and abandonment*,"[92] transfer under the new law "means the transfer made by any person belonging to the Scheduled Tribe of lands in his *ownership and possession* to a person other than a member of the Scheduled Tribe."[93] The particular meaning given to the word transfer in the earlier Act was clearly aimed at recognizing and addressing the particular nature of transactions and the circumstances in which such transfers in fact took place between tribals and nontribals. By introducing the concepts of ownership and possession, the new law critically reverses the burden of proof, placing an evidentiary burden on Adivasis that most of them are unlikely to be able to meet. How would Amma, who for example, thinks through relationships of belonging, prove ownership and possession of her ancestors in a civil suit? What kind of legal claim can statements like "we worked for ourselves" be translated into? Yet she would have to find a way to do this, if she decides to make a claim under the new law. The burden of proof is squarely on the dispossessed now, as section 8 of the 1975 Act that placed the burden of proving a transfer to be valid on the person who claimed it to be so, is missing in the new law.

[91] *The Kerala Restriction on Transfer by and Restoration of Lands to the Scheduled Tribes Act*, 1999, sections 5 & 6.

[92] *The Kerala Scheduled Tribes (Regulation of Transfer of Land and Restoration of Alienated Land) Act*, 1975, section 2(g) [emphasis added].

[93] *Kerala Restriction on Transfer by and Restoration of Lands to the Scheduled Tribes Act*, 1999, sections 2(g) [emphasis added].

Restoration of land that had been used and occupied by the Adivasis, and has admittedly been taken from them, is no longer an issue. As Ottukan said, "the law is like that." The "permanent solution" to theft of tribal lands is that all, especially those from whom it was taken, must forget the theft. The now impoverished and landless Adivasis can certainly submit applications for land, not the one that was taken from them, but for some other land. The state will give them land somewhere, as and when it is available. Unfortunately, as everyone in Kerala repeatedly and anxiously points out, there is no more land for anyone anymore. Even if there were lands that could be given to Adivasis, no thought appears to have been given to the loss of livelihood, cultural practices, and identity that accompany displacement of Adivasi communities from their traditional lands.[94]

Given that the new law undid what had been promised earlier, this legislation was unacceptable to the Adivasis who in 1999 were still awaiting the restoration of land prescribed, and in many cases already ordered, under the 1975 law. Two separate organizations challenged the constitutional validity of the Act of 1999 before the Kerala High Court.[95] The central government, also a party in the cases, supported the "stand of the tribals" in its response.[96] In August 2000 the High Court declared the provisions challenged by the petitioners as discriminatory, arbitrary, and ultra vires.[97] The court also noted that the enactment basically seeks to nullify a judicial decision.[98] It therefore directed that the state of Kerala implement the orders of restoration made under the 1975 Act. In the court's view the new law destroyed "a vested right accrued to the members of Scheduled Tribes" under the provisions of the 1975 Act.[99] Its enactment exhibited a "colorable exercise of power" by the legislature.[100] State of Kerala appealed to the Supreme Court of India.

Even as the debate on the legality of the new law continued in courts, Adivasi groups and their supporters continued to protest against the government's

94 For an account of such losses, see M. Sasikumar, "Towards Muthanga and After: The Tribal Movements for Land in Kerala," in *Land and Forest Rights of the Tribals Today*, ed. R. M. Sarkar, (New Delhi: Serials Publications, 2006), 132–142.

95 The two organizations were the Kerala state unit of the Peoples Union of Civil Liberties and Niyamvedi.

96 *State of Kerala* v. *Peoples Union for Civil Liberties*, para. 24. It is worth noting that Bhartiya Janata Party that led the coalition that formed the government in the center in 1999 had not won any seats in Kerala. The Congress Party and the Communist Party were leading in Kerala at the time. The Communist Party was also leading the state government at the time.

97 Ibid., para. 25.

98 Ibid., para. 68.

99 Ibid., para. 26.

100 Ibid.

failure to restore land. In 2001, the Adivasi-Dalit Action Council led an agitation outside the state secretariat in Kerala that lasted for 48 days.[101] In order to "settle the agitation by the tribals," the chief minister of the state called a meeting on October 16, 2001 during which an "agreement" was reached between the state and the Adivasi leaders after a "detailed discussion."[102] The document signed by the chief minister, the chief secretary, the principal secretary, and another officer of the Scheduled Tribes and Scheduled Castes Welfare Department addressed several issues. It was decided that the "distribution" (not restoration) of land to Adivasis "would start on 1st January 2002."[103] To tide over the initial period before the land thus "distributed" could begin to generate income, "job opportunities and enterprises" would be provided to tribal families for the first five years.[104] Two other significant decisions were also taken at this meeting: firstly, that the state of Kerala would approach the central government for having the areas occupied by the Adivasis in the state declared as "Scheduled Areas" and secondly that the "involvement of the tribals would be ensured in the planning and implementation of projects related to them."[105]

This agreement is a significant event that suggests a fundamental departure from the long-standing Adivasi demand for restoration of *alienated* lands. After over five decades of struggle for the lands that have been fraudulently or forcefully taken from them, the Adivasi leaders present in the meeting appear to have agreed to what was perhaps seen as a more workable outcome at the time – land for all Adivasis in the state as well as a promise of consultation on matters that affect lives of the Adivasis. It is clear, however, that the Adivasi leaders did not give up their opposition to the Act of 1999. This is suggested by the fact that one of the promises the government made in that agreement was that the Act would "be implemented only as per the final verdict of the Supreme Court" in the appeals against the High Court's decision.[106] In 2001 the Adivasi leaders perhaps did not foresee how the compromises made then would affect the outcome in the appeal in the Supreme Court of India. That decision was not handed down until 2009.

101 R. Krishnakumar, "A Conflict in the Forest," *Frontline* 20:5 (2003), accessed August 11, 2014, http://www.frontline.in/static/html/fl2005/stories/20030314003603700.htm.

102 See Bhaskaran, "Text of the Agreement between the Government and the Agitation Committee of the Tribals," in *Mother Forest: The Unfinished Story of C.K. Janu*, trans. N. Ravi Shankar (New Delhi: Kali for Women, 2004), 59–61.

103 Ibid., 59.

104 Ibid., 60.

105 Ibid.

106 Ibid., 60.

6.3.2. *Muthanga*

In the mean time, after the state of Kerala failed to honor its other promises, several Adivasi families led by the *Adivasi Gothra Mahasabha* (Adivasi Grand Assembly), moved into the Muthanga range of the Wayanad Wildlife Sanctuary in January 2003 by way of protest. According to an account published at the time, the Adivasis "declared 'self-rule' in the area," and also denied entry into the area to non-Adivasis including state officials.[107] They also began to cultivate the land as "they had nowhere else to go."[108] This occupation continued for 45 days during which time both the State Forest Department and "some environmental groups" protested against the government's inaction against this "encroachment" on "fragile forest tracts."[109]

According to available reports, on February 17th, a "mysterious" fire erupted near the Adivasi settlement in the forest.[110] There are conflicting accounts of the cause of this fire. A group of twenty-one people that included forest officials as well as unspecified others, who visited the area to enquire about the fire, were allegedly taken hostage by the Adivasis. The Adivasis claimed that these people had confessed to starting the fire. They allowed them to leave after the District Collector of Wayanad agreed to record the statements of the "hostages" as to the circumstances in which they were "held captive."[111]

The situation appears to have escalated around this time, even as particular facts and causes are disputed by all concerned. There is indication that non-Adivasi residents began protesting against the encroachment and denial of entry into the "tribal land" and there were increased demands for the arrest of Adivasi leaders.[112] The state government finally arrived at the decision to evict the Adivasis. It maintains that this decision was conveyed to the occupants of the forestland.[113]

On February 19th, a police operation to evict the Adivasis from the forest began. This action turned "increasingly brutal and insensitive," especially after some Adivasis, who were reported to be armed with bows, arrows, and sickles, allegedly "captured a police constable and a forest official" and threatened to kill them unless the forcible eviction stopped.[114] The police reportedly went

107 Krishnakumar, "A Conflict in the Forest."
108 Ibid.
109 Ibid.
110 Ibid.
111 Ibid.
112 Ibid.
113 Ibid.
114 Ibid.

"berserk from then on."[115] They opened fire and kicked and beat up fleeing Adivasi men, women, children, and elders. Huts and other belongings were set on fire. Several Adivasis as well as policemen were injured, and according to the police two men died: an Adivasi man and a police constable. This number was disputed by the Adivasis and the opposition parties, who alleged that the number of Adivasi victims was much higher.[116] One source suggests that sixteen people died in Muthanga.[117]

Several Adivasi men and women were also arrested in Muthanga. Some of those arrested were accompanied by their children while in custody.[118] The events in Muthanga later led to arrests of some Adivasis who were not present in the area at the relevant time.[119] C. K. Janu, the Adivasi woman who has actively led the struggle for land in Kerala and had been invited to inaugurate the launch of the sit-in agitation against Coca-Cola in Plachimada, was not present in Muthanga on the day the events described above took place. But she subsequently surrendered to prevent further harassment of the Adivasis by the police. She has alleged that she was tortured by the local police while in custody.[120] The police have, however, refuted all this and claim to have arrested her through their own efforts.[121]

The events in Muthanga resulted in an inquiry by the National Human Rights Commission. The criminal investigation that was initially handled by the local state police was subsequently handed over to the Central Bureau of Investigation, which was also directed to investigate the allegations of custodial torture against the local police.[122] The Adivasis have all along maintained that they entered the forestland by way of protest against the breach of the agreement of October 2001 by the government. A final resolution is yet to be seen, even as criminal proceedings against the Adivasis charged with offences ranging from criminal trespass to illegal detention, conspiracy, and murder continue.[123]

115 Ibid.

116 Ibid.

117 Rath, "Introduction," 45.

118 C. K. *Janu* v. *Director, Central Bureau of Investigation*, December 4, 2008, unreported decision of the High Court of Kerala in WP(C). No. 32732 of 2003(V), para. 18.

119 Ibid.

120 Ibid., paras.16, 27.

121 Ibid., para. 28.

122 For more on this and other related issues considered by the Kerala High Court, see *C. K. Janu* v. *Director, Central Bureau of Investigation*, 2008.

123 Ibid. See also *P. Viswambharam* v. *State of Kerala*, November 10, 2010, unreported decision of the High Court of Kerala in Crl.MC.No.2264 of 2008.

The incident in Muthanga is only one episode in the long, mainly peaceful, Adivasi struggle for alienated lands in Kerala, however, the violence associated with it has significantly changed the non-Adivasi attitudes toward Adivasis in the state. Most significantly, it gave an easy way out to the government by shifting the focus away from its inaction toward fulfilling the terms of the agreement of October 2001 toward the need to address the "law and order" situation in the state. This concern for maintaining public order also appears to have figured prominently in its arguments before the Supreme Court in its appeal pertaining to the 1999 Act mentioned above.[124]

6.3.3. *The Legalities of "Paper Owners"*: State of Kerala *v.* People's Union for Civil Liberties

On July 21, 2009, the Supreme Court of India upheld the validity of the *Kerala Restriction on Transfer by and Restoration of Lands to the Scheduled Tribes Act, 1999*, accepting several of the arguments advanced by the state.[125] It is clear from the judgment that it is an admitted fact that the lands in question are in fact "tribal lands," that is, lands traditionally owned, occupied, possessed, and used by peoples who are classified as members of the Scheduled Tribes in Kerala. The fact that these lands are now in possession of nontribals is also not disputed. It also cannot be denied that a law of the state was not acted upon for decades to the detriment of its intended beneficiaries.

Whereas the fact of transfer of land is not disputed, the fraudulent nature of the transactions, acknowledged clearly in the 1975 Act, and in the statement of its objects and reasons, is not something the Supreme Court goes into in its decision. In fact, if one were to read only the judgment, it would seem that all these lands were in fact sold by members of Scheduled Tribes for good consideration to *bone fide* buyers who just happened to be nontribal. If this is a presumption made by the court, the judgment does not offer any clues as to the basis for it.

This is not, however, the only presumption that appears to have been made here. One argument advanced by the state of Kerala in the court is that since the "tribals" had not themselves filed any petition, "it must be presumed that they were not aggrieved by the provisions of the 1999 Act."[126] The basis of this presumption, if any were offered to the court, is not revealed in the judgment. How such a presumption can be made about Adivasis who repeatedly

[124] See *State of Kerala & Anr.* v. *People's Union for Civil Liberties*, para. 147.
[125] Ibid.
[126] *State of Kerala & Anr.* v. *People's Union for Civil Liberties*, para. 8.

approach the police to complain about not being able to cultivate their lands, only to be turned away with advice to not create trouble, is not clear. Surely the state of Kerala and its representatives in court were not unaware of the realities of Adivasis who have to save money for weeks before they can afford to forgo a day's wage and the bus fare to visit the nearest legal aid office. Sometimes, they decide to spend that money on buying rice instead, especially since they are repeatedly told that the law is "like that" and nothing can be done. The judgment does not reveal whether the state was asked to provide any evidence in this regard, or whether the petitioners were given a chance to rebut this presumption. Moreover, even if an opportunity had been provided, whether the resources available to the petitioners would have enabled them to tender evidence to rebut the presumption is another matter altogether.[127]

Another presumption the Supreme Court felt it could "safely" make is that the members of the Scheduled Tribes in Kerala are educated and that "most of them are serving various institutions in the State of Kerala and/or other parts of India."[128] This "safe presumption" was no doubt inspired both by the image of Kerala as a "model state" in India generally, as well as the state's specific submission that "the literacy rate of the tribals of Kerala is 57%."[129] If the fact that most Adivasis I spoke with in Palakkad could not read the consent forms printed in Malayalam is any indication, it is highly unlikely that most Adivasis from Kerala are spending comfortable lives in the service of the "various institutions" in the country.[130]

Moreover, other data that were either not placed before the court or not considered by it also tells its own story. For example, the literacy rate for non-Adivasis in Kerala is 89.81 percent.[131] What does this difference of nearly 33 percent indicate? Other data show that the Adivasi "population" in Kerala is "overwhelmingly rural" and therefore more likely to be dependent on land and forests.[132] The percentage of Adivasis that are counted as living "below poverty line," that is, the poorest of the poor, in rural Kerala in 1999/2000 was 24.2 percent – a much higher percentage than any other social group in the state.[133] The state and the court, while making their presumptions, may have had in mind the few Adivasis who manage to work and study their way into

[127] For the ways in which access to resources impacts parties in a litigation, see Galanter, "Why the 'Haves' Come Out Ahead."
[128] *State of Kerala & Anr.* v. *People's Union for Civil Liberties*, para. 34.
[129] Ibid., para. 153.
[130] Ibid., para. 167.
[131] *Kerala State Development Report* 2008, 356.
[132] Ibid.
[133] Ibid., 357.

universities. There are definitely some who do. A professor narrated to me the story of one such Adivasi student who has been accepted at a university in Kerala, but is unable to cope with coursework that is all in the English language. Not having had a chance to previously attend (the expensive) schools where the medium of instruction is English, or grow up in a family or neighborhood where English is the language of everyday conversations, the student is not only struggling with coursework but is very likely also struggling for social acceptance in an unkind environment.[134] The professor, who narrated the story and shared his own frustration with the situation and his personal efforts to do something, indicated that the student is likely to drop out.

Although unexamined presumptions about "tribals" in Kerala may have enabled the court to distance itself from lived realities and to write the judgment as it did, they are not the primary basis for it. In upholding the validity of the 1999 Act, the court relied on legal principles. Firstly, it relied on a mass of precedents to hold that as long as a legislature is competent to enact a particular law, its motives for doing so are irrelevant. In the Supreme Court's opinion, once the legislative competence of the Kerala state legislature had been upheld, the doctrine of "colorable legislation" could not have been invoked by the High Court while deciding the case. With the focus on technical interpretation of procedures, the fact that most of the people who form the legislature belong to landowning castes in the state is immaterial. The fact that the dispossessed did not have any say in the making of this new law is not relevant. That this new law seriously affects the rights of "tribals who enjoy the protection of Constitution of India" was also not relevant in the opinion of the Supreme Court.[135] The historical injustices that led to inclusion of provisions for their protection in the Constitution would also appear to be irrelevant by that logic.

Most significantly, the Supreme Court held that the dispossessed had no rights to restoration of their lands. In this the court basically agreed with the state, which had argued that the "members of the Scheduled Tribes had no fundamental or common law right to obtain restoration of possession of their lands which had already been alienated."[136] The court did not disagree with this. In fact, it also cited in this regard the precedent in *Narmada Bachao*

[134] See for example Anoop Kumar, "The Death of Anil Meena," *The Indian Express*, March 14, 2012, accessed August 11, 2014, http://www.indianexpress.com/news/the-death-of-anil-meena/923471/0.

[135] *State of Kerala & Anr.* v. *People's Union for Civil Liberties*, para. 82.

[136] Ibid., para. 34.

Andolan v. *Union of India and Others* handed down by the Supreme Court in 2000,[137] where it held that the "displacement of the tribals and other persons would not per se result in the violation of their fundamental or other rights."[138] Expressed in the language of "assimilation," "betterment," and "progress," the opinion of that court was that the displaced would be better off than they were in their "tribal hamlets."[139]

One reason why the court felt no constitutional rights could come to the aid of the Adivasis demanding restoration of their lands was that these lands were not located in what are declared as Scheduled Areas elsewhere in the country, and are governed by the special provisions contained in the Fifth Schedule of the Constitution of India.[140] Ironically, a suggestion had been made to the Dhebar Commission by the government of Kerala (and some other state governments) to declare the areas with a high percentage of "tribal population" in the state as Scheduled Areas, in hope of receiving more funds from the central government for the development of these areas.[141] After giving the proposal some "serious consideration," and noting that the process of scheduling additional areas was likely to create additional burden on the administration, the Commission proposed an alternative to declaring additional Scheduled Areas.[142] This alternative approach proposed by the Commission included protection of their "rights in land," and "in forests," as well as "protection of their way of life," including their "religious beliefs" and "customs" through enactment of necessary laws by state governments.[143] The Commission had also recommended that until such legislation

[137] *Narmada Bachao Andolan* v. *Union of India*.

[138] Ibid., para. 62. This is perhaps what an Adivasi representative in the Constituent Assembly had feared when he had demanded that any discussion on a proposed fundamental right guaranteeing every citizen a right to acquire land and settle anywhere in the country take into consideration the views of Adivasis who feared losing lands they had traditionally lived on. Had the Adivasis' right to not be alienated from their lands been recognized as an inalienable right at the time the Constitution was framed, it would perhaps have not been as easy to hold that they had no legal right to seek restoration of alienated lands. See Parmar, "Undoing Historical Wrongs."

[139] *Narmada Bachao Andolan* v. *Union of India*, para. 62.

[140] See *Constitution of India*, Fifth Schedule. Part C of the Schedule defines Scheduled Areas as any areas that are declared as such by the president of the country. The phrase is borrowed from the colonial administration and was used to demarcate areas traditionally occupied by tribes. The Schedule authorizes the governor of each state where Scheduled Areas exist to regulate the transfer of property in such areas. See also "Criteria for Scheduled Areas" in *Dhebar Commission's Report*, 60.

[141] *Dhebar Commission's Report*, 65.

[142] Ibid., 66.

[143] Ibid., 66–67.

was enacted, "tribal land should be regarded as on inalienable tenure and the registration authorities should be directed not to register transfer of land by tribals to non-tribals."[144]

The 1975 Act was in fact such a law enacted as an alternative to declaring Scheduled Areas in Kerala. The repeal of that Act means that Adivasis in the state can avail neither the constitutional provisions applicable to Scheduled Areas for protecting their lands nor the legislation that was meant to fulfill a similar purpose in areas not declared as Scheduled Areas. This crucial fact was left out from the law's story.

Having determined the general unavailability of a right to restoration of lands under the Indian Constitution or the common law, the court turned to the specific rights available under the 1975 Act. In this regard, the court opined that any rights that were "conferred upon" the tribals under the 1975 Act "were statutory in nature," and could not be raised "to the exalted status of Constitutional rights."[145] Thus, any "right which may be conferred by a statute can also be taken away by another."[146]

The Supreme Court also disagreed with the view of the High Court of Kerala (which had ruled against the state) that certain "vested rights" had accrued in favor of the tribals under the 1975 Act. Through a long analysis of the nature of "vested" and "prescriptive" rights to property, the Supreme Court arrived at the conclusion that the current non-Adivasi holders of the Adivasi lands had a right to the property they hold. Their right is protected by Article 300A of the Constitution, that prescribes that no person be "deprived of his property save by authority of law."[147] Moreover, their right is also protected because, the court declared: "[i]t is a human right."[148] The Adivasis from whom they had taken the lands, on the other hand, had no right to restoration, either constitutional or human. The fact that restoration had already been ordered in many cases did not mean the Adivasis had acquired a "vested" right, according to the Supreme Court. A vested right to get back the possession of their lands would have "accrued" to the "tribals," the court held, had they paid the compensation determined under the 1975 Act. Since no such compensation was paid to the current holders of land, no right of restoration had accrued.[149]

[144] Ibid., 67.
[145] *State of Kerala & Anr. v. People's Union for Civil Liberties*, para. 85.
[146] Ibid.
[147] Ibid., para. 123.
[148] Ibid.
[149] Ibid.

Here again, a crucial fact that seems to have been missed is that the Act provided for the compensation to be paid out of loans to be advanced by the state, because it was known to the state that the dispossessed Adivasis do not have any other way to make these payments to get back their own lands. But the same state had for two decades been busy defying court orders to implement the Act. The "settlers," on the other hand, who were refusing to restore possession, would not have accepted the money even if an Adivasi had managed to offer it. The judgment does not indicate whether these facts were considered by the court.

In passage after passage of careful deliberation on prescriptive and indefeasible rights to property, the doctrine of eminent domain, rights of "vendors," "vendees," and subsequent *bona fide* purchasers, and the difference between land that lies in Scheduled Areas versus that which does not, one fact is conspicuous by its absence: It is an admitted position that most, if not all, of these transfers were effected through fraud or force. As indicated in the report of the Dhebar Commission and acknowledged by the state itself while enacting the 1975 Act, the "property" in question are lands that were initially occupied and used by tribals and were taken over by nontribals through various, often fraudulent, means. Contrary to the court's observation that these transactions were valid under existing law at the time, and only made invalid by the 1975 Act, the Act was in fact passed *in recognition of* the fraudulent and forcible dispossession of tribals. The wrongful taking of Adivasi lands preceded the Act, which was an attempt, however inadequate, to address a past and continuing injustice.

Finally, the Supreme Court also accepted the state's position that the new Act was based on the new "ground realities."[150] Foremost among these was that the new law was necessary to "avert a conflict between tribals and non-tribals."[151] Moreover, the state claimed that it had consulted various "tribal organizations."[152] According to it, "many" of these organizations did not insist on restoration of "the very same land" that had been alienated.[153] The state had also held discussions with the "present occupants of the alienated tribal lands."[154] Several of these, according to the state, were "small landholders who were in possession and enjoyment of property which had belonged to tribal community."[155] As many of them have resisted restoration, even through

[150] *State of Kerala & Anr.* v. *People's Union for Civil Liberties*, para. 86.
[151] Ibid., para. 137.
[152] Ibid.
[153] Ibid.
[154] Ibid.
[155] Ibid., para. 169.

violence, their insistence on keeping the "very same lands" requires some attention, but is left unexplored. Why these "settlers" could not be given land elsewhere by the government is never explained anywhere.

In the end, the state claimed to have amended the law keeping in mind the interests of all concerned. That this law in the end allows nontribals, who have either wrongfully taken land from tribals or inherited lands so taken by their ancestors, to keep the land is perhaps seen as nothing more than a coincidence. Moreover, the Supreme Court accepted the state's position that the 1999 Act is in fact more beneficial to the dispossessed tribals. Not only did the 1975 Act "not really serve the purpose of ameliorating the problems of the scheduled tribes," the state had argued, but its implementation was also likely to "lead to [a] law and order situation" in the state.[156] In committing itself to giving some land to the tribals, albeit not that which was taken from them, as well as a commitment to set up dedicated funds for tribal "welfare," the state had come up with the best solution – a "permanent" one in its own words – to the tribal demands for restoration of their lands.

It appears from the judgment that the issue of tribal rights to lands traditionally used and occupied by them and to their "culture connected with their lands," was urged before the court to some extent.[157] In this regard, the court felt that the "elected representatives of the people" were in the best position to determine if dislocation could cause more harm.[158] The fact that more than 98 percent of "the people" who elect these representatives in Kerala are non-Adivasis seems to be of relevance here, but it is not considered. The judgment notes that in making its decisions, the state had considered the fact that the tribals had in fact "been out of possession of their lands for decades."[159] The premise here appears to be that whatever "culture" had connected them to the land was already lost. Moreover, as held in the Supreme Court decision in the *Narmada* case mentioned above, and approvingly cited in this judgment, displacement "per se" does not result in violation of any rights, despite availability of research that suggests otherwise.[160]

In conclusion, the court also notes that the position of those members of tribes who "are still living in the jungle [forest] and are dependant on the

[156] Ibid., para. 147.
[157] Ibid., paras 139 and 154.
[158] Ibid., para. 139.
[159] Ibid.
[160] See for example Rath, "Introduction," 45–46. Rath suggests that displacement is one of the "most disastrous aspects" of large-scale development projects in the country. Some of these disastrous effects noted by the author are loss of women's autonomy, destruction of "valuable community life," and undermining of "cultural practices."

products thereof" was different from those "who have become a part of the mainstream."[161] There is no reference in the judgment to the 5 percent Adivasis in Kerala still classified by the state as "primitive" tribes.[162] It is therefore not clear who the court was referring to as those who live in the forests. But "tribals" generally in Kerala, it had already been "safely presumed," based on the literacy figures quoted above, fall in the latter category, that is, those who are part of the "mainstream." This is another ground that disentitles them to restoration of their lands – tribals who are not *really* tribal would not want to get back the same land.

Finally, neither the formerly favored doctrine of minimal interference with tribal polities[163] nor the domestic or international law relating to Indigenous peoples could do anything for the dispossessed. The former, according to the court "is no longer valid" owing (inexplicably) to "passage of time."[164] In respect of the ILO Convention 169 of 1989,[165] and the U.N. Declaration on the Rights of Indigenous Peoples,[166] the court noted that firstly, "the notion of autonomy contained in the 1989 Convention has been rejected by India," and secondly, neither the Convention nor the U.N. Declaration are binding.[167]

This is the nature of "the law" that Ottukan knows cannot help them. It is the law of the people who C. K. Janu, the prominent Adivasi leader in Kerala, calls the "paper-owners" of their lands.[168] "Nothing can be done," Ottukan had said.[169] Unlike me, he did not need to read the judgment handed down by the Supreme Court of India to learn this. He lives the realities of this law.

6.4. ADIVASI PASTS AND PRESENTS

All the narratives presented in this chapter – the oral and written histories, the stories of dispossession, and the law's narrative of Adivasi lands – are central to

[161] *State of Kerala & Anr.* v. *People's Union for Civil Liberties*, para. 168.
[162] *Kerala State Development Report*, 356.
[163] This was the position favored by Nehru. See Jawaharlal Nehru, "The Tribal Folk," in *The Tribal People of India* (New Delhi: Government of India Press, 1973), 1. For the five principles enunciated by Nehru, see S. C. Dube, "Development Designs and Tribal People," in *Antiquity to Modernity in Tribal India: Continuity and Change Among Indian Tribes*, vol 1, ed. S. C. Dube (New Delhi: Inter-India, 1998), 11–12.
[164] *State of Kerala & Anr.* v. *People's Union for Civil Liberties*, para. 158.
[165] *Indigenous and Tribal Peoples Convention No. 169*, Geneva, June 27, 1989.
[166] *United Nations Declaration on the Rights of Indigenous Peoples* (September 13, 2007) A/RES/61/295. General Assembly Resolution 61/295. A/RES/61/295.
[167] *State of Kerala & Anr.* v. *People's Union for Civil Liberties*, para. 158.
[168] Bhaskaran, *Mother Forest*, 48.
[169] Interview with Ottukan.

understanding what the protests against Coca-Cola mean to the Adivasis who started them because these pasts are integral to their lives in the here-and-now. Their dispute with Coca-Cola, and their objections to its operations, cannot be adequately understood or addressed without a meaningful engagement with these narratives. As pointed out earlier, they also illustrate the simultaneous existence of multiple worlds of rights and wrongs, and the mistranslations as stories of justice and injustice travel across these worlds.

For a people who worked for themselves for centuries, the transformation into people in need of the state's protection or into applicants for various welfare schemes has not been easy. C. K. Janu, leader of the Adivasi struggle for alienated tribal land in Kerala, offers a striking and moving account of this journey in an account published in 2004.[170] She notes how "her people" who had never known hunger before all their lands were taken over, are now "caught up in applying to whomever and for whatever."[171] As "paper-owners" of lands traditionally occupied by them increased, the Adivasis were given more and more applications to fill out, and entire departments of people to help fill them.[172]

Amma, the elderly Adivasi woman, narrated a similar story of her life. After the land they had always cultivated was gone, Amma who did not know any other work, tried to sell woven bags and baskets for some time. But nobody uses those bags any more. Later she opened a small shop and was able to make ends meet for a while before "settlers" set up bigger shops in the area. Now she sells matted palm leaves for a living. Life has been difficult, but she does not complain much, except about "the company." Her neighbors, the "settlers" who live on land that once belonged to her family, are good people according to her. They too have suffered because of the company, she says. The Gounder who is cultivating their land (by illegally denying them access) too has suffered because of the company. He is only cultivating their land for now. She believes he will return it, although she is not sure when.

In the meantime, people like her – dispossessed and impoverished – can avail themselves of many programs instituted by the state. Adivasis in the area speak about people who sometimes visit the hamlets to tell them about government schemes that members of the Scheduled Tribes are eligible to apply, such as loans for constructing houses or pension schemes. They often cannot read or do not know how to fill out the applications or even where and how to submit them. People like Subramaniam help them fill out and

170 Bhaskaran, *Mother Forest*.

171 Ibid., 32.

172 For reference to "paper-owners" see ibid., 48.

submit the applications. Sometimes they get approved, especially when the applicant is able to provide documentary evidence of name, age, tribe, and so on. Sometimes it takes longer for the applications to result in anything of substance.

They cannot grow the grains they traditionally grew in these parts anymore, but can apply for cards that allow them to buy rice from "ration shops" (retailers who stock and sell grains at a price fixed by the government, typically lower than the market price). These retailers do not always give them the entire quantity of rice that they are entitled to buy at the subsidized rate, but it is one of the things they say nothing can be done about. Women are also eligible to apply for a "widows' pension," something I learnt about the day Maariamma asked me why I did not ask any questions about the pension.[173] She suggested I write about that too. Maariamma and some other women in the area have applied for the pension, but they do not know when they might get any. Before this they had applied for other documents, such as proofs of their identities and certificates that confirmed that their husbands were dead. Some women in the hamlet get a pension of Rs. 120 ($2.50 approx.) per month. The postman who brings it takes Rs. 10 (about 20 cents) from each of them. If they object, he will not bring the money anymore. They would rather he bring it, even if it is less than what they are entitled to. Maariamma awaits the day her application will get approved.

The Kerala Scheduled Tribes Department (earlier known as the Tribal Welfare Department), with its vision of "education, employment, and empowerment" of tribals has set up many such "welfare schemes" that members of the Scheduled Tribes are eligible to apply for.[174] The Tribal Development Office in Palakkad administers these programs and schemes directly or through the *grama panchayats*. In addition to organizing "trade fairs" for promoting "tribal art forms and medicine," the department provides loans for buying land and building homes. Some schemes offer assistance to members of Scheduled Tribes who wish to acquire skills such as tailoring; others provide assistance to buy a cow. The department also provides "free rations to all tribals" during the annual Onam festival.[175] Twelve kilos of rice are distributed to each family under this program.

Although all the officers of the department I met were non-Adivasis, the department employs some Adivasis as temporary employees. The department

[173] Interview with Maariamma.

[174] See Government of Kerala, Department of ST Development, accessed March 15, 2011, www.kerala.gov.in.

[175] Ibid.

describes about a thousand of them employed across the state as its "backbone."[176] These young Adivasi women and men, known as "Tribal Promoters," typically have had basic formal education up to grade 10 or 12. They are employed for terms of less than one year. They mainly serve as links between the communities and the administrators, visit Adivasi hamlets and help "identify needs" of the communities.[177] They also spread word about the various schemes, identify eligible members, and help them fill out applications. At times, they even help Adivasis access health care by taking them to nearby hospitals when required.

According to an officer of a local Tribal Development Office, there is no paucity of funds for implementing its various schemes aimed at removing the "backwardness" of tribals.[178] Their problems lie elsewhere. To begin with, there is some concern about the effectiveness of all these schemes. The concerned officer told me that there is "no system for monitoring in the field."[179] Not having "enough staff" is another concern.[180] When asked about Tribal Promoters, the officer expressed dissatisfaction with the entire program. It is not very "effective," the officer said without offering any specific reason, other than that "some [tribal promoters] are lazy."[181] Some, however, "do well" – the ones who are "active."[182]

For Adivasis, as for many others more generally in the country or elsewhere, access to formal education holds the promise of change for a better future. Maariamma said more than once that since the kids cannot go to the forest like before, they need education and jobs. With the agricultural lands shrinking rapidly, ensuring that their children acquire newer and more acceptable skills has become a priority for parents in the hamlets. Amma is happy that her children were able to go to school, even though they could not pass grade 10. One of her daughters, herself a mother of two bright kids, hopes to learn about computers in a government run school in a nearby town. They have heard about government subsidies for women who enroll in such courses.

Almost every Adivasi I spoke with talked about their desire to ensure their children have access to formal education. It is something that came up in all

176 Ibid., 13.

177 Ibid.

178 Conversation with an officer, who declined a request for an interview, but he agreed to meet with me and provided useful information about the department and its programs during our brief conversation.

179 Ibid.

180 Ibid.

181 Ibid.

182 Ibid.

kinds of ways during conversations. Like one afternoon in the *samara pandal* when Maariamma asked me to take back with me a two-and-a-half-year-old boy, who was there that day with his mother, so he could study. "You take him with you. Make him study up to [grade] ten, and then send him back to us," she had said. His mother, sitting next to me at the time, did not say anything, but decided instead to look at her toes. She looked at me after, having found my voice again, I said I hoped for him to study too, but perhaps he would be happier with his mother. I think her smile meant she agreed.

After numerous conversations about education in the hamlets, I was surprised at a Tribal Development Department officer's remark regarding the Adivasis' lack of interest in education and its correlation to their high rates of unemployment. "They don't show interest in studying further," he had said.[183] According to him, many of them "don't study even if they have an opportunity."[184] This perceived unwillingness to study, along with what he describes as their "reluctan[ce] to work in distant places," is the reason why they are unable to find jobs.[185] It is hard to understand how the response that the Adivasis "don't like to" work in "distant places" explains higher Adivasi unemployment in *this* region as compared with that of other communities.[186] But that, and a shrug, is all he had to offer by way of an explanation. Perhaps he has never thought it necessary to search for any other reason.

Each of Vijaynagar and Plachimada has an *anganwadi* preschool. The teachers in both these places appeared to be sincere and committed. Their genuine care for the students showed in many ways during the time I spent in the hamlets. There are secondary and high schools a short bus ride away. The Tribal Development Office offers a lot of information about the various scholarships, stipends, and tuition fee assistance specifically for Adivasis. But I did not meet or learn about a single Adivasi teacher, teaching assistant, staff member, or administrator. A question about that elicited the same response – a frown, a shrug, a look that seemed to ask "how is that relevant?" It is relevant, at least to Adivasis such as Ottukan who said there were hundreds of schools for members of Scheduled Castes and Scheduled Tribes, but they are all managed by other communities. The communities to which the students belong have no say in the management, curriculum, or goals of these schools.

I was reminded then of an earlier conversation in the *samara pandal*, the day I learnt about the Adivasi "language" that is not spoken in the presence

[183] Interview with Govind.
[184] Ibid.
[185] Ibid.
[186] Ibid.

of non-Adivasis, the one that their children are ashamed of, because everyone speaks proper Malayalam or Tamil.[187] Some women worry that it will be lost soon along with the lives it represents. Maya, a young mother, said their language was their culture. What if the language could be taught in schools with other things, I asked. Everyone laughed at that. The teachers do not know the language, one of them said, wondering secretly, I am sure, at the ignorance of outsiders. My suggestion that one of them could teach it was met with silence. As I looked around trying to interpret that silence, Maya had said, almost in a whisper: "yes, that would be good." An older woman present there asked how anyone among them could be a teacher. No one had passed grade ten, she reminded everyone.

Access to education is a major area of focus for the Scheduled Tribes Department, and it has instituted a number of programs toward this end. There are provisions for free education to younger children, scholarships and stipends for students enrolled in primary, secondary, and high schools. There are also special incentives by way of awards for students who score high grades. An important component of the department's education programs are the *ashramam* or residential schools. These schools provide accommodation, food, and education to children who belong to, in the words of an officer, "primitive tribes" in Kerala. The officer proudly informed me that there is more demand for these schools than the department can meet. The department advertises the schools, but students already enrolled in the schools also spread the word.

In her memoir, C. K. Janu remembers a time from her childhood when some children from her area, including her "little sister," were taken to one such school:

> [I]t was some time during those days that people came to take children to the Hostel in Maananthavadi. many children were taken away. all ages. my little sister went to School like that. can't remember where I was then working in the fields catching fish in the stream grazing cattle hiding in the forest or digging for roots. can't be sure.[188]

Her sister studied in that school up to grade three.[189] Janu taught herself to read from the books her sister brought back from the school. She had been perplexed by the lessons on agriculture, chemical manures, pictures of

[187] I have been unable to determine whether this reference is to a different language or dialect. A local teacher confirmed that the Adivasis in the area speak a different language, which is neither Malayalam nor Tamil, but certainly contains many words from these two languages.

[188] Bhaskaran, *Mother Forest*, 6.

[189] Ibid., 23.

"machines tilling fields," and women in a paddy field. Her people knew, she says, all about transplanting paddy and harvesting. They did not need to learn this from books. At the time, she notes, they had thought these lessons were meant for the teachers.[190]

One such residential school has been set up near Palakkad town. All the students in this school are members of "primitive tribes" who live in forests and hills where there are no schools. No visitors are allowed in the premises without permission. The man I met in the school's main office spoke pleasantly for a few minutes until he learnt I was a researcher. He said he was not allowed to speak to anyone without prior permission of his superiors, none of whom were around that day. He became increasingly aggressive after that and asked us to leave. Some non-Adivasis who live near the school believe it is a good school for the Adivasi children, but they mentioned that the students have no interaction with anyone in the neighborhood. The only time they are seen outside is when they walk out in rows to visit a local Hindu temple or for tutorials. That is all I managed to learn as I was unable to speak with anyone from the school that day or later.

At first this reaction did not make any sense, especially since I had not asked to speak with any students. All I had been hoping for was some information about the school and its programs. Since no printed material was available, I had hoped somebody in the office could tell me about their recruitment policies and curriculum, as well as offer the department's perspectives on the strengths and weaknesses of the program. The reaction of the man I met in the office had been completely unexpected. Later, faced with complete silence, I began to search for information on my own. This was when I first came across reports alleging neglect, poor conditions, sexual abuse, and pregnancies in "tribal hostels" elsewhere in the state.[191]

Back in Plachimada, while speaking about the various issues the Adivasis wanted to be addressed, Ottukan, one of the leaders of the struggle against Coca-Cola, spoke about a residential school for Adivasi children nearby. The non-Adivasi warden of the residence has been convicted for illegally cultivating *ganja* (marijuana) in the past. The community is deeply troubled by the fact that such a man is managing the place. They are also concerned

[190] Ibid.

[191] For example, see Jos Chathukulam and M. S. John, "Issues in Tribal Development: The Recent Experience of Kerala," Rath, *Tribal Development*, 184; D. Jose, "Kerala's Tribal Hostels Converted to Prostitution Dens," *Rediff News*, July 10, 2000, http://www.rediff.com/news/2000/jul/10jose.htm; Payal Kapadia, "The Savaged Tribes," *Outlook*, July 10, 2000, http://www.outlookindia.com/article.aspx?209685.

about the complete lack of access and transparency about what goes on in the place. Ottukan suggested that the requirement for prior permission to visit such schools from the tribal departments, which can take up to a week to come through, is to ensure things are in order for visitors. "We sometimes go in forcefully with students," he said. They have even taken reporters inside with them at times.

Had someone from the school spoken with me, I might have learned other things about the school. Anything that could have indicated that somebody in the well-funded department run by polite men and women who claim to be committed to removing the "backwardness" of "tribals," had taken note of the incidents reported in newspapers and concerns expressed by the Adivasis in the area; something that showed that these schools are not destroying lives; perhaps an assurance that the department is working to ensure that the rows of children I saw seated in their classrooms through the windows in that school would one day leave the place unharmed, with their bodies, minds, and spirits unbroken would have given me hope.

I left without any such reassurance. Based on what I have learned since, the reality of these schools, and their impact on entire generations of Adivasis, has not even begun to be recognized or acknowledged in Kerala. To an Adivasi, this is what these residential schools have come to mean:

> Every summer, buses from big schools arrive to pick up impoverished children. They are, without any remorse, turned into sinners in the confines of the hostels. They return as people who have lost their minds, as the poorest of the poor. Some get lost in city nights. They become the stuff of *cinima* stories or statistics. Real colonies are created that way.[192]

Clearly there is a disconnect here. Why is it that schools that officers in the Tribal Development Offices speak so proudly about are seen as places from where Adivasis return having "lost their minds"? Everything that Janu mentions in her account of these schools – from a curriculum she sees as pointless, to places that further impoverish her people, perhaps by destroying their culture and ability to live in their communities again – points to an urgent need for re-examining where things have gone wrong.

6.5. CONCLUSION

The several recognized as well as eclipsed narratives of the past and present presented here are inseparable from the violation experienced by the Adivasis

[192] Bhaskaran, *Mother Forest*, 51.

because of the presence of Coca-Cola and their demands for the closure of its plant. This particular separation from lands around which their lives and livelihoods were centered for centuries is connected to other separations at other times. The dispute in Plachimada can neither be adequately understood nor addressed without a meaningful engagement with these narratives. This is, however, easier said than done as the extended Adivasi accounts included here illustrate the diverging epistemologies and approaches to meaning. These Adivasi stories give powerful emphasis to the different worlds of rights and wrongs that Adivasis, lawyers, and activists inhabit, and illustrate (among other things) the degree to which indigenous epistemology differs from that of the state in not basing meaning and action on a separation of "law" from everything else. A just outcome of such disputes, however, requires that these unacknowledged differences and eclipsed narratives of displacement, dispossession, impoverishment, exclusion, and denial of any say in matters that affect their lives fundamentally be taken seriously in understanding the meanings of the Adivasi opposition to Coca-Cola as well as similar mobilizations elsewhere.

7

Conclusion

In the Introduction I acknowledged that understanding all the stories about the dispute in Plachimada, as well as writing about them, has been extremely difficult. As I look back at this challenging journey of learning and unlearning, two aspects stand out as the most difficult: walking away from a place where so many everyday injustices demand an urgent response without offering anything more than a promise to tell stories that were shared with me; and coming to terms with the conclusion of a project that is, in fact, far from concluded. As I continue to learn from the many stories and encounters, I summarize here some important issues this book attempts to draw attention to and point to some vital questions that deserve attention.

In juxtaposing the multiple accounts of the dispute in Plachimada, I have tried to shed light on critical differences between these accounts. These accounts reveal the practices and processes of translation as the many committed supporters of Adivasi protests, the lawyers and judges who have shaped the legal dispute and the media that has ensured the dispute does not disappear from public view, re-present the dispute. In doing so, they reorganize the narratives to meet the demands of their target audiences or target languages of rights and formal state law. This retelling of the stories is at times a result of the translators' own relationship with the popular human rights or legal languages as either their creators or adherents, and at other times a result of strategy in the quest for final, achievable results. More often than not, this re-presentation of the dispute with a different focus and emphasis is done with the best intentions to ensure justice for those who began the protests and have been most affected by the dispute.

Despite this, Adivasi accounts of the dispute with Coca-Cola as well as the issues that matter the most to them remain eclipsed in the available accounts. What is obscured in the process of translation of their stories into the stronger and readily accepted popular and legal narratives are the meanings and significance of the opposition to the Coca-Cola plant for the Adivasis who began the protests. It is easy when faced with multiple narratives to give into the temptation of identifying the one true story. My goal, however, has not been to suggest that only one of the accounts presented here is valid, but rather to emphasize the differences in these various accounts, and the significance of the differences. My aim is to understand how meanings are gained and lost as narratives originating in one normative universe encounter another, how the actors involved attempt to bridge the differences, and how in a world of unequal languages, some have the power to eclipse others.

Just as the popular and legal accounts of the dispute are determined by particular normative worlds, the meanings of the Adivasi protests and the wrongs they seek to draw attention to in their opposition to Coca-Cola are closely linked to who they are, the lives they live in the place they live, and the stories they tell. The Adivasis' insistence on the closure of the Coca-Cola facility is inadequately understood when separated from the realities of their everyday lived experiences and the narratives that shape their normative universe. Without recognizing and taking seriously the Adivasi narratives of their past, present, and future, we cannot begin to understand either the violence experienced by them or formulate an adequate response to such injustice.

The violations that the Adivasis have experienced because of Coca-Cola's presence amidst their homes, on lands and wells that their lives and livelihoods are connected to are much more serious than those represented in the narrow claims put forward on their behalf. The dispute draws attention to the issues of depletion and pollution of water by Coca-Cola, but Adivasi protests in Plachimada and other such struggles in many other parts of the world are misconstrued if understood as events in themselves, unconnected to past local struggles or global forces. The violence of separation of Indigenous peoples from their water, lands, and homes is related to the much larger issues of dispossession and exclusion that cannot be adequately addressed either by any monetary compensation for losses incurred in the recent past or by deciding the question of rights of a village council or the legality of its decision to cancel Coca-Cola's license. These outcomes, even if achieved, can only serve as a barely adequate beginning of what can only be a long process of addressing old and new wrongs, and not a final resolution as hoped by some in this instance.

As is clear from themes that recur in Adivasi stories presented especially in Chapters 5 and 6, alienation from land, subordination of local economies, the emotional and cultural aspects of displacement as well as its impact on livelihood, and the denial of a voice are all issues that are critical to the Adivasis. Coca-Cola's presence and approach has only served to accelerate the processes that have been distancing Adivasis from their lands, water, and familiar ways of life. It is these processes that connect Plachimada to other places in India and elsewhere in a world searching for newer lands and resources in order to meet its ever increasing demands and to the complicated questions of development and progress. These are also the processes that connect Plachimada to other times when similar quests for land and resources had led to colonization of a large part of the world.

My purpose in presenting these Adivasi and other stories is not to give them a set of fixed meanings, or to close down further interpretation. This is in fact an invitation to take seriously these and other such stories. It is an invitation for further and wider engagement with them and the role that formal state law plays in shaping them in particular ways. While traveling in Kerala and in other parts of India, I met women and men who, upon learning that my project was about a dispute that involved Coca-Cola and Adivasi protestors, reacted in one of two ways. One was the old and tiresome question about whether I wanted the Adivasis to continue living in forests. Plachimada is not a forest, of course, but such questions, as elsewhere in the world, are not based on anything other than a belief that whether or not "tribals" must live in a forest is all there is that needs to be determined. They are also based on the extremely problematic arrogance that it is one of "us" who will decide this issue. The other reaction, related to the first one, is about development. Despite its many achievements in the fields of human and social development, Kerala has been criticized for its failure to attract industry and capital. This lack of industrial development is what in popular belief lies behind the increasing unemployment, alcoholism, and suicides in the state. The point, made to me in different ways by different people, was that since industrial units have to be set up somewhere, why not in Plachimada? I often asked if they would pose the same question if Coca-Cola had chosen to locate amidst their homes. Some responses revolved around how expensive the parts of town they lived in were. Sometimes the response, after a brief pause, was that in fact they would feel differently if they were the ones who lost their homes. Several, however, protested that this was an oversimplification that serves no purpose.

I admit that I do not have answers to the complicated issues faced by the residents of Kerala or their elected representatives, or those faced by others in other parts of the world where lands and water bodies are being taken over for various development projects accompanied by promises of job creation and prosperity for all. That does not, however, change the fundamental question of justice involved here that, put simply, is one of denial of voice. It is this injustice of exclusion, of losing all that they hold dear to make way for "development" that does not take their priorities into account and, as in the past, is not likely to benefit them in any way,[1] without having any say in the matter at all, that Adivasi protests like the one in Plachimada draw attention to. There is unfortunately very little serious engagement or debate over these issues in the country today.

It is not unless this injustice is acknowledged that the central government and the Government of Kerala, who have so far not even arrived at any consensus over the issue of financial compensation, will be able to turn their minds to other important questions that have not even begun to be asked yet, such as: What happens when Coca-Cola leaves Plachimada? Will the existing bottling plant be replaced by another industrial unit that perhaps does not pollute, as a non-Adivasi respondent suggested to me? Should the land be acquired by the government, perhaps to build an educational institution, as another non-Adivasi respondent suggested? Why do the Adivasis in Plachimada respond to this question with silence? How must we translate these silences?

A meaningful response to the dispute must address these questions. Will those Adivasis who lost their daily-wage work on lands they had always cultivated be employed by whoever replaces the company? Will the young men who were forced to leave the place in search of employment be able to return to their families? Will the older members of the Adivasi communities who were always able to work on the lands before be able to find employment and be self-reliant again? Can any of these separations from familiar lands and lives be reversed? These are all questions no one seems to be interested in, least of all courts that tend to distance themselves from social and political contexts and focus instead on the technical questions of law they feel more comfortable addressing even as they attempt to dispense justice.

As emphasized throughout, in presenting these multiple accounts, my goal is also to point to the importance of the processes of translation that determine speeches and silences to justice and to search for just outcomes. This is in fact a connection anyone who spends some time in courts of law or with litigants generally is unlikely to miss. More than the fact of losing a case, what frustrates and bothers many litigants as unjust is the denial of an opportunity to tell their story as they want to. Not surprisingly, an opportunity of being heard by a decision-making authority is a fundamental principle of natural justice protected by courts in India as well as in other jurisdictions committed to the rule

[1] For an argument that Adivasis have not benefitted from past large-scale development projects, see Rath, "Introduction."

of law. It is for this reason the Supreme Court of India needs to be concerned about the absence before it of Adivasi accounts of the dispute in Plachimada. It may not, in the end, succeed in addressing itself to them in their language, and may ultimately choose to assert its own language, but in acknowledging their stories, in trying to translate and respond, it would have to also acknowledge the limits of its own language and narratives.

Bibliography

LEGISLATION

Constitution of India, 1950.

The Kerala Land Reforms Act, 1963.

The Kerala Scheduled Tribes (Regulation of Transfer of Land and Restoration of Alienated Land) Act, Act 31 of 1975.

The Scheduled Caste and Scheduled Tribe (Prevention of Atrocities) Act, 1989.

The Kerala Restriction on Transfer by and Restoration of Lands to the Scheduled Tribes Act, 1999.

The Kerala Panchayat Raj (Conduct of Cases and Payment of Fees to Legal Advisors) Rules, 2003.

The Scheduled Tribes and Other Traditional Forest Dwellers (Recognition of Forest Rights) Act, 2006.

JURISPRUDENCE

C. K. Janu v. Director, Central Bureau of Investigation, 4 December 2008, unreported decision of the High Court of Kerala in WP(C). No. 32732 of 2003(V).

Hindustan Coca-Cola Beverages Pvt. Ltd. v. Perumatty Grama Panchayat, 2005(2) KLT 554.

Kailas & Ors v State of Maharashtra, [2011] 1 SCR 94.

Narmada Bachao Andolan v. Union of India, 2000 INSC 518; AIR 2000 SC 3751.

P. Viswambharam v. State of Kerala, 10 November 2010, unreported decision of the High Court of Kerala in Crl.MC.No. 2264 of 2008.

Perumatty Grama Panchayat v. State of Kerala, 2004 (1) KLT 731.

State of Kerala & ANR v. People's Union for Civil Liberties, Kerala State Unit & ORS, (2009) 8 SCC 46.

ARCHIVAL MATERIAL

Buchanan, Francis. *A Journey from Madras through the Countries of Mysore, Canara, and Malabar*. London: T. Cadell and W. Davies, 1807.

Cherian, P. J. ed. *William Logan's Malabar Manual – 1887*, Volume 1. Thiruvananthapuram: Kerala Gazetteers Department, 2000.

The Cochin Village Panchayat Regulation, Regulation V of 1089 M.E. (1914 C.E.) Kerala State Archives, Ernakulam.

Constituent Assembly Debates (Proceedings), India, December 9, 1946–January 24, 1950.

The Imperial Gazetteer of India. Oxford: Clarendon Press, 1908, vol. X.

Iyer, Ananthakrishna, L. K. *Cochin Tribes and Castes*. Madras: Publication for the Government of Cochin by Higginbotham & Co. London, Luzas & Co., 1909–1912.

Menon, C. Achyuta. *The Cochin State Manual*. Thiruvanantapuram: Kerala Gazetteers Department, 1911.

Pillai, T. K. Velu. *The Travancore State Manual*, vol. 4. Travancore: Government of Travancore, 1940.

Shortt, J. "Account of the Hill Tribes of Neilgherries." (April 11, 1868), In Home Department Proceedings, Hon'ble R. S. Ellis, C.B., Chief Secretary to the Government of St. Fort George, to E. C. Bayley, Esquire, Secretary to the Government of India, No. 305, New Delhi, National Archives.

Thornton, Edward. *A Gazetteer of the Territories under the Government of the Viceroy of India 1799–1875*. Revised and edited by Roper Lethbridge and Arthur N. Wollaston. London: Allen & Co., 1886.

Thurston, Edgar. *Castes and Tribes of Southern India*. Madras: Government Press, 1909.

REPORTS

Centre for Development Studies. *Human Development Report*. Thiruvananthapuram: Government of Kerala, 2005.

Government of India, Planning Commission. *Kerala State Development Report*. New Delhi: Academic Foundation, 2008.

Investigations on the Extraction of Groundwater by M/s Hindustan Coca-Cola Beverages Private Limited at Plachimada, February 11, 2005.

Report of the High Power Committee. Presented to the Government of Kerala on March 22, 2010.

Report of the Scheduled Areas and Scheduled Tribes Commission 1960–61, Volume I.

SECONDARY MATERIAL: BOOKS AND CHAPTERS

Amin, Shahid. "Approver's Testimony, Judicial Disourse: The Case of Chauri-Chaura." In *Subaltern Studies V: Writings on South Asian History and Society*, edited by Ranajit Guha, 166–202. Delhi: Oxford University Press, 1987.

Appiah, Kwame Anthony. "Thick Translation." In *Translation Studies Reader*, edited by Lawrence Venuti, 417–429. Florence: Routledge, 1999.

Asad, Talal. "The Concept of Cultural Translation in British Social Anthropology." In *Writing Culture: The Poetics and Politics of Ethnography*, edited by James Clifford and George E. Marcus, 140–164. Berkeley: University of California Press, 1986.

Bankowski, Zenon and Geoff Mungham. *Images of Law*. London: Routledge Direct Editions, 1976.

Bassnett, Susan and Andre Lefevere. "Introduction." In *Translation, History and Culture*, edited by Susan Bassnett and Andre Lefevere, 1–13. London: Pinter Publishers, 1990.
Baviskar, Amita. "The Politics of Being 'Indigenous'." In *Indigeneity in India*, edited by Bengt G. Karlsson and T. B. Subba, 33–50. London: Kegan Paul, 2006.
Baxi, Upendra. *The Future of Human Rights*, 2nd ed. New Delhi: Oxford University Press, 2006.
Benjamin, Walter. "Task of the Translator: An Introduction to the Translation of Baudelaire's Tableux Parisiens." Translated by Harry Zohn. In *Translation Studies Reader*, edited by Lawrence Venuti, 15–22. Florence: Routledge, 1999.
Berreman, Gerrald D. *Behind Many Masks: Ethnography and Impression Management in a Himalayan Village*. New York: Society for Applied Anthropology, 1962.
Bhaskaran. *Mother Forest: The Unfinished Story of C.K. Janu*. Translated by N. Ravi Shankar. New Delhi: Kali for Women, 2004.
Blomley, Nicholas K. *Law, Space, and the Geographies of Power*. New York: Guildford Press, 1994.
Borrows, John. *Recovering Canada: The Resurgence of Indigenous Law*. Toronto: University of Toronto Press, 2002.
Cain, Maureen. "The Symbol Traders." In *Lawyers in a Postmodern World: Translation and Transgression*, edited by Maureen Cain and Christine B. Harrington, 15–48. Buckingham: Open University Press, 1994.
Chakrabarty, Anjan and Anup Dhar. *Dislocation and Resettlement in Development: From Third World to World of the Third*. Oxford: Routledge, 2010.
Chakrabarty, Dipesh. "History and the Politics of Recognition." In *Manifestoes for History*, edited by Keith Jenkins et al., 77–87. London: Routledge, 2007.
Charlesworth, Hillary. "The New Jurisprudences." In *Beyond the Disciplines: The New Humanities*, edited by K. K. Ruthven, 121–134. Canberra: Australian Academy of the Humanities, 1992.
Chathukulam, Jos and M. S. John. "Issues in Tribal Development: The Recent Experience of Kerala." In *Tribal Development in India: The Contemporary Debate*, edited by Govinda Chandra Rath, 182–202. New Delhi: Sage, 2006.
Davies, Margaret. *Asking the Law Question*. Sydney: Law Book Co., 1994.
Derrida, Jacques. *Monolingualism of the Other or the Prethesis of Origin*. Stanford, CA: Stanford University Press, 1996.
"Letter to a Japanese Friend." In *Derrida and Difference*, edited by David Wood and Robert Bernasconi, 1–5. Warwick: Parousia Press, 1985.
DeVault, Marjorie. *Liberating Method: Feminism and Social Research*. Philadelphia, PA: Temple University Press, 1999.
Drummond, Susan G. *Mapping Marriage Law in Spanish Gitano Communities*. Vancouver: UBC Press, 2006.
Dube, S. C. "Development Designs and Tribal People." In *Antiquity to Modernity in Tribal India: Continuity and Change Among Indian Tribes*, vol. 1, edited by S. C. Dube, 1–26. New Delhi: Inter-India, 1998.
Elwin, Verrier. "Do We Really Want to Keep Them in a Zoo." In *The Tribal People of India*. New Delhi: Government of India Press, 1973.
The Aboriginals, 2nd ed. London: Oxford University Press, 1944.

Escobar, Arturo. "The Making and Unmaking of the Third World through Development." In *The Post-Development Reader*, edited by Majid Rehnema and Victoria Bawtree, 85–93. London: Zed Books, 1997.

Foster, Hamar, Benjamin L. Berger, and A. R. Buck. *The Grand Experiment: Law and Legal Culture in British Settler Societies*. Vancouver: UBC Press, 2008.

Foucault, Michel. *Society Must be Defended: Lectures at the Collège De France*. New York: Picador, 2003.

Geertz, Clifford. "Local Knowledge: Fact and Law in Comparative Perspective." In *Local Knowledge: Further Essays in Interpretive Anthropology*, edited by Clifford Geertz, 167–234. New York: Basic Books, 1983.

Ghosh, Amitav. *The Hungry Tide*. Boston: Houghton Mifflin, 2006.

Ghurye, Govind S. *The Scheduled Tribes*, 3rd ed. Bombay: Popular Press, 1963.

Griffiths, Anne. "Doing Ethnography: Living Law, Life Histories, and Narratives from Botswana." In *Practicing Ethnography in Law: New Dialogues, Enduring Methods*, edited by June Starr and Mark Goodale, 160–181. New York: Palgrave Macmillan, 2002.

Guha, Ramachandra. "The Unquiet Woods: Ecological Change and Peasant Resistance in the Himalaya." In *The Ramachandra Guha Omnibus*. New Delhi: Oxford University Press, 2005.

Guha, Ranajit. "Chandra's Death." In *Subaltern Studies V: Writings on South Asian History and Society*, edited by Ranajit Guha, 135–165. Delhi: Oxford University Press, 1987.

Guha, Sumit. *Environment and Ethnicity in India, 1200–1991*. London: Cambridge University Press, 1999.

Haksar, Nandita. "Law and the Self-Management of Tribal Societies in North-East India." In *Antiquity to Modernity in Tribal India: Tribal Self-Management in North-East India*, vol. 2, edited by Bhupinder Singh, 161–198. New Delhi: Inter-India, 1998.

Hall, Stuart. "Cultural Identity and Diaspora." In *Contemporary Postcolonial Theory: A Reader*, edited by Padmini Mongia, 110–121. London: Arnold, 1996.

Haraway, Donna. "Situated Knowledges: The Science Question in Feminism and the Privilege of Partial Perspectives." In *Simians, Cyborgs, and Women*, edited by Donna Haraway, 183–202. New York: Routledge, 1991.

Hardiman, David. *The Coming of the Devi: Adivasi Assertion in Western India*. Delhi: Oxford University Press, 1987.

Harding, Sandra. "Rethinking Standpoint Epistemology: What Is Strong Objectivity?." In *Feminist Perspectives on Social Research*, edited by Sharlene N. Hesse-Biber and Michelle Yaiser, 39–58. New York: Oxford University Press, 2004.

Harrington, Christine B. "Outlining a Theory of Legal Practice." In *Lawyers in a Postmodern World: Translation and Transgression*, edited by Maureen Cain and Christine B. Harrington, 49–69. Buckingham: Open University Press, 1994.

Herring, Ronald J. *Epistemic Brokers, Authoritative Knowledges, and a Diffusion of Opposition to Biotechnology*. Cambridge: Cambridge University Press, 2010.

Imai, Shin and Kathryn Buttery. "Indigenous Belonging: A Commentary on Membership and Identity in the United Nations Declaration on the Rights of Indigenous People." In *Oxford Commentaries on International Law: A Commentary on the United Nations Declaration on the Rights of Indigenous Peoples*, edited by Marc Weller and Jessie Hohmann. Oxford University Press, Forthcoming.

Karlsson, Bengt G. and T. B. Subba, eds. *Indigeneity in India*. London: Kegan Paul, 2006.

Koonan, Sujith. "Groundwater: Legal Aspects of the Plachimada Dispute." In *Water Governance in Motion: Towards Socially and Environmentally Sustainable Water Law*, edited by P. Cullet et al., 159–198. New Delhi: Cambridge University Press, 2010.

Kuhiwczac, Piotr. "Translation as Appropriation: The Case of Milan Kundera's 'The Joke'." In *Translation, History and Culture*, edited by Susan Bassnett and Andre Lefevere, 118–130. London: Pinter Publishers, 1990.

McCracken, Grant. *The Long Interview*. New Delhi: Sage Publications, 1988.

McCrudden, Christopher. "A Common Law of Human Rights?: Transnational Judicial Conversations on Constitutional Rights." In *Human Rights and Legal History*, edited by Katherine O'Donovan and Gerry R. Rubin, 29–65. Oxford: Oxford University Press, 2000.

Meehan, M. "Law and Literature: Reworking the Master-Plot." In *Beyond the Disciplines: The New Humanities*, edited by K. K. Ruthven, 109–120. Canberra: Australian Academy of the Humanities, 1992.

Mehta, Lyla and Anand Punja. "Water and Well-being: Explaining the Gap in Understandings of Water." In *Waterscapes: The Cultural Politics of a Natural Resource*, edited by Amita Baviskar, 188–210. New Delhi: Permanent Black, 2007.

Merry, Sally Engle. "Changing Rights, Changing Culture." In *Culture and Rights*, edited by Jane K. Cowan et al., 31–55. Cambridge: Cambridge University Press, 2001.

Mertz, Elizabeth. *The Language of the Law School: Learning to "Think Like a Lawyer*. Oxford: Oxford University Press, 2007.

Miller, Bruce G. *Oral History on Trial: Recognizing Aboriginal Narratives in the Courts*. Vancouver: UBC Press, 2011.

Mosse, David. "Ecology, Uncertainty and Memory: Imagining a Pre-colonial Irrigated Landscape in South India." In *Waterscapes: The Cultural Politics of a Natural Resource*, edited by Amita Baviskar, 213–247. New Delhi: Permanent Black, 2007.

Murickan, Jose and M. K. George. *Development-Induced Displacement: Case of Kerala*. New Delhi: Rawat Publications, 2003.

Nair, K. N., Paul Antonyoto and Vineetha Menon. *Water Insecurity, Institutions and Livelihood Dynamics: A Study in Plachimada, Kerala, India*. Delhi: Daanish Books, 2008.

Naples, Nancy A. "The Insider/Outsider Debate: A Feminist Revisiting." In *Feminism and Method: Ethnography, Discourse Analysis, and Activist Research*, 49–66. New York: Routledge, 2003.

Nehru, Jawaharlal. "The Tribal Folk." In *The Tribal People of India*. New Delhi: Government of India Press, 1973.

Palmater, Pamela D. *Beyond Blood: Rethinking Indigenous Identity*. Saskatoon: Purich Publishing Ltd., 2011.

Prakash, Gyan. "True Stories." In *Bonded Histories: Genealogies of Labour and Servitude in Colonial India*. Cambridge: Cambridge University Press, 1990.

Radhakrishna, Meena. *Dishonoured by History: "Criminal Tribes" and the British Colonial Policy*. Delhi: Orient Longman, 2001.

Ramachandran, Bindu. "Displacement of Land and Identity Crisis: Tribal Situation Today in Wayanad, Kerala." In *Land and Forest Rights of the Tribals Today*, edited by R. M. Sarkar, 152–158. New Delhi: Serials Publications, 2006.

Ramazanoglu, Caroline and Janet Holland. *Feminist Methodology: Challenges and Choices*. London: Sage Publications, 2002.

Rath, Govinda Chandra. "Introduction." In *Tribal Development in India: The Contemporary Debate*, edited by G. C. Rath, 45–46. New Delhi: Sage, 2006.

Rich, Robert M. "Sociological Paradigms and the Sociology of Law: An Overview." In *The Sociology of Law: A Conflict Perspective*, edited by Charles E. Reasons and Robert M. Rich, 954–966. Toronto: Butterworths, 1978.

Sachs, Wolfgang, ed. *The Development Dictionary: A Guide to Knowledge as Power*. New York and London: Zed Books, 1992.

Santos, Boaventura DeSousa. *Towards a New Legal Common Sense: Law Globalization and Emancipation*, 2nd ed. London: Butterworths, 2002.

Sarkar, R. M., ed. *Land and Forest Rights of the Tribals Today*. New Delhi: Serials Publications, 2006.

Sasikumar, M. "Towards Muthanga and After: The Tribal Movements for Land in Kerala." In *Land and Forest Rights of the Tribals Today*, edited by R. M. Sarkar, 132–142. New Delhi: Serials Publications, 2006.

Skaria, Ajay. *Hybrid Histories: Forests, Frontiers and Wildness in Western India*. New Delhi: Oxford University Press, 1999.

Smith, Linda Tuhiwai. *Decolonizing Methodologies: Research and Indigenous Peoples*. Dunedin: University of Otago Press, 1999.

Spradley, James P. *The Ethnographic Interview*. New York: Holt, Rinehart and Winston, 1979.

Spivak, Gayatri. "Politics of Translation." In *The Translation Studies Reader*, edited by Lawrence Venuti, 397–416. London: Routledge, 2000.

"Can the Subaltern Speak?" In *Marxism and the Interpretation of Culture*, edited by Cary Nelson and Lawrence Grossberg, 271–313. Chicago: University of Illinois Press, 1987.

Starr, June and Mark Goodale. *Practicing Ethnography in Law: New Dialogues, Enduring Methods*. New York: Palgrave Macmillan, 2002.

Sundar, Nandini. *Subalterns and Sovereigns: An Anthropological History of Bastar (1854–2006)*, 2nd ed. New Delhi: Oxford University press, 2007.

"Village Histories: Coalescing the Past and the Present." In *History and the Present*, edited by Partha Chatterjee and Anjan Ghosh, 144–182. New Delhi: Permanent Black, 2002.

Surendranath, C. "What the World Water Conference Reminds." Translated by Praveen Hariharan. In *Plachimada: Water Exploitation and Peoples Resistance*, edited by A. Vasuvedan. Kozhikode: Mathrubhoomi Books, 2005.

Suresh, Mayur and Siddharth Narrain. Eds., *The Shifting Scales of Justice: The Supreme Court in Neoliberal India*. New Delhi: Orient Black Swan, 2014.

Thompson, E. P. *Customs in Common: Studies in Traditional Popular Culture*. New York: The New Press, 1993.

Whigs and Hunters: The Origin of the Black Act. New York: Pantheon Books, 1975.
Tymoczko, Maria. "Translation in Oral Tradition as a Touchstone for Translation Theory and Practice." In *Translation, History and Culture*, edited by Susan Bassnett and Andre Lefevere, 46–55. London: Pinter Publishers, 1990
Vansina, Jan. *Oral Tradition as History*. Wisconsin: University of Wisconsin Press, 1985.
Vasudevan, A., ed. *Plachimada: Water Exploitation and Peoples Resistance*. Translated by Praveen Hariharan. Kozhikode: Mathrubhoomi Books, 2005.
Veluthat, Kesavan. *The Early Medieval in South India*. New Delhi: Oxford University Press, 2009.
White, James B. *Justice as Translation: An Essay in Cultural and Legal Criticism*. Chicago: University of Chicago Press, 1990.
Winichakul, Thongchai. *Siam Mapped: A History of the Geo-Body of a Nation*. Honolulu: University of Hawaii Press, 1994.
Xaxa, Virginius. *State, Society, and Tribes: Issues in Post-Colonial India*. New Delhi: Pearson Longman, 2008.

SECONDARY MATERIAL: ARTICLES

Aiyer, Ananthakrishnan. "The Allure of the Transnational: Notes on Some Aspects of the Political Economy of Water." *Cultural Anthropology* 22:4 (2007): 640–658.
Bayly, Susan. "Hindu Kingship and the Origin of Community: Religion, State and Society in Kerala, 1750–1850." *Modern Asian Studies* 18:2 (1984): 177–213.
Benton, Lauren. "Beyond Legal Pluralism: Towards a New Approach To Law in the Informal Sector." *Social Legal Studies* 3 (1994): 223–242.
Bhabha, Homi. "The Voice of the Dom: Retrieving the Experience of the Once-Colonized." *Times Literary Supplement* 4923 (August 8, 1997): 14–15.
Bijoy, C. R. "Forest Rights Struggle: The Adivasis Now Await a Settlement." *American Behavioral Scientist* 51 (2008): 1755–1773.
"Kerala's Plachimada Struggle: A Narrative on Water and Governance Rights." *Economics and Political Weekly* (October 2006): 4332–4339.
Bijoy, C. R. and K. Ravi Raman. "Muthanga: The Real Story: Adivasi Movement to Recover Land." *Economic and Political Weekly* (May 2003): 1975–1982.
Boothman, Derek. "Critique and Semantic Modification in Gramsci's Approach to Paradigmatic Translation." *Italian Culture* 24–25 (2006–2007): 113–140.
Borchgrevink, Axel. "Silencing Language: Of Anthropologists and Interpreters." *Ethnography* 4 (2003): 95–12.
Brown, Wendy. "Suffering Rights as Paradoxes." *Constellations* 7 (2000): 230.
Cain, Maureen. "The General Practice Lawyer and the Client: Towards a Radical Conception." *International Journal of the Sociology of Law* 7 (1979): 331–354.
Cook, Amelia and Jeremy Sarkin. "Who Is Indigenous? Indigenous Rights Globally, in Africa, and Among the San in Botswana." *Tulane Journal of International and Comparative Law* 38 (2009–2010): 94–97.
Coulthard, Glen. "Subjects of Empire: Indigenous People and the Politics of Recognition in Canada." *Contemporary Political Theory* 6 (2007): 437–460.

Cover, Robert M. "Obligation: A Jewish Jurisprudence of the Social Order." *Journal of Law and Religion* 5 (1987): 65–74.

"Violence and the Word." *Yale Law School Journal* 95:8 (1986): 1601–1629.

"Folktales of Justice: Tales of Jurisdiction." *The Capital University Law Review* 14 (1984–1985): 179–203.

"Foreword: Nomos and Narrative." *Harvard Law Review* 97 (1983–1984): 4–68.

Davies, Margaret. "The Ethos of Pluralism." *Sydney Law Review* 27 (2005): 87–112.

Devika. J. "The Capabilities Approach in Vernacular: The History in Kerala." *Economic and Political Weekly* 26–27 (26 June 2010):

Derrida, Jacques. "Force of Law: The Mystical Foudation of Authority." *Cardozo Law Review* 11 (1989–1990): 920–1046.

Fawcett, Barbara and Jeff Hearn, "Researching Others: Epistemology, Experience, Standpoints and Participation." *Social Research Methodology* 7:3 (2004): 201–218.

Felstiner, William L. F., Richard L. Abel, and Austin Sarat. "The Emergence and Transformation of Disputes: Naming, Blaming, Claiming ..." *Law and Society Review* 15:3–4 (1980–1981): 631–654.

Foucault, Michel. "The Subject and Power." *Critical Inquiry* 8:4 (1982): 777–795.

Fuller, Lon. "Human Interaction and the Law." *The American Journal of Jurisprudence* 14 (1969): 1–36.

Galanter, Marc. "When Legal Worlds Collide: Reflections on Bhopal, the Good Lawyer, and the American Law School." *Legal Education* 36 (1986): 292–310.

"Justice in Many Rooms: Courts, Private Ordering and Indigenous Law." *Journal of Legal Pluralism* 19 (1981): 1–47.

"Why the 'Haves' Come Out Ahead: Speculations on the Limits of Legal Change." *Law and Society Review* 9:1 (1974): 95–160.

Ganesh, K. N. "Ownership and Control of Land in Medieval Kerala: Janmam-Kanam Relations During the 16th–18th Centuries." *Indian Economic Social History Review* 28 (1991): 299–321.

Ghosh, Kaushik. "Between Global Flows and Local Dams: Indigenousness, Locality, and the Transnational Sphere in Jharkhand, India." *Cultural Anthropology* 21:4 (2008): 501–534.

Guha, Ramachandra. "Adivasis, Naxalites and Indian Democracy." *Economic and Political Weekly* 42:32 (2007): 3304–3312.

Gupta, Akhil and James Ferguson. "Beyond 'Culture': Space, Identity and the Politics of Difference." *Cultural Anthropology* 7:1 (1992): 6–23.

Habib, Irfan. "The Formation of India: Notes on the History of an Idea." *Social Scientist* 25:7/8 (1997): 3.

Harris, Mark. "Mythologising 'Recollections of Squatting in Victoria': Law's Intersection with Colonial Memory." *Law, Social Justice and Global Development Journal* 1 (2003): 1–14.

Herring, Ronald J. "Persistent Narratives: Why Is the 'Failure of Bt Cotton in India' Story Still with Us?" *AgBioForum* 12:1 (2009): 14–22.

Huisman, Kimberly. "'Does This Mean You're Not Going to Come Visit Me Anymore?': An Inquiry into an Ethics of Reciprocity and Positionality in Feminist Ethnographic Research." *Sociological Inquiry* 78:3 (2008): 372–396.

Merry, Sally Engle and Rachel E. Stern, "The Female Inheritance Movement in Hong Kong: Theorizing the Local/Global Interface." *Current Anthropology* 46:3 (2005): 387–409. Comments by Masamichi Inoue.

Kjosavik,Darley J. and N. Shanmugam. "Property Rights Dynamics and Indigenous Communities in Highland Kerala, South India: An Institutional-Historical Perspective." *Modern Asian Studies* 41:6 (2007): 1183–1260.

Kleinhans, Martha-Marie and Roderick A. MacDonald, "What Is Critical Legal Pluralism?" *Canadian Journal of Law and Society* 12 (1997): 25–46.

Koonan, Sujith. "'Legal Implications of Plachimada: A Case Study.' International Environmental Law Research Centre, working paper 5, 2007. Kothari, Smitu. 'Whose Nation? The Displaced as Victims of Displacement.'" *Economic and Political Weekly* 31:24 (1996): 1476–1485.

Kurien, Prema. "Colonialism and Ethnogenesis: A Study of Kerala, India." *Theory and Society* 23:3 (1994): 385–417.

Kurup, Apoorv. "Tribal Law in India: How Decentralized Administration is Extinguishing Tribal Rights and Why Autonomous Tribal Governments Are Better", *Indigenouds Law Journal* 7 (2008–2009): 87–126.

Leiten, G. K. "The Human Development Puzzle in Kerala." *Journal of Contemporary Asia* 32:1 (2002): 47–68.

Lowie, Robert H. "Native Languages as Ethnographic Tools." *American Anthropologist* 42:1 (1940): 81–89.

MacDonald, Roderick A. "Custom Made – For a Non-Chirographic Critical Legal Pluralism." *Canadian Journal of Law and Society* 26 (2011): 301–327.

Mawani, Renisa. "Law's Archive." *Annual Review of Law and Social Science* 8 (2012): 337–365.

"Imperial Legacies (Post) Colonial Identities: Law, Space and the Making of Stanley Park, 1859–2001." In Making Law Visible: Past and Present Histories and Postcolonial Theory, edited by Nan Seuffert and Catharine Coleborne, *Law Text Culture* 7 (2003): 98–141.

Mead, Margaret. "Native Languages as Fieldwork Tools." *American Anthropologist* 41:2 (1939): 181–205.

Mellisaris, Emmanuel. "'The More the Merrier?' A New Take on Legal Pluralism." *Social and Legal Studies* 13:1 (2004): 57–79.

Merry, Sally E. "Transnational Human Rights and Local Activism: Mapping the Middle." *American Anthropologist* 108:1 (2006): 38–51.

"Legal Pluralism." *Law and Society Review* 22 (1988): 869–896.

Merry, Sally E. and Rachel E. Stern, "The Female Inheritance Movement in Hong Kong: Theorizing the Local/Global Interface." *Current Anthropology* 46:3 (June 2005): 387–410.

Mertz, Elizabeth. "Teaching Lawyers the Language of Law: Legal and Anthropological Translations." *John Marshall Law Review* 34 (2000–2001): 91–117.

Mickelson, Karin. "Rhetoric and Rage: Third World Voices in International Legal Discourse." *Wisconsin International Law Journal* 16 (1997–1998): 353.

Omvedt, Gail. "Disturbing Aspects of Kerala Society." *Bulletin of Concerned Asian Scholars* 30:3 (1998): 31–33.

Parayil, Govindan. "The 'Kerala Model' of Development: Development and Sustainability in the Third World." *Third World Quarterly* 17:5 (1996): 941–957.

Parayil, Govindan and T. T. Sreekumar. "Kerala's Experience of Development and Change." *Journal of Contemporary Asia* 33:4 (2003): 465–492.

Prakash, B. A. "Agricultural Development in Kerala from 1800 AD to 1980 AD: A Survey of Studies." Centre for Development Studies, Trivandrum, working paper 220, June 1987.

Parmar, Pooja. "Undoing Historical Wrongs: Law and Indigeneity in India." *Osgode Hall Law Journal* 49:3 (2012): 491–525.

"Revisiting the Human Right to Water." *Australian Feminist Law Journal* 28 (2008): 77–96.

Pue, W. Wesley. "Globalization and Legal Education: Views from the Outside-In" *International Journal of the Legal Education* 8:1 (2001): 87–102.

Quigley, Michael. "Language of Conquest, Language of Survival." *The Canadian Forum* 52:723 (1982): 14–15.

Rajagopal, Balakrishnan. "Counter-hegemonic International Law: Rethinking Human Rights and Development as a Third World Strategy." *Third World Quarterly* 27:5 (2006): 767–783.

Raman, K. Ravi. "Transverse Solidarity: Water, Power, and Resistance." *Review of Radical Political Economics* 42:2 (2010): 251–268.

Randeria, Shalini. "The State of Globalization: Legal Plurality, Over-lapping Sovereignties and Ambiguous Alliance between Civil Society and the Cunning State in India." *Theory, Culture and Society* 24:1 (2007): 1–33.

Sakai, Naoki. "Translation." *Theory Culture and Society* 23 (2006): 71–86.

Santos, Boaventura DeSousa. "The Heterogenous State and Legal Pluralism in Mozambique." *Law and Society Review* 40 (2006): 39–76.

Sharafi, Mitra. "Justice in Many Rooms since Galanter: De-romanticizing Legal Pluralism through the Cultural Defense." *Law and Contemporary Problems* 71 (2008): 139–146.

Skaria, Ajay. "Some Aporias of History: Time, Truth and Play in Dangs, Gujarat." *Economic and Political Weekly* 34:15 (1999): 897–904.

Spivak, Gayatri. "Translation as Culture." *Parallax* 6:1 (2000): 13–24.

Teubner, Gunther. "The Two Faces of Janus: Rethinking Legal Pluralism." *Cardozo Law Review* 13 (1991–1992): 1443–1462.

Thapar, Romila. "The Theory of Aryan Race and India: History and Politics." *Social Scientist* 24:1 (1996): 3–29.

Venn, Couze. "Translation: Politics and Ethics." *Theory Culture and Society* 23 (2006): 82–84.

Webber, Jeremy. "Legal Pluralism and Human Agency." *Osgoode Hall Law Journal* 44 (2006): 167–198.

White, James Boyd. "Law as Language: Reading Law and Reading Literature." *Texas Law Review* 60 (1981–1982): 415–430.

Wolfe, Patrick. "Settler Colonialism and the Elimination of the Native." *Journal of Genocide Research* 8:4 (December 2006): 387–409.

Xaxa, Virginius. "Transformation of Tribes in India: Terms of Discourse." *Economic and Political Weekly* 34:24 (June 1999): 1519–1524.

"Tribes as Indigenous People of India." *Economic and Political Weekly* 34:51 (December 1999): 3589–3595.

SECONDARY MATERIAL: NEWS ARTICLES, MAGAZINES, AND INTERNET SOURCES

"Water Not a Private Property, Says Plachimada Declaration." *The Hindu* (January 24, 2004). Accessed: February 18, 2015 http://www.hindu.com/2004/01/24/stories/2004012402321300.htm.

"500 Arrested in Rally Against Coca-Cola in India." *India Resource Centre* (June 9, 2005). Accessed: November 30, 2005. http://www.indiaresource.org/

"500 Anti–Coca-Cola Demonstrators Arrested in India." *Newswire* (June 2005). Accessed: November 30, 2005. http://www.ens-newswire.com/ens/jun2005/2005-06-09-02.html.

"Anti-Coke Agitators Held, Released Later." *The Hindu* (June 9, 2005). Accessed: September 20, 2010. http://www.thehindu.com/2005/06/09/stories/2005060903050700.htm.

"Anti Coca-Cola Agitation – Plachimada: 1000 Historical Days." Compiled by Haritha Bhumi. Translated by Praveen Hariharan. *Keraleeyam* 1:7 (January 2005): 29–40.

"Coca-Cola Not Disclosing Full Liabilities in India, Misleading Shareholders: Company Challenged at Shareholders Meeting." (April 19, 2006). Accessed: February 18, 2015 http://www.indiaresource.org/news/2006/1055.html

"Coke Rejects Conditional License." *The Hindu* (June 10, 2005). Accessed: September 21, 2010. http://www.thehindu.com/2005/06/10/stories/2005061002380700.htm.

"Check Exploitation of Groundwater: Achuthanandan." *The Times of India* (February 6, 2006). Accessed: May 15, 2006. http://timesofindia.indiatimes.com/articleshow/1402847.cms.

"Chief Secretary to Look into Official's Controversial Statement on Coca-Cola." *The Hindu* (May 26, 2010). http://www.thehindu.com/news/states/kerala/article438655.ece.

"Editorial." Translated by Praveen Hariharan. *Keraleeyam* 4–6 (January 2007).

"High Court of Kerala Quashes the Ban on Coca-Cola in Kerala." *New Delhi* (September 22, 2006). Accessed: April 7, 2007. http://www.coca-colaindia.com/quality/fact_sheet.asp.

"Kerala High Court quashes ban on Coca-Cola, Pepsi." September 23, 2006
http://www.thehindu.com/todays-paper/tp-national/tp-kerala/kerala-high-court-quashes-ban-on-cocacola-pepsi/article3079639.ece

"Interview: N. P. Johnson Chairman, Co-ordination Committee, Plachimada." Translated by Jiss Verkey. *Keraleeyam* 129 (April 2008):19–20. See also Nizar Ahmed. "Justice through Decentralized Democratic Struggle." *Keraleeyam* 129 (April 2008): 41–43.

"Jananeethi Report on the Amplitude of Environmental and Human Rights Ramifications." (July 2002). Accessed: October 6, 2010. http://www.jananeethi.org/jananeethi/majorevents.htm

"Plachimada Stir Completes 2000 Days." *The Hindu* (October 13, 2007). Accessed: June 23, 2008. http://www.thehindu.com/2007/10/13/stories/2007101362600600.htm.

"Naxalism Biggest Threat to Internal Security: Manmohan." *The Hindu* (May 24, 2010). Accessed: August 3, 2010 http://www.thehindu.com/news/national/article436781.ece.

"Kerala Court Lifts Cola Ban: Coke, Pepsi Relieved." (September 22, 2006). Accessed: September 21, 2010. http://www.siliconindia.com/shownews/Kerala_court_lifts_cola_ban_Coke_Pepsi_relieved-nid-33226.html.

"Kerala House Passes Bill to Form Plachimada Tribunal." *The Hindu* (February 24, 2011). Accessed: February 18, 2015 http://www.thehindu.com/news/cities/Thiruvananthapuram/article1485861.ece.

"Named for Naxal 'Nexus', Delhi Prof, NGO Call Chhattisgarh Police Fascist." *The Indian Express* (July 13, 2010). http://www.indianexpress.com/news/named-for-naxal-nexus-delhi-prof-ngo-call-chhattisgarh-police-fascist/645692/.

"Speak Out Winner: Mylamma." *Outlook* (October 11, 2005). Accessed: November 4, 2010. http://www.outlookindia.com/article.aspx?228877.

"The Problem of Solid Waste at Plachimada: An Evaluation.". *Keraleeyam* (August 2005): 4–24.

"The Coca-Cola Company 2010 Annual Review." Accessed: August 2, 2011. www.annualreview.thecoca-colacompany.com.

"Tribunal to Adjudicate Compensation to People Affected by Coca-Cola Plant." *The Hindu* (June 30, 2010). Accessed: February 18, 2015 http://thehindu.com/news/cities/Thiruvananthapuram/article493750.ece.

Anand, S. "Industry Is a Human Vocation." Translated by Praveen Hariharan. *Keraleeyam* 1:5 (January 2005); Divya K., "The Peoples Establishment at Plachimada: A Special Study about Perumatty Panchayat." *Keraleeyam* 1:7 (January 2005): 66.

Fletcher, Matthew L. M. "Tribal Membership and Indian Nationhood." *Social Science Research Network*. Accessed: August 3, 2014. http://papers.ssrn.com/sol3/papers.cfm?abstract_id=2129813.

Jayaraman, Nityanand. "Coca Cola Parches." *Global Policy* (May 28, 2002). Accessed: September 21, 2010. http://globalpolicy.org/component/content/article/162/28046.html.

Jose, D. "Kerala's Tribal Hostels Converted to Prostitution Dens." *Rediff News* (July10, 2000). http://www.rediff.com/news/2000/jul/10jose.htm.

Kapadia, Payal. "The Savaged Tribes." *Outlook* (July 10, 2000). http://www.outlookindia.com/article.aspx?209685.

Kumar, Anoop. "The Death of Anil Meena." *The Indian Express* (March 14, 2012). Accessed: August 11, 2014. http://www.indianexpress.com/news/the-death-of-anil-meena/923471/0.

Krishnakumar, R. "A Conflict in the Forest." *Frontline* 20:5 (2003). Accessed: November 11, 2010. http://www.4lonnet.com/4l2005/stories/20030314003603700.htm.

Mathew, Vijith and Eed Muhammed Haneefa. "The Plachimada Issue in Views of Social Work Students." Translated by Jiss Verkey. *Keraleeyam* (April 2008).

Menon, Mukundan C. "A Fact File on Tribal Land." *NCHRO*. Accessed: August 10, 2014. http://www.nchro.org/index.php?option=com_content&view=article&id=43:a-fact-file-on-tribal-land&catid=17:campaigns&Itemid=27s.

Paikada, Sunny/ Janaadhikaara Rashtriya Samithi, "The Politics and Future of Plachimada." Translated by Jiss Verkey. *Keraleeyam* 129 (April 2008): 33–35. Laxman, Narayan. "Coca-Cola's Response Disappoints Plachimada Activists." *The Hindu* (April 23, 2010). Accessed: August 5, 2014. http://www.thehindu.com/opinion/op-ed/article408788.ece.

Nair, C. Gauridasan. "Industries Department Slams Plachimada Report." *The Hindu* (June 29, 2010). Accessed: August 5, 2014. http://www.thehindu.com/2010/06/29/stories /2010062954230400.htm.

Nigam, Aditi. "Model Bill for Permit System, Stiff Fines to Regulate Groundwater Use." (n.d.), http://www.thehindubusinessline.com/industry-and-economy/government-and-policy/article2313846.ece.

Radhakrishnan, M. G. "Capital Convert." *India Today* (August 28, 2006). Accessed: September 14, 2010. http://www.indiatoday.com/itoday/20060828/kerala .html.

Shiva, Vandana. "Building Water Democracy: People's Victory Against Coca-Cola in Plachimada." (May 13, 2004). Accessed: February 18, 2015 https://zcomm.org/zcommentary/building-water-democracy-peoples-victory-against-coca-cola-in -plachimada-by-vandana2-shiva/

Surendranath, C. "Coca-Cola: Continuing Battle in Kerala." *India Resource Center* (July 10, 2003). Accessed: July 3, 2012. http://www.indiaresource.org/campaigns/coke/2003/continuingbattle.html.

Venugopal, P. N. "End of Plachimada Battle. Or Is It?" *India Together* (April 30, 2010). Accessed: August 5, 2014. http://www.indiatogether.org/2010/apr/env-plachmada .htm.

Waite, John. "Face the Facts: Coca-Cola Update 02.01.04. Transcript." BBC Radio 4. http://www.bbc.co.uk/radio4/youandyours/yy_20040102.shtml.

WEBSITES

The Coca-Cola Company, http://www.thecoca-colacompany.com.

Backward Classes Bureau under the Ministry of Social Justice and Empowerment, http://socialjustice.nic.in/aboutdivision4.php.

Communist Party of India (Marxist), http://cpim.org/.

Democratic Youth Federation of India, http://www.dyfi.in/, http://www.dyfikerala.net/.

Government of Kerala, Department of ST Development, www.kerala.gov.in .

Government of India, Office of Registrar General and Census Commissioner, Census Data 2001, www.censusindia.gov.in.

Jamaat-e-Islami Hind, Kerala, www.jihkerala.org.

Kerala State Industrial Development Corporation, http://www.ksidc.org/.

India Resource Centre, http://www.indiaresource.org/about/index.html.

Ministry of Panchayati Raj, Government of India, www.panchayat.gov.in.

Ministry of Tribal Affairs, Statistical Profile of Scheduled Tribes in India (Government of India, 2010), www.tribal.nic.in.

National Commission for Backward Classes, http://www.ncbc.nic.in/.

National Backward Classes Finance and Development Corporation, http://www .nbcfdc.org.in/main.html.

Rashtriya Swayamsevak Sangh, http://www.rss.org/.

Solidarity Youth Movement, www.solidarityym.org.

Swadeshi Jagaran Manch, http://www.swadeshionline.in/.

Index

Books in the Series

Diseases of the Will
Mariana Valverde

The Politics of Truth and Reconciliation in South Africa: Legitimizing the Post-Apartheid State
Richard A. Wilson

Modernism and the Grounds of Law
Peter Fitzpatrick

Unemployment and Government: Genealogies of the Social
William Walters

Autonomy and Ethnicity: Negotiating Competing Claims in Multi-Ethnic States
Yash Ghai

Constituting Democracy: Law, Globalism and South Africa's Political Reconstruction
Heinz Klug

The Ritual of Rights in Japan: Law, Society, and Health Policy
Eric A. Feldman

The Invention of the Passport: Surveillance, Citizenship and the State
John Torpey

Governing Morals: A Social History of Moral Regulation
Alan Hunt

The Colonies of Law: Colonialism, Zionism and Law in Early Mandate Palestine
Ronen Shamir

Law and Nature
David Delaney

Social Citizenship and Workfare in the United States and Western Europe: The Paradox of Inclusion
Joel F. Handler

Law, Anthropology and the Constitution of the Social: Making Persons and Things
Edited by Alain Pottage and Martha Mundy

Judicial Review and Bureaucratic Impact: International and Interdisciplinary Perspectives
Edited by Marc Hertogh and Simon Halliday

Immigrants at the Margins: Law, Race, and Exclusion in Southern Europe
Kitty Calavita

Lawyers and Regulation: The Politics of the Administrative Process
Patrick Schmidt

Law and Globalization from Below: Toward a Cosmopolitan Legality
Edited by Boaventura de Sousa Santos and Cesar A. Rodriguez-Garavito

Public Accountability: Designs, Dilemmas and Experiences
Edited by Michael W. Dowdle

Law, Violence and Sovereignty among West Bank Palestinians
Tobias Kelly

Legal Reform and Administrative Detention Powers in China
Sarah Biddulph

The Practice of Human Rights: Tracking Law Between the Global and the Local
Edited by Mark Goodale and Sally Engle Merry

Judges Beyond Politics in Democracy and Dictatorship: Lessons from Chile
Lisa Hilbink

Paths to International Justice: Social and Legal Perspectives
Edited by Marie-Bénédicte Dembour and Tobias Kelly

Law and Society in Vietnam: The Transition from Socialism in Comparative Perspective
Mark Sidel

Constitutionalizing Economic Globalization: Investment Rules and Democracy's Promise
David Schneiderman

The New World Trade Organization Knowledge Agreements: 2nd Edition
Christopher Arup

Justice and Reconciliation in Post-Apartheid South Africa
Edited by François du Bois and Antje du Bois-Pedain

Militarization and Violence against Women in Conflict Zones in the Middle East: A Palestinian Case-Study
Nadera Shalhoub-Kevorkian

Child Pornography and Sexual Grooming: Legal and Societal Responses
Suzanne Ost

Darfur and the Crime of Genocide
John Hagan and Wenona Rymond-Richmond

Fictions of Justice: The International Criminal Court and the Challenge of Legal Pluralism in Sub-Saharan Africa
Kamari Maxine Clarke

Conducting Law and Society Research: Reflections on Methods and Practices
Simon Halliday and Patrick Schmidt

Planted Flags: Trees, Land, and Law in Israel/Palestine
Irus Braverman

Culture under Cross-Examination: International Justice and the Special Court for Sierra Leone
Tim Kelsall

Cultures of Legality: Judicialization and Political Activism in Latin America
Javier Couso, Alexandra Huneeus, and Rachel Sieder

Courting Democracy in Bosnia and Herzegovina: The Hague Tribunal's Impact in a Postwar State
Lara J. Nettelfield

The Gacaca Courts and Post-Genocide Justice and Reconciliation in Rwanda: Justice without Lawyers
Phil Clark

Law, Society, and History: Themes in the Legal Sociology and Legal History of Lawrence M. Friedman
Robert W. Gordon and Morton J. Horwitz

After Abu Ghraib: Exploring Human Rights in America and the Middle East
Shadi Mokhtari

Adjudication in Religious Family Laws: Cultural Accommodation, Legal Pluralism, and Gender Equality in India
Gopika Solanki

Water On Tap: Rights and Regulation in the Transnational Governance of Urban Water Services
Bronwen Morgan

Elements of Moral Cognition: Rawls' Linguistic Analogy and the Cognitive Science of Moral and Legal Judgment
John Mikhail

A Sociology of Constitutions: Constitutions and State Legitimacy in Historical-Sociological Perspective
Chris Thornhill

Mitigation and Aggravation at Sentencing
Edited by Julian Roberts

Institutional Inequality and the Mobilization of the Family and Medical Leave Act: Rights on Leave
Catherine R. Albiston

Authoritarian Rule of Law: Legislation, Discourse and Legitimacy in Singapore
Jothie Rajah

Law and Development and the Global Discourses of Legal Transfers
Edited by John Gillespie and Pip Nicholson

Law against the State: Ethnographic Forays into Law's Transformations
Edited by Julia Eckert, Brian Donahoe, Christian Strümpell, and Zerrin Özlem Biner

Transnational Legal Process and State Change
Edited by Gregory C. Shaffer

Legal Mobilization under Authoritarianism: The Case of Post-Colonial Hong Kong
Edited by Waikeung Tam

Complementarity in the Line of Fire: The Catalysing Effect of the International Criminal Court in Uganda and Sudan
Sarah M. H. Nouwen

Political and Legal Transformations of an Indonesian Polity: The Nagari from Colonisation to Decentralisation
Franz von Benda-Beckmann and Keebet von Benda-Beckmann

Pakistan's Experience with Formal Law: An Alien Justice
Osama Siddique

Human Rights under State-Enforced Religious Family Laws in Israel, Egypt, and India
Yüksel Sezgin

Why Prison?
Edited by David Scott

Law's Fragile State: Colonial, Authoritarian, and Humanitarian Legacies in Sudan
Mark Fathi Massoud

Rights for Others: The Slow Home-Coming of Human Rights in the Netherlands
Barbara Oomen

European States and Their Muslim Citizens: The Impact of Institutions on Perceptions and Boundaries
Edited by John R. Bowen, Christophe Bertossi, Jan Willem Duyvendak, and Mona Lena Krook

Religion, Law and Society
Russell Sandberg

The Experiences of Face Veil Wearers in Europe and the Law
Edited by Eva Brems

The Contentious History of the International Bill of Human Rights
Christopher N. J. Roberts

Transnational Legal Orders
Edited by Terence C. Halliday and Gregory Shaffer

Lightning Source UK Ltd.
Milton Keynes UK
UKHW050612131219
355159UK00029B/308/P

9 781107 081185